Executive Coaching

Executive Coaching

Developing Managerial Wisdom in a World of Chaos

Richard R. Kilburg

American Psychological Association
Washington, DC

Published by
American Psychological Association
750 First Street, NE
Washington, DC 20002

Copies may be ordered from
APA Order Department
P.O. Box 92984
Washington, DC 20090-2984

In the U.K., Europe, Africa, and the Middle East, copies may be ordered from
American Psychological Association
3 Henrietta Street
Covent Garden, London
WC2E 8LU England

Typeset in Meridien by Harlowe Typography, Cottage City, MD

Printer: United Book Press, Inc., Baltimore, MD
Cover Designer: Naylor Design, Washington, DC
Technical/Production Editor: Jennifer Powers

Library of Congress Cataloging-in-Publication Data

Kilburg, Richard R., 1946–
Executive coaching : developing managerial wisdom in a world of chaos / Richard R. Kilburg.
p. cm.
Includes bibliographical references and index.
ISBN 1-55798-648-7 (alk. paper)
1. Executives—Training of. 2. Business consultants—Handbooks, manuals, etc. I. Title: Developing managerial wisdom in a world of chaos. II. Title.

HD30.4 .K54 2000
658.4'07124—dc21 99-059663

British Library Cataloguing-in-Publication Data
A CIP record is available from the British Library.

Printed in the United States of America
First Edition

To my son, Benjamin,
God bless our muse and our hard work.

Contents

Preface

The decision to write a book leads logically to a series of other, much more intricate choices. Early in my career, I attended my first workshop on management concepts and skills. I remember it as being full of useful information and providing a satisfying and helpful experience. However, the only concrete piece of advice that remains stuck in my mind even today was a remark made by one of the instructors in an off-handed response to a long-forgotten question by a fellow classmate. He said, "in management, you live far longer with your yeses than you do with your noes." And so it is with a book. It contains my yes answers about what to include about executive coaching given the page limits of this book.

I began the journey toward this volume some 7½ years ago when I accepted the challenge and invitation of Jimmy Jones, who had become the new vice president of human resources at Johns Hopkins University, to build an organizational unit that would deal with issues involving change management at the university. I initially rejected his suggestion to create an organization development (OD) unit, arguing instead for an integrated human services model that would incorporate an OD function. After months of negotiations and wrestling, we finally agreed on the initial design for our Office of Human Services, which would house our employee assistance program (EAP), training and education, OD, diversity, and worklife programs. We are now in the latest version of that structure, and OD remains a core component of our ability to help the institution and its people cope with and adapt to the myriad challenges that life in modern American organizations can produce.

Early in the construction of our OD service, my colleague Emma Stokes and I created a list of client services. We specifically included leadership coaching as part of what we would offer because we both recognized the value and importance of working closely with individuals and small teams of leaders who carried both the responsibility and the authority for directing the line operations of the vast array of functions of the university and its affiliated institutions. Johns Hopkins is the largest private employer in Maryland, with close to 30,000 faculty and staff involved in its worldwide endeavors. And so we began to work hard and very close to some of the most brilliant, hard-working, and intensely motivated people in the world. They became our clients, and in a sense, we became their students.

In 1994, I decided to write about some things that I was learning and practicing. I followed the advice of my colleague and former teacher Tony Broskowski, who once said in a graduate school class, "I think it's always wise to write about what you do professionally. It's really the best way to learn about what is really going on." In 1995, I called Skip Leonard, who, as editor of *Consulting Psychology Journal: Practice and Research*, was leading a revival of that most important resource for practitioners in the field. I proposed a special edition devoted to executive coaching. He responded enthusiastically, and together we created the fall 1996 edition, which still stands today as the best compilation of articles describing and discussing the practice of coaching in the consulting industry. Several other articles and workshops later, I confronted the obvious. I had reached the point where I should probably compile everything that I was writing, thinking, and doing into a book. I approached Gary VandenBos, my long-time friend and colleague who directs APA's publishing empire, and proposed the project. He responded enthusiastically and put me in touch with Susan Reynolds, acquisitions editor, who guided me through the proposal and contract. It was then that I really had to decide what to write.

The material on coaching has continued to expand tremendously in the 1990s. It is now difficult to stay abreast of, as new books appear monthly. National conferences are held several times a year. Clinicians and helping professionals of every stripe are being encouraged to jump into the field. Two national organizations have been formed, and in the inevitable way that markets and entrepreneurs often work, certification of "coaches" has begun. As I have observed these developments, I have been most impressed by what people are not really writing and lecturing about, namely, how difficult and complex this all is. I have found that most of the available material is technique-oriented and does not really talk about what coaches confront when helping clients in their leadership roles. I have been especially concerned that most practitioners have either forgotten what psychotherapy and behavior therapy can tell us about the process of changing individual behavior or that they never learned those lessons in the first place. As a result, I decided that this book would focus on just those issues. I have tried to logically compile the material I produced through the mid-90s and put it in a conceptual framework emphasizing systems and psychodynamic theories that incorporates features of complexity theory and recent work on the development of human wisdom. I hope that it will be useful to consultants who are actually coaching managers or leaders but are getting stuck in the complexity of it, or to those people who are trying to learn how to coach. I have not tried to include all the techniques and methods so well described by other authors, although the literature review does provide an excellent gateway to what is currently available. I also describe and amplify the conceptual material through case vignettes. Finally, I've provided some exercises and descriptions of methods that I use routinely and to good effect. With the page limitations of this book, I was not able to do everything that I wanted to, but I am generally pleased with the results. I believe that readers of this volume will come to understand better what coaches really do with clients in the sticky, exciting, and troubled world of leading and managing modern organizations. I hope that you, my readers, will be encouraged, challenged, and supported by what you find in these pages. And now to live with my yeses.

Acknowledgments

I have already acknowledged some of the key people who led and helped me to produce this book, but I would also like to highlight several others. My assistant Chanda Marvin has helped me with a variety of tasks related to this work, and I could not get through the average day without her. Harry Levinson, probably the earliest pioneer in applying psychodynamic concepts to the world of management and leadership, has been my colleague, mentor, and inspirational force for decades. He encouraged me to write about what I was doing at Johns Hopkins. I hope that he will be pleased with the results. My colleagues in our OD and diversity program provide me with constant stimulation and support. In particular, Emma Stokes, my longtime collaborator; Cecy Kuruvilla, our in-house expert on multiculturalism and systems change; and Geno Schnell, our director of OD, who has put systems theory to work on a day-to-day basis, continue to inspire and push me to do better in everything that I practice. Catherine Fitzgerald, my newfound friend and colleague, has made invaluable contributions to this book and my professional life with her ideas, challenging questions, and exploring mind and spirit. She reads more than anyone I know and truly comprehends what she discovers. She has made me and this book better, and I am grateful to her. My current supervisor, Audrey Smith, vice president for human resources at the university, has been incredibly supportive of my many professional activities including the production of this volume. I continue to greatly enjoy working with and for her. The editorial staff at the American Psychological Association have truly made this book possible. They are world-class professionals. Special thanks to Susan Reynolds, Acquisitions Editor, Shelly Wyatt, Development Editor, and Jennifer Powers, Technical/Production Editor, my most supportive shepherds during the production process. Finally, my clients inside and outside of the university have inspired and taught me for years. I appreciate the opportunity to serve them and to repay their invitation into their lives and work with this book.

In the last word, I want to thank my son, Ben Kilburg, who is an artist, a friend, and a source of continuing amazement and joy in my life. As I watch and share in his creative journeys, I continue to be nourished in taking my own.

Executive Coaching

1 Introduction to Executive Coaching

The Case of Ann and Stephen

As I walked across campus for my two o'clock appointment with Ann and her supervisor, Stephen, I felt the familiar tension and sense of dread that always comes when I know that the consulting situation I face will undoubtedly produce intense conflict between clients and that they will depend on me to help them overcome their natural tendencies for mutual misunderstanding, aggression, and injury. I had worked with the two of them for over a year. The initial request for services came from Ann, a frontline manager in a financial production unit, who faced significant interpersonal conflict, productivity problems, employee turnover, and challenges to her managerial style with her 6-person team. After 6 months of activity and significant progress in her unit, Ann requested that our work extend to include her relationship with Stephen, with whom she found it almost impossible to conduct a civil conversation.

Although small, Ann's unit played a critical role in the overall process of managing the organization's finances because many other departments depended on the accuracy of the transactions it performed. Everyone in the related departments constantly scrutinized the unit members' work and responded with instant, unbridled, public criticism to both Stephen and Ann when errors were made or deadlines missed. Both of them felt under the microscope and under the gun. Ann's unit depended on the accuracy and timeliness of the information that departments sent her team for processing. As long as everything worked, the situation usually remained under control. When someone detected and reported an error, often "all hell broke loose."

I knew going into the meeting that Ann had experienced another major battle with Stephen the previous week when he without notice unilaterally changed his mind about supporting her request for additional training. Ann reported the fight to me in our regularly scheduled coaching session. She openly fretted that she had crossed the line with Stephen in their verbal battle, but she felt justified because he had deliberately provoked her with his authoritarian decision and his refusal to listen to her state her educational needs. The reality of the situation argued for Ann's position, because the evening courses for which she had registered would not involve time off from work. Initially supportive, Stephen had signed the appropriate papers for Ann to receive tuition assistance. He later changed his mind, demanded the papers be returned to him, and said that she needed additional education in other areas. Ann did not disagree with this assessment, but she pointed out that at several times in the past he had refused to support her requests for the training he now proposed. During our session, Ann stated that she thought she might be fired over the incident.

I assumed that the session would be full of tension and conflict. I met with the two of them approximately six times before, and they had come a long way in recognizing how they pushed each other into conflict positions, injured themselves in the process, and then avoided further contact and projected the blame for the problems on to one another. Both Ann and Stephen found it easy to regress into open interpersonal combat. Under pressure, Stephen quickly retreated into a detached, very intellectualized, obsessive, and argumentative interaction pattern that resulted in Ann feeling dismissed, defeated, and routinely humiliated. Extremely skilled at shifting debate tactics and remaining emotionally aloof, he was very difficult to reach in any interpersonal or emotional sense. Ann typically responded by pointing out all of the contradictions in his directives to her, his constant changes of procedure, his inability to listen to what she repeatedly told him, and his overall lack of support when problems arose in the work of her unit. Faced with his detachment and argumentativeness, she often regressed either into a silent withdrawn fury or into open displays of incendiary criticism that left him furious and frustrated.

In our previous sessions, we explored this pattern and Ann and Stephen's personal contributions to the problems they encountered. Individual differences in personality, communication styles, and gender dynamics all played major roles in the difficulties they encountered with each other. As a result of coaching, they both reported significant improvements in their interactions and ability to work together. In the sessions, they became more able to listen to each other, to inhibit the worst of their regressive tendencies, and to create productive solutions to very difficult and seemingly intractable problems in the work for which they were responsible.

In my individual coaching sessions with Ann, we successfully uncovered several dynamics that contributed to the difficulties in her work with Stephen. First, she became aware that she experienced tremendous waves of anxiety and shame whenever she interacted with him. The power of these emotional storms often left her so devastated that it took days for her to recover. As a result, she had developed a pattern of avoiding him whenever possible. Second, in her interactions with Stephen, she quickly became defensively enraged as a result of his behavior and the other emotional states she experienced. Her anger became so powerful that she seemed unable to hear his honest attempts to support her and understand the nature of the problems that she faced. Whenever the defensive anger reached a threshold of expression, she either withdrew into sullen, uncooperative silence, or she attacked Stephen verbally. Finally, in one very productive coaching session, Ann was able to connect the pattern of conflict at work with the history of interpersonal and emotional trouble she experienced in her family of origin. She described years of utter frustration and depressing loneliness as she struggled to relate to her mother whom she described as emotionally aloof, extremely critical, nonsupportive, and verbally abusive. As she tearfully related this history to me, Ann was able to draw the parallels to her relationship with Stephen without prompting from me.

Against this background, I approached and knocked on Stephen's door, which was closed for the first time since I bagan working with them. Ann opened the door, and a tidal wave of nonverbal tension washed over me. Ann seemed flushed, with her face drawn into a tight frown. Her hair was slightly disheveled, and her eyes actively searched for a way out of the room. Stephen sat in his chair like a stone statue. He too was flushed, and his body looked compressed, as though he had an enormous weight pressing him deeper down into his chair. After I sat, Stephen took the lead and explained that he had just handed Ann a letter terminating her employment. He outlined several options including her leaving at once; remaining in the position while she searched for another job; and strangely enough, the possibility of demoting her to a more technical position that she had occupied for years before her promotion.

With tears in her eyes, Ann handed me the letter. It was short, and it described the ongoing performance problems in her unit, the necessity to make a leadership change, and the willingness to provide reasonable support to her in the transition. It is of interest to note that the letter came from their supervisor. In response to my questions, Stephen described the process he had undergone in the previous week.

"I met with all of the key customers of Ann's unit, and although several of them were quite understanding and supportive of the changes she has been making, the majority of them reported that the problems continued, and that they found working with Ann very difficult. Faced with this feedback, our mutual boss informed me that he believed a change was in everyone's best interest." Stephen's voice was choked with quiet tension.

"I can't believe that people said that they were unwilling to work with me," Ann challenged.

"I met with everyone individually, and the majority do feel that way. Despite my efforts to describe the excellent progress you've made in filling vacancies, developing your new team, and addressing the production problems, they remained quite critical. And, our boss was not willing to listen to me. Believe me, I tried to argue with everyone. Personally, I think this is the last thing that we need to do right now."

We then spent several minutes discussing the likely effects on the staff, particularly their morale and cohesion. Ann indeed had worked hard to successfully rebuild and train her team in the preceding months. They had surmounted many of their production problems, but they still had numerous troubles, particularly with the accuracy of the data they received from other units. Stephen seemed overwhelmed at the thought of tackling these issues himself. He spoke openly about the likely impact of Ann's firing or demotion on his own chances for a promotion, stating strongly that the situation might ultimately lead to the derailment of his career in the organization.

"Would you be willing to consider the option of taking the other position?" he asked Ann defensively, while looking at me with a glimmer of hope in his eyes.

"I've been dedicated to this organization and have made enormous sacrifices to build my team. I've worked many weekends by myself over the past 6 months trying to hold the operation together as we recruited, and taken precious time away from my family . . ." said Ann.

At that point, Ann lost control and began to weep openly. She searched for a tissue, which Stephen found for her. "I'm sorry, I really didn't want to cry!" Ann's voice ached with emotion, and her body heaved with sobs that she tried vainly to control.

Stephen seemed at a loss about what to do. He tried to push Ann to make a decision about taking the demotion. At that point, I intervened and strongly suggested to both of them to avoid making any decisions in the powerful emotional currents of the moment. I also suggested that Ann gather herself together and go home. I stated in strong terms that she would need time to incorporate the meaning of their supervisor's decision, as well as to work through what she wanted to do. I pointed out to Stephen that even if she made a decision in the heat of the moment, she could not be held to it given the intensity of the emotional strain that she obviously was experiencing. Stephen agreed with me, and through her tears, Ann asked if she could talk privately to me about a related problem. Stephen seemed grateful for the opportunity to withdraw and immediately left us alone in his office.

Ann then told me about a meeting she had scheduled for that afternoon with the leader of the organization. We discussed the pros and cons of trying to take the meeting in her current emotional state, and Ann saw wisdom in canceling the meeting, because she would probably be unable to interact in a constructive manner. I suggested to her that she try to regain her composure as best she could and beat the traffic home. She got up with tears in her eyes, as did I, and I crossed the room and took her hand.

"I'm sure that you will land very safely, and that the prospects for your career will be untarnished by this event," I said.

"I know that I contributed to this happening," she replied. "It's just that I thought that I had made such good progress during this last year, working with you and learning things that I never did in my family." Again, she started to sob openly.

Choked by my own strong emotional responses to her words and the event itself, I could find nothing to say. I simply patted her hand and tried to look into her eyes in as reassuring a fashion as I could muster in the moment. We walked out of the office together and down the hall.

"Can I meet with you until I leave?" Ann asked as she turned to mount the stairs that would take her to her office.

"Of course," I replied.

As I walked out of the building and to the garage where I had parked my car, I trembled openly. I felt an enormous sadness for both Stephen and Ann, and I shared in the violent sting of humiliation at our collective failure. I frantically searched for a way out of the mess, for some brilliant ploy that would turn the situation around and provide the three of us with at least some temporary reprieve. Simultaneously, I struggled to accept that this experience again reinforced my awareness of the powerful Darwinian forces and complex psychodynamic elements of human, organizational life over which I had very limited control.

I considered the possibility of a private appeal to the supervisor who made the decision, someone whom I knew from other consulting assignments in the organization. Upon reflection, I rejected the thought because I knew the person well enough to know that a reconsideration would not be possible. I thought about an appeal to the highest level of administration in the division, but I also knew that those individuals were completely distracted by other momentous organizational issues and that they would be unlikely to do anything other than make a telephone call to reassure themselves that the decision had been carefully taken. I knew that there were real and continuing production problems in the unit for which Stephen and Ann bore some responsibility. I also knew that Ann had contributed significantly to the adverse outcome by her behavior in the 2 years prior to the start of our work together and through a number of recent interactions with key clients in which she had regressed to her previous response patterns when they attacked or challenged her.

I reviewed several other options, but I rested on the fact that Ann and Stephen would, under the best of circumstances, make uneasy allies, and that they were unlikely ever to develop a true working partnership. As I thought about Ann's career, it became obvious that with a little help from Stephen, she could proudly identify many powerful and important contributions she had made to the organization. After 3 years in her current position, she could and probably would be able to find and land in a similar position or perhaps even step up to greater responsibilities in a different organization with a more supportive supervisor. I took several days to consider the various options, and eventually, I resolved to take no immediate action that would challenge the situation. Rather, I would try to support Ann in her efforts to find another job and to incorporate and solidify as many of her personal and professional lessons as possible. I would also reach out to Stephen to try to reassure and support him as he continued to struggle with the very real organizational problems faced by the unit for which he was responsible.

Problems in Coaching Theory and Practice

I began this book with a dramatic, real-world example of coaching with managers and leaders because it illustrates some of the most entrenched and difficult problems that practitioners face in this type of work. Leadership and followership issues are often at the heart of any effort to create change in an organization. Lewin's (1997) classic theory of "unfreezing, changing, and refreezing" the enterprise in a change process assumes that consultants really do modify the behavior of the people involved as a prelude to movement. Recent theoretical developments from the application of complexity theory to the practice of management and consultation by Stacey (1996), Vaill (1991), Wheatley (1992), and others go much further. These developments suggest that people in modern organizations face constant internal and external pressure to change. As with Stephen and Ann, often these changes are nonlinear and catastrophic in nature, resulting in tremendous upheaval, significant organizational carnage, and disruptions in personal and professional lives that can be dangerous to people. In many enterprises today, the unrelenting pace and pressures challenge the physical and emotional resources of everyone. In some organizations, people are reduced to a survivalist mentality because their worlds have lost many—if not most—of the characteristics of predictability and stability on which they depend psychologically and physically, for example, the type of organization, the organization's clientele, and the nature of the work involved.

Those of us in the consulting field know and understand these trends. We also know that when these complex and chaotic pressures are brought to bear in any organization, it is often as though a powerful weapon was being aimed at people, their colleagues and friends, and their relationships with each other. The worst of these environments pressure people emotionally and interpersonally to such a high degree that employees often seem like victims in a modern version of a concentration camp. To be sure, their physical lives are not in jeopardy on a moment-to-moment basis, but their identities as human beings are threatened as the organization demands total dedication and complete commitment to the welfare of the enterprise over everything. In many organizations today, stockholders, the financial community, leaders, and the cultures they create imply that delivering anything else will lead to job loss, the organizational equivalent of psychological and physical elimination.

With this in mind, it is no wonder that studies of leadership derailment (Hogan, Curphy, & Hogan, 1994) have reported that 50% of people in executive positions fail at some time in their careers. Other studies (Marks & Mirvis, 1998) strongly suggest that the causes of the majority of failures in mergers and acquisitions are found in the clash of assumptions, values, and behaviors brought by the people who are forced together by leaders who most often decide to make major changes based solely on economic and competitive fundamentals. Evidence of the trail of human carnage created by modern organizations can be found in virtually every neighborhood, often behind the tidy lawns and painted shutters of well-kept, middle-class homes, homes occupied by people who, because of what has happened to them at work, are trying to maintain or rebuild lives that feel fragmented and threatened at best and devastated and devoid of meaning at worst. It seems to me that leaders in organizations often ignore the fact that there are no enterprises without people. This occurs despite the reality that every human being who has been in some type of significant relationship understands completely that people cannot simply be ordered to behave in a certain way without suffering potential consequences.

The previous case vignette illustrates this point well. In a complex, difficult, and ever-changing organizational situation, a leader and a key reporting manager struggle with the real job of trying to perform financial operations that are crucial to the organization. They are ill suited to work together, and both lack the managerial training, key interpersonal skills, and personal and professional self-awareness that would enable them to get past these deficiencies. As in most organizations, they were promoted to their positions based on their extraordinary technical performances in previous jobs. Little consideration was given to whether they were truly prepared to perform at higher levels or to work with each other, and neither received as much as an hour of training for their new positions. In addition, components of their behavior and fundamental issues in their psychodynamic structures and processes created nearly constant conflict whenever they met and tried to work together. The leaders of the organization gave no consideration to any of these issues when they put these two people in a structure they had reorganized in an effort to improve efficiency and performance. Stephen and Ann's best efforts to make fundamental and constructive change in the organization resulted in two continuous years of overt and covert conflict and misery for everyone involved, the termination of employment for one of the organization's most valued and critical employees, and serious damage to the promotional potential of the manager who remained in the business unit. In addition, the unit itself continued to underperform in precisely the same ways despite the reorganization. This is hardly the kind of outcome that any rational business strategist would plan, yet it is typical in many organizational initiatives.

Time and again, I witness these types of difficulties in organizations as I am called in to help people improve production, solve intractable conflict, and assist them in figuring out where they are going next. As I move from one client to the next, I am struck by the similarities I find and by the presence of a number of core problems that present major challenges to everyone involved, challenges that must be met if the people and the organizations are to grow and prosper. These are challenges that consultants must surmount if they are to provide truly lasting assistance to their clients.

Unpredictable and Complex Human Behavior

The first challenge involves the complexity and predictability of human behavior in individuals, dyads, groups, and organizations of various size. The assumptions of logical positivism and rational analysis suggest strongly or even require us to believe and assert that behavior at any of these levels can be described, understood, predicted, and ultimately controlled. That stance, reassuring in many ways, demands that we collect and analyze data, identify problems, design interventions, and evaluate outcomes. Failure often remains unanticipated in the initial blush of optimism that launches any change management project. The stench and sting of a failed consultation engagement only force their way into the practitioner's awareness as an initiative unfolds catastrophically and proceeds to take everyone by surprise. The usual suspects identified as the causes of the trouble are resistance in the members of the target organization and unanticipated side effects of the change process. In reality, the trouble most often resides in models of individual and organizational behavior that are overly simplified.

Let us assume that a careful analysis of a large modern organization would demonstrate that there are hundreds of thousands if not millions of variables that contribute in some way to the success or failure of the enterprise. If we further assume that many of these variables interact in both observable and nonobservable ways, we can begin to understand that true prediction and control are elusive. In the previous case example, Ann proved much more able to predict her near-term future than I. Although her dismissal did not catch me by complete surprise, I did believe that she and her team had fixed many of the problems in their operation and were on the way to a much higher and more consistent level of performance. I understood that she was experiencing difficulties with some of her colleagues, but I remained completely unaware that they were organizing to have her fired. Similarly, Ann knew that aspects of her behavior contributed to the problems she experienced in job settings. Despite this awareness, she consistently struggled and often failed in the moment to either know what she was doing wrong or to change her approach even when she did have a fundamental grasp of what she needed to do. The complex underlying organization and psychodynamics of her behavior in her interactions with Stephen and other colleagues remained elusive at best and completely hidden from her view at worst. Consultants are called on to operate effectively with clients in these convoluted, unpredictable, and sometimes unknowable situations, and our training, conceptual models, and professional skill are often insufficient in the face of a chaotic organizational landscape. I have come to believe that only the development of true wisdom in both consultants and clients will enable them to cope effectively with the complex, unstructured, and ever-changing world of modern organizations.

INFLUENCE OF PSYCHODYNAMIC PROCESSES AND STRUCTURES

A second challenge, closely related to the first, involves the degree to which both conscious observable and unconscious invisible psychodynamic processes and structures influence behavior in individuals, dyads, groups, and organizations. Ann and Stephen's case illustrates this issue. Over the course of several coaching sessions before the debacle described earlier, Ann revealed to me that she played a unique role in her family. Her father treasured and encouraged her intellectual development. Indeed, she successfully pursued much higher levels of education than any of her siblings. She viewed herself as her father's favorite, and she thought that her best skills were very much like his. However, her relationships with her birth mother and her stepmother from her father's second marriage were stormy at best. These important women in her life were described as critical, unpredictable, and dangerous in the sense that she never knew when they would attack her verbally. In our session described briefly in the opening case vignette, we talked about the trouble she often encountered in working with Stephen. I asked her of whom he reminded her. "My mother," she blurted out without hesitation and in complete surprise. Subsequent discussions illuminated the degree to which Stephen truly did share many personality and interpersonal style traits with her mother. During these dialogues, Ann began to recognize that she often behaved with Stephen as if he were her mother, despite the reality. She was able to identify that these were the worst times between them and that their interactions at those times were characterized by open, bitter conflicts in which they called each other names; exchanged mutual taunts and sometimes threats; and then retreated into a detached isolation from each other accompanied by uneasiness, guilt, shame, smoldering resentment, and an absence of any mutual effort to identify and solve the organization's problems.

The point here is that both of these otherwise smart, talented, and committed professionals had evolved a pattern of behavior at work that was highly destructive. Neither of them truly knew why they acted in that way, nor could they predict when the vicious pattern would emerge and transport them to a place neither of them wanted or intended to go. Both suffered significantly from their troubles, and the organization consistently underperformed to their embarrassment and their supervisors' and customers' constant frustration. The unconscious dynamics proved elusive until the coaching process started, and change, although greatly desired by both of them, had been truly impossible until then. If individuals have such difficulty mastering these dimensions of behavior, how then are organizations that are structured and operated on the assumption that they are completely rational and predictable entities to cope with these unseen yet very real influences?

CREATIVE ASPIRATIONS AND REGRESSIVE PROCESSES

The third challenge flows logically from the first two. Ann and Stephen's case illustrates a major individual and organizational paradox operating in organizations. Everyone involved in the situation experienced a humiliating failure in which the people and the specific subunit as a whole routinely and with chaotic unpredictability regressed into a suboptimal state of performance. They demonstrated that they were mostly powerless to change the course of their regressive behavior, even when they knew what was happening. Simultaneously, each manager espoused the conscious motivation and values associated with the desire to pursue creativity, growth, freedom, and choice for him- or herself and for the organization as a whole. Individuals and organizations can ill afford this "escape from freedom," a pattern described by Eric Fromm (1941) in his classic with the same title, in a world that moves ever more rapidly and demands more from each of us with every passing day.

Business books, magazines, and journals routinely call on leaders and managers to be courageous champions of change and progress. Indeed, the modern lore of leadership virtually worships the person who steps into a managerial role and proceeds to turn around an organization in trouble. Almost no other pattern of behavior so ensures promotional opportunities and rewards. And yet, every consultant knows that the majority of managers are merely stewards of the status quo. If they stretch at all, they reach for the safe, incremental step that produces no real change in the homeostatic state of the enterprise. If they aim at all, they set their sights low, knowing that they are most likely to "succeed" by not producing spectacular failure. Yet, organizations and their people constantly yearn for and need leadership that will push them to new levels of creativity and growth. Investors, analysts, and other stakeholders increasingly demand extraordinary performance on a routine basis. I believe that enterprises and people who solve the paradox of creative aspirations versus regressive results will consistently outperform those that do not.

INABILITY TO INFLUENCE HUMAN AND ORGANIZATIONAL BEHAVIOR

A fourth challenge for consultants coping with these other problems resides in our realistic ability to influence behavior in individuals and organizations. To be sure, we have learned a number of hard-won technical lessons over the past 50 years of practical efforts to change the status quo. We have relentlessly pursued innovative techniques and concepts in the desire to help. Everyone that I know in the field professes frustration when their interventions do not result in the desired change. At a recent professional meeting, a group of colleagues and I mutually and quietly acknowledged the gut-wrenching anxiety we experience whenever we are invited into a new consulting engagement. The work is demanding, difficult, and often produces disastrous results.

Recently, I had the privilege of watching part of a 4-day workshop being delivered by a highly competent facilitator from a fairly well-known company. Thirty-five people sat in a room set up classroom style and listened intently to a lecture that focused on the importance of and methods to change their behavior for themselves and for the sponsoring corporation. They were engaged fully and working hard as individuals and as a class. The cost of the workshop was approximately $40,000 plus hotel, travel, and meals for each participant. The event was part of a long-term change initiative supported by the highest levels of leadership in the corporation, who had themselves been the first group through the workshop. The company had already spent several million dollars on the project over several years and put thousands of employees through the workshops.

Over lunch, I had the opportunity to discuss the workshop with one of the participants. He told me that he had been sent by his supervisor, who had attended an identical intervention conducted by the same consulting company at a different location 3 months before the one we were discussing.

"I was tremendously impressed by how the experience changed my boss," he said.

"What did you notice?" I asked.

"He delegated much more often. He seemed to really want to trust our whole team. He controlled his angry outbursts well, so that we had more opportunity to talk about what was going on in our business unit. Everyone felt a lot better."

"Pretty impressive gains from a 4-day workshop," I replied.

"I only hope that he can hold onto them."

"What do you mean?"

"After about 2 weeks, his old behaviors began to creep back in. Last week it was as though he never attended in the first place. I hope I can avoid that when I get back home. I hope I can maintain the changes I feel I really want and need to make."

Further candid discussion with this honest man revealed that many attendees reported similar experiences with their own colleagues. In the atmosphere of the formal workshop where the behavioral norms and contingencies supported change, participants could and did demonstrate the ability to modify highly problematic behaviors. In fact, in some situations in which the majority of members in a business unit attended, they were often able to clear up long-standing problems and commit to new ways of interacting. However, once back at their offices, many, if not most, participants reported the same tendency to slide into the previous behavioral patterns despite their recognition that these patterns were ineffective and even harmful.

What then was the sponsoring company getting for its tremendous investment in time and money? In subsequent discussions with other corporate staff, the long-term outcome of the whole consultation effort seemed to depend on maintaining the presence of the consultants who continued to press the various business units to maintain their commitments to behavioral change. The original intent of the change project was never to create a permanent dependency on the consultation firm; however, that dependency was becoming readily apparent to many people in the firm. The clients themselves really wanted to change the nature of their organization and the ways in which their managers and staff interacted. They wanted an organization that valued people, encouraged innovation and creativity, and rewarded leadership and risk taking, outcomes that any management or consultation team could readily endorse. However, this example demonstrates that our ability as consultants to deliver long-term outcomes for organizations and people often is compromised by the nature of human behavior as manifested by individuals, groups, or whole organizations and by our own unwillingness to discuss the complexity and difficulties of change with our clients.

Imagine, if you will, a conversation with a potential client in which you tell him or her that the likely outcomes of the project under discussion are that the company will spend a lot of money, realize some short-term gains, make many people unhappy and defensive, and have no long-term impact on whether they will make money. What consultant in his or her right mind would do that? And yet, in the absence of any controlled variable research done with identical interventions and with the presence of a plethora of articles expressing reservations about what we are doing, it seems as though these are precisely the kinds of meetings and discussions we ought to be having with clients. The lessons of change management projects focus our attention on how difficult they are to conduct and how hard the outcomes are to predict.

"SHADOW SIDE" OF HUMAN BEHAVIOR

This brings us to the fifth challenge, the "shadow side" of human behavior. The case of Ann and Stephen clearly illustrates the complexities faced by people trying to change themselves. Even when they are motivated to commit time and energy to the process, and are willing to do the difficult work involved, they can still fail. The power and structure of Ann and Stephen's interactions made it difficult for them to do what they both said they wanted publicly to me and to each other. Even after they began to understand the structure of their relationship and they successfully practiced behaving differently in my presence, they reenacted their long-standing pattern whenever either one momentarily turned away from their newer behaviors. They had not yet developed the ability to stop themselves at the beginning or in the middle of a vicious regressive slide and maneuver to safer and more virtuous ground. Although I had hopes that they would eventually be able to, they clearly never got the opportunity. After over 2 years of poor performance and problems, their supervisor simply pulled the plug on Ann and on the change initiative.

Stephen clearly had no conscious desire to behave in a way that reinforced Ann's previous experiences with her family. He simply did his best. Ann, frustrated and at her wit's end in trying to improve the situation, turned to me for coaching and began the process of understanding what she contributed to the situation. She had made concrete changes in her behavior based on her growing knowledge of herself, but these came too little and too late for her customers, her boss, and his supervisor.

I firmly believe that consultants must have at least a rudimentary understanding of the nature and extent to which unconscious forces shape behavior for individuals, groups, and organizations. I also believe that consultants must be able to manage their own emotional and psychodynamic responses to clients and change initiatives and to assist their clients in doing the same. In situations in which I have seen individual clients and teams of leaders willing and able to explore these dimensions of a change process as well as the technical aspects of what they are trying to accomplish, I have observed both accomplishment of the specific goals of the change strategy and the maintenance of the gains made over several years. The ability to weave the knowledge and skills of psychodynamic and emotional management into the ongoing challenges and tasks of leading, managing, and changing organizational systems greatly adds to the likelihood that any consultation project will succeed. The reverse is also true. Namely, in the absence of this ability, long-term outcomes and even short-term gains will prove ephemeral in change initiatives with organizations in conflict and at various stages of chaotic regression.

LACK OF TRAINING

The sixth challenge for consultants derives directly from the previous point. Very few people in the change management industry have formal training or experience in helping individuals, dyads, or groups to learn about and change behaviors influenced by the shadow side. The best training and experience available can be obtained in programs preparing mental health professionals to work with people with severe emotional and interpersonal problems. However, these programs rarely, if ever, provide their students with the experience of applying the knowledge and skills they learn with people not experiencing such problems. They also rarely consider that most of people's lives are experienced in relationships within their workplace. Although the consulting field has been blessed with a significant number of mental health practitioners who have made major contributions to theory and practice, most of the field still lacks even the most rudimentary knowledge in these areas.

I am not arguing that consultants must be trained as mental health professionals to be successful. On the contrary, I do not think that the majority of therapists could work successfully as consultants or coaches in organizational contexts. There are many attitudes, values, behavioral patterns, and personality traits that would make it difficult for them to adapt their ideas and methods to the typical corporate setting. Rather, I am arguing that the average consultant who is working closely in coaching individuals, dyads, or management teams can benefit greatly from an increased knowledge of the unconscious dimensions and processes that influence behavior regardless of the setting. An increase in this knowledge can radically improve the ability of consultants to maneuver in difficult, conflict-ridden situations, and therefore can help clients produce better long-term results both for themselves and their companies.

LACK OF RESEARCH

The last challenge derives directly from the previous six. There is a true absence of good, controlled-variable research that demonstrates the successful application of clinically based methods and theories to changing the behavior of individuals and groups in organizational applications. To be sure, there has been a great deal written, and the field is replete with case examples and illustrations of these techniques being applied. However, most of this material concentrates on interventions with individual client organizations, and no true effort is made to provide control conditions for the experiments. No comparison can be made with the mental health field in which thousands of such studies have been conducted and the results critically reviewed. We have no consulting interventions that compare to systematic desensitization of phobias, the cognitive–behavioral treatment of affective disorders, or other forms of empirically validated treatments. We cannot reasonably discuss the likely outcomes or side effects of open space technology, process reengineering, organizational assessment, downsizing, or even coaching for individuals or teams. We can say that "in our experience, some case examples suggest," or "there is some empirical evidence that supports," weak endorsements of our efforts and suggestions at best.

Nevertheless, large numbers of individuals and organizations will continue to turn to us for help. The stresses, strains, and problems associated with trying to work constructively and productively with groups of human beings will always confound and frustrate leaders and members of work teams. The critical dependence of companies on the effective performance of key individuals will be even higher in the current era of lean, mean organizations with minimum redundancy and less capacity to tolerate even temporary lapses in performance. So, until our rather slim base of university research scientists interested in these problems and issues can produce the necessary studies, practitioners will continue to muddle through in the complex and wondrous world of organizational consultation and executive coaching.

Goals and Structure of This Book

Given the challenges described above and the complexity illuminated in the case of Ann and Stephen, we are left with a significant gap between the growing understanding of the importance of complexity theory, human behavior, and the psychodynamic aspects of organizational and managerial life and the lack of practical guidance for how consultants or coaches can and should work with executives and managers on issues, performance problems, and dimensions of human behavior that have shadow components. This book is dedicated to narrowing that gap. The goals to be pursued in the following chapters include:

- Provide practical and useful concepts to help consultants or coaches improve their awareness and understanding of how chaotic processes and structures and psychodynamic issues and problems can influence organizational and executive behavior and performance.
- Explore some concrete methods for using these concepts in coaching activities designed to change the behavior of executives and help them develop more human wisdom to apply in their work.
- Expand the applicability of complexity theory and psychodynamic theory and methods derived from therapeutic experience into the realm of everyday human life.

The plan of the book flows from these goals. The next several chapters explore aspects of several consultation cases and how to use them to understand some conceptual frameworks that apply systems, complexity, and psychodynamic theory and principles to organizational and managerial issues. These chapters also illuminate how methods and techniques developed largely in clinical settings can be applied in efforts to coach executives and management teams. The final chapters of the book take up specific problems and methods associated with working with patterns of emotions, thoughts, defenses, and conflicts experienced by managers in organizational life. I hope that when you have finished exploring these materials you will be better prepared to both understand and work constructively with the chaotic, shadow side of individual and organizational behavior in current and future consultation and coaching projects.

Systems and Psychodynamics: Concepts for Coaches

2

Modern approaches to organization development and coaching practice are primarily based on the conceptual foundations of general systems theory as it is applied to human organizations and behavior (Beckhard, 1969; French & Bell, 1990; Goodman and Associates, 1982; Kilburg, 1995; Lawrence & Lorsch, 1969; Lippitt, 1969). Interventions based on this approach most often include organizational diagnosis, process consultation, sociotechnical and structural changes, team building, coaching, and other training technologies. The emphasis is always on trying to make the organization and its various components more rational, supportive, and effective in enabling the managers and other employees to do their work. Experienced consultants also know that even the most well-designed interventions and sophisticated systems analyses can fail in the face of protracted resistance to change by the members of an organization. Many organizational development (OD) practitioners and coaches find the insights and methods offered by modern psychodynamic theory useful for extending their appreciation of the complexity of organizational and executive behavior and for supporting their work in highly resistant and emotionally charged situations. Little consideration of the psychodynamic issues and approaches is given in standard OD textbooks, yet a number of scholars and practitioners have pushed the limits of understanding and application of psychodynamic theory in organizational practice (Baum, 1987; Czander, 1993; Diamond, 1993; Hirschhorn,

1988; Hunt & McCollom, 1994; Kernberg, 1998; Kets de Vries & Miller, 1987; Levinson, 1972, 1981, 1991; Schwartz, 1990).

What follows is an overview of the basic concepts of general systems and psychodynamic theories applied to the practice of executive coaching and organization development. This information is applied to several case examples to illustrate how both systems and psychodynamic approaches can be integrated by the practicing coach or consultant in real-world applications. Without such a foundation, I believe that anyone working as a coach or consultant with managers in organizations will soon become hopelessly lost and confused while trying to assess what is truly happening in this most complex and difficult world.

Figure 2.1 presents a 17-dimensional model that illustrates the complexity any consultant faces when working in an organization. The dimensions around the perimeter of the circle represent the major components of general systems theory interwoven with the principal elements of modern psychodynamic theory. Table 2.1 lists these dimensions in the psychodynamic and systems categories. Figure 2.1 also demonstrates how these dimensions interact with and flow through the various levels of organizations from the individuals who constitute them to the groups, work groups, organizational substructures, and organizations as a whole. In modern megaorganizations that are

FIGURE 2.1

A 17-Dimensional Model of Psychodynamic and Organizational Systems

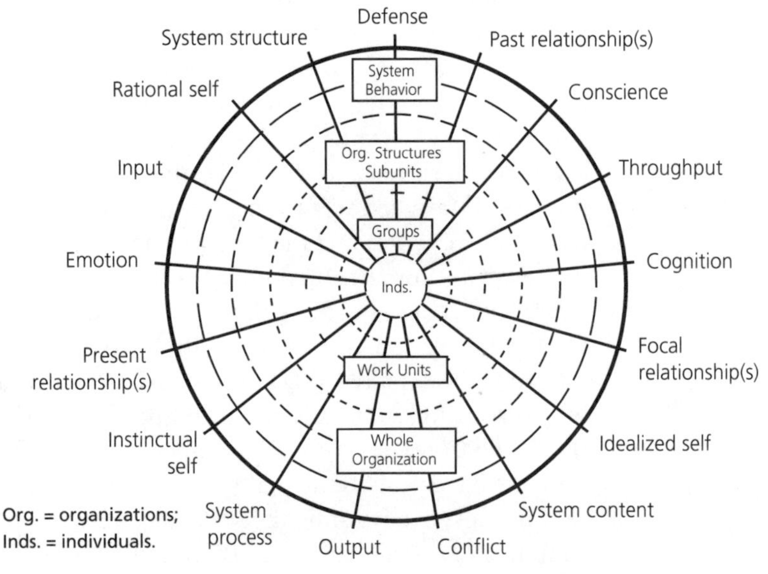

Org. = organizations; Inds. = individuals.

TABLE 2.1

Key Elements of Psychodynamic and Systems Models

Psychodynamic elements	Systems elements
Rational self	System structure(s)
Instinctual self	System process(es)
Conscience	System content(s)
Internalized self	Input elements
Conflict	Throughput elements
Defense	Output elements
Emotion	
Cognition	
Past relationship(s)	
Present relationship(s)	
Focal relationship	

comprised of hundreds of thousands and sometimes millions of people, there can be myriad levels of structure with which a consultant must be concerned. Figure 2.1 illustrates the need to be alert to each dimension because it shows that they are all constantly interacting and dramatically influencing the events of organizational life. The balance of this book demonstrates that the figure is a tremendous simplification of the actual complexity at work in organizational life.

General Systems Elements

The principal elements of general systems theory have been well described by Kuhn (1974), S. G. Miller (1972), and Von Bertalanffy (1968) and are well known to most organizational practitioners. These elements are applied in nearly every modern textbook on organizational behavior and management (Bedian & Zammuto, 1991; Kreitner, 1992; Schermerhorn, Hunt, & Osborn, 1994). For the purposes of this book, I have compressed the model into six major dimensions, comprising the structure, process, and content of any system and their input, throughput, and output components (see Figures 2.2 and 2.3). As coaches and consultants we are constantly trying to unravel these dimensions in organizations through our diagnostic and intervention work.

As recommended by Levinson (1972), Lawler, Nadler, and Cammann (1980) and others, consultants are required to assess and reach a sophisticated understanding of the organizations in which they work.

FIGURE 2.2

Basic System Components of Structure, Process, and Content

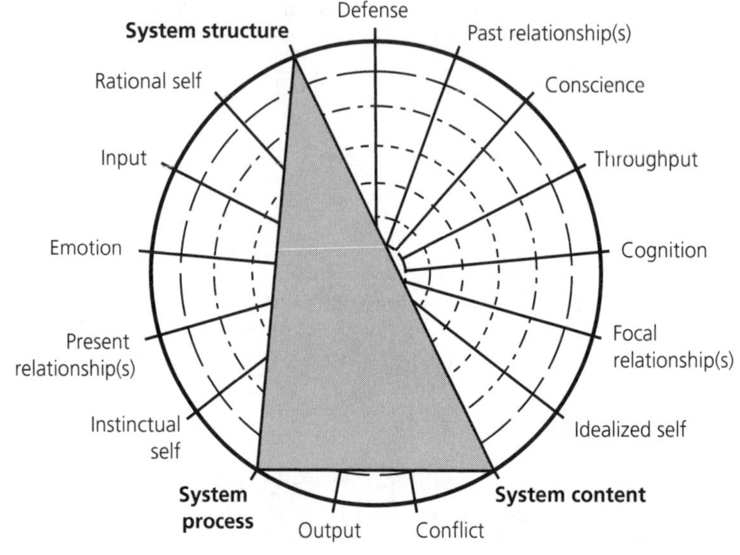

The six major dimensions of general systems focus attention on key components of organizations and allow consultants to structure what would otherwise be incomprehensible. Table 2.2 shows this complexity by providing an array of elements of formal and informal organizational structure in a matrix that would allow a practitioner to map any of these elements onto the input, throughput, or output systems of any organization. Structural elements range from tasks to be done to roles and jobs for individuals and finally to the missions, values, and cultures of organizations. Traditional elements of structure such as hierarchy, departmentation, networks, degree of centralization or decentralization, and characteristics of the organizational or environmental niche and fit are also displayed. Informal structure includes elements such as interests, relationships, favor or debt structures, political alliances, and various forms and types of meetings. These elements are joined through their structural focus, which starts inside the individual and moves through groups, organizational units, organizations, and into the environment external to the organization at local, regional, national, international, and global levels.

Table 2.3 provides a similar overview of the key elements of organizational processes in the input–throughput–output matrix. The ele-

FIGURE 2.3

Traditional Systems Model Showing Input, Throughput, and Output Elements

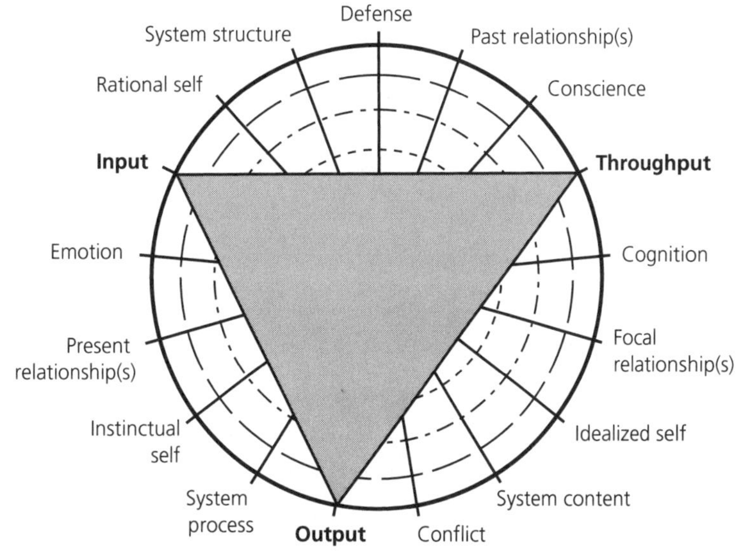

ments include leadership, followership, decision making, goal setting, communication, transaction (in the sense of general systems terminology, meaning an exchange of matter or energy), motivation, information systems, control processes, resource allocation, socialization, human resources processes, resource acquisition, organization, change, and life cycles. These terms are abstract, and they do little justice to the complexity of the processes involved in running a modern manufacturing company or university health system. Nevertheless, the table shows the complexity of many of the process elements with which we are commonly concerned.

Similarly, Table 2.4 shows an array of some of the key elements of the content of organizational systems. The titles of many traditional departments of institutions are listed, such as research and development, engineering, manufacturing, marketing, purchasing, human resources, finance, safety, planning, maintenance, communications, facilities management, general management, and transportation. Each represents a composite of many other elements that comprise the whole, and any one or all can represent a stiff challenge to the consultant on assignment.

TABLE 2.2

Key Elements In Organizational Structure

Element	Input systems	Throughput systems	Output systems
Formal structure			
Detectors[a]			
Effectors[a]			
Selectors[a]			
Tasks			
Knowledge, skills, abilities			
Roles			
Jobs			
Rules			
Standards			
Norms			
Policies			
Procedures			
Mission(s)			
Plans/Goal(s)			
Values			
Culture			
Hierarchy			
Networks			
Meetings			
Schedules			
Departmentation (Levels/Work and task groups)			
Differentiation/Integration (Centralization/Decentralization)			
Environmental and economic niche			
Informal structure			
Interests			
Relationships			
Favors/Debts			
Mutual support			
Political/Organizational alliances			
Meetings			
Structural focus			
Intraindividual			
Individual			
Group			
Organizational unit			
Intraorganizational			
Whole organizational			
Interorganizational			
Local			
Regional			
National			
International			
Global			

[a]Kuhn, A. (1974). *The Logic of Social Systems.* San Francisco: Jossey-Bass.

Psychodynamic Elements

Psychodynamic theory has evolved over the past century into a flexible and useful tool for psychologists, consultants, and coaches. In the proper hands, it can provide complex explanations for the motivations and behaviors of individuals, groups, and families and also assistance in resolving an ever-increasing number of human problems. It is impossible in the confines of this chapter and even within this book to provide a thorough description and explanation of psychodynamic theory. However, the 17-dimensional model allows us to focus on some major elements that can be useful to consultants and coaches. What follows is a summary of these elements based on the work of Davanloo (1980), S. Freud (1964), C. S. Hall and Lindzey (1970), and many others and as summarized and adapted by Czander (1993), Langs (1973, 1974), and others. I elaborate on these basic concepts in subsequent chapters and illustrate how they can be integrated into executive coaching.

Figure 2.4 depicts the major psychological substructures identified by Sigmund Freud. In the figure I substitute the terms *rational self* for *ego, conscience* for *superego, instinctual self* for *id,* and *idealized self* for *ego ideal* to reduce the dependence on the psychoanalytic jargon that many professionals find to be unusable. Table 2.5 presents the organizing principles, primary methods of operation, and major goals for each substructure. Classic psychodynamic theory states that these structures exist within the mind of each human being and that their organizing principles or functions are different. The instinctual self is organized around the pleasure principle, and it seeks to reduce tension and to do what feels good. Its main goals are gratification and reduction of the pressure that results from evolutionary and biologically based drives and psychological and social needs. The rational self is organized by the reality principle, and it seeks what will lead a person to better adaptation in the world or solutions that will work either in the short or long term. Its goal is a person's survival in biological, social, and psychological terms. The conscience is organized by the moral principle, and it pushes the person to do what is right or what will avoid shame and guilt. Its goal is to help the person maintain social order and cohesion in his or her world. Finally, the idealized self contains the characteristics of role models and other important people experienced by a person and the unconscious and conscious fantasies concerning how the person would like to be experienced by others. It is organized along a continuum involving idealization at one end and devaluation on the other. The behavior of an individual's role models and other interpersonal experiences combined with elements from other people's values, thoughts, wishes, and ideals (that can be projected into an individual)

TABLE 2.3

Key Elements In Organizational Process

Element	Input systems	Throughput systems	Output systems
Leadership (visioning, power utilization, delegation, discipline, supervision, external monitoring, Mintzberg's roles)			
Followership (participation, loyalty, task analysis, and fulfillment)			
Problem solving/Decision making/Entrepreneurship (strategies, tactics, alignment/fit)			
Goal setting			
Succession management			
Communication (direction, content, distortion, disclosure, feedback, volume, timing)			
Transaction (exchanges of real energy, matter)			
Group process (addition/loss, conflict, deviance, morale, norms, values, harassment, discrimination, diversity, fight–flight, pairing, dependency)			

Motivation

Information and evaluation systems

Control processes
(policies, procedures, rules, standards, plans, roles, functions)

Resource allocation

Acculturation/Socialization
(modeling, transference, identification, internalization, education, training, learning)

Human resources processes

Resource acquisition and development

Organization

Change
(growth, decay, differentiation, integration, progressive independence, progressive centralization, revolution, evolution, development, adaptation, assimilation, accommodation, homeorhesis, homeostatis, equilibrium, emergence, causality, formality, chaos, nonlinear system change)

Life cycles
(products, markets, organizations, individuals, groups)

TABLE 2.4

Key Elements In Organizational Content

Element	Input systems	Throughput systems	Output systems
Research and development			
Engineering			
Manufacturing/Production/ Service delivery			
Marketing/Sales/Distribution			
Purchasing			
Human resources			
Finance/Accounting			
General management			
Planning			
Safety/Security			
Information systems			
Maintenance			
Communications			
Facilities management			
Transportation			

FIGURE 2.4

Classic Psychodynamic Structure of the Mind

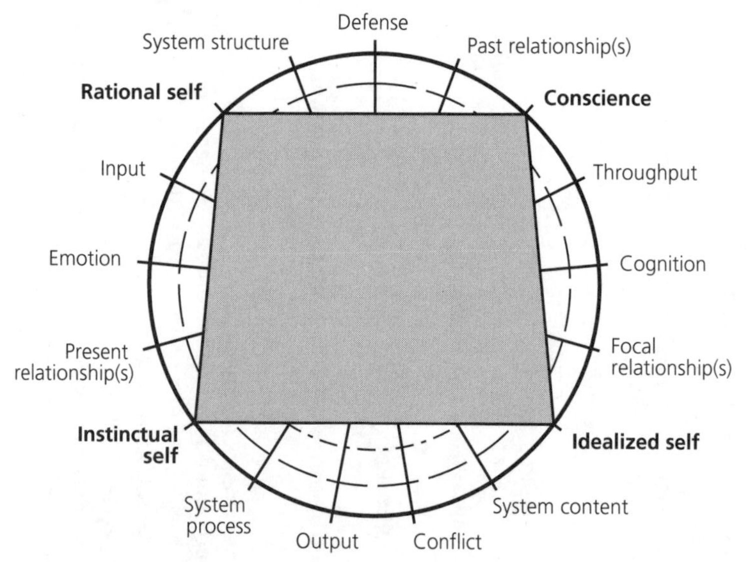

TABLE 2.5

Classic Psychodynamic Structure of the Mind

Element	Instinctual self (Id)	Rational self (Ego)	Conscience (Superego)	Internalized self (Ego ideal)
Organizing principle	Pleasure principle	Reality principle	Moral principle	Idealization–devaluation principle
Primary method of operation	Do what feels good or reduces tension	Do what works or what leads to better adaptation	Do what is right or what will avoid shame and guilt	Do what helps to live up or down to internal models and incorporated projections
Major goal	Gratification	Survival	Maintaining social order/cohesion	Striving

are brought into the idealized self by the individual either consciously, as in the hero worship of an admired figure, or unconsciously, as when we find ourselves saying or doing something that reminds us of someone whom we do not care to emulate. These parts of the idealized self are valued or devalued, and they are often used as standards against which people judge their worth as human beings. The goal of the idealized self is to provide a model of how the person should behave, live, and experience the self in the world. It is often used as an ally or target in the conflicts that emerge between the other parts of psychological structure.

It is easy to see how the internal structures identified here can conflict with each other, based on their organizing principles, methods of operation, and goals. Psychodynamic theory suggests that these conflicts can occur at the conscious or unconscious level and that the movement of people through their normal developmental cycles presents an enormous range of opportunities for such conflict to manifest itself. The emergence and existence of this conflict leads to much of the misery that human beings and their organizations experience.

Figure 2.5 presents a quadrangle comprised of four elements—conflict, defense, emotion, and cognition—first suggested by Davanloo (1980). The difficulties and tensions arising from an individual's efforts to manage his or her daily life and to surmount the challenges presented by the tasks of normal developmental cycles are addressed by the structures and in the ways described above. Table 2.6 illustrates the complexity of human conflicts in a matrix that identifies the content or issue that can start or drive a conflict and the focus of the conflict either on the tasks of external adaptation to the surrounding world or of internal adaptation to psychological lives. The table also demonstrates the types of conflict that can arise following Hilgard and Marquis's (cited in Kimble, 1961) categories: approach–approach, avoidance–avoidance, approach–avoidance, and multiple approach–avoidance. The contents or issues of conflicts can be varied and complex, ranging from external dangers to internal wishes, demands, emotions, mastery issues, achievement, attachment, separation, control, values, and change. The four psychological structures, following their own goals and organizing principles, can each adopt different positions on these issues leading to major problems in the individual's efforts to manage in the external or his or her internal world.

Table 2.7 presents a summary of many of the mechanisms of psychological defense and adaptation that have been identified so far (Conte & Plutchik, 1995; A. Freud, 1966; Valliant, 1977). Five levels of mechanisms are identified:

FIGURE 2.5

Internal Components of Psychodynamic Models

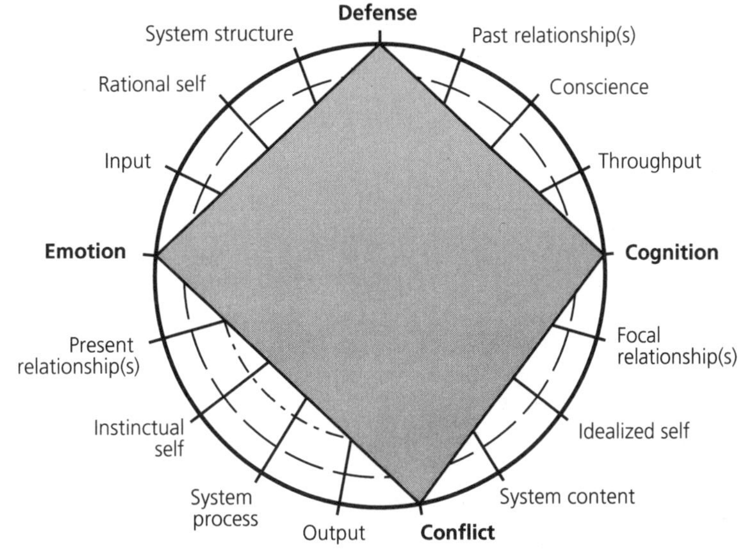

1. primitive mechanisms of denial, splitting, distortion, and delusional projection
2. immature mechanisms such as fantasy, projection, passive–aggressive behavior, acting out, dissociation, and derealization
3. neurotic mechanisms such as intellectualization, repression, reaction formation, displacement, dissociation, and detachment
4. mature mechanisms such as sublimation, altruism, suppression, anticipation, humor, curiosity, work, play, wisdom, and love
5. complex patterns of defenses and behaviors such as games, rituals, cultures, cognitive distortions, and psychodynamic patterns.

Analyzing data from the table suggests that there are three major purposes for these defenses: equilibration of the person's internal and external worlds; avoidance of pain, suffering, or psychological work on conflicts; and mastery of the internal and external world. Defenses also can be focused on emotions, wishes, conflicts, behaviors, other defenses, or particular events or memories.

TABLE 2.6

Types of Conflict Faced by Executives

Content/Issue	External adaptation				Internal adaptation			
	Approach–approach	Avoidance–avoidance	Approach–avoidance	Multiple approach–avoidance	Approach–approach	Avoidance–avoidance	Approach–avoidance	Multiple approach–avoidance
Dangers, trauma								
Wishes, impulses, drives, fantasies, inhibitions, aspirations, goals, objectives								
Demands, pressures, challenges								
Emotional responses								
Fear								
Anger								
Sadness								
Shame								
Joy								
Curiosity								
Surprise/Shock								
Sex								
Psychodynamic and adaptation themes								
Feeding–devouring, being devoured, sensory incorporation, voyeurism								
Mobility–mastery–achievement, environmental manipulation, autonomy/omnipotence, physical confidence, display, exhibitionism, helplessness, powerlessness, control, knowledge, skills, abilities								
Attachment–trust interpersonal affiliation, relatedness, love, symbiosis, unity, identification, morale, merger/partnership, envy, jealousy, self–not/self, good me–bad me, internaliza-tion, idealization, dependence, birth, engulfment, mirroring, narcissistic perfection, grandiose self, ideal object								
Change–emergence, birth, death, differentiation, integration,								

transitional objects

Organizational issues. Structure–restructure, processes, contents (products, services, people, policies, procedures, technology, markets, strategy, capital, land, factories, other resources and assets), power, politics, hierarchy, ideology, culture, climate, leadership, followership, stage of development, timing, location

Group dynamics. Membership, boundaries, stage of development, limits, norms, deviance, conformity, roles, jobs, tasks, clarity, leadership, followership, inclusion, exclusion, power, influence, control, communication, problem solving, conflict management, diversity, diversity management

Interpersonal relationships. Personal, professional, dimensions (control–accountability, authority, dexterity, responsibility, emotion–approval, bonding, fairness, respect, satisfaction, trust, operation–accuracy of information, availability of resources, capacity, ease of operation, knowledge, responsiveness, structure–flexibility, formality, openness)[a]

Legal environment. Laws, regulations, case law, contracts, torts, liability

Spiritual issues. Morals, ethics, moral reasoning and philosophy, religion and religious beliefs and influences

Special issues. Boundaries, limit setting and maintenance, creating conflict, deliberate deviance, disobedience, acting out

[a]This material was adapted from *Relationship Dynamics: Theory and Analysis,* by J. Musgrave and M. Anniss, 1996, New York: Free Press.

TABLE 2.7

Mechanisms of Psychological Defense and Adaptation

	Goal/Purpose			Focus					
Type	Equilibration	Avoidance	Mastery	Emotion	Wish/desire	Conflict	Behavior	Defense	Event/memory
1. Primitive mechanisms (psychosis, dreams, normal childhood)									
Denial									
Splitting									
Distortion									
Delusional projection									
2. Immature mechanisms (severe depression, personality disorders, adolescence)									
Fantasy. Schizoid withdrawal, denial through fantasy									
Projection. Projective identification									
Hypochondriasis									
Passive–aggressive behavior. Masochism, turning against the self									
Acting out. Compulsive delinquency, criminality, sadism, perversion									
Dissociation. Extreme									
Derealization									
3. Neurotic mechanisms (common in everyone)									
Intellectualization. Isolation, obsessive behavior, compulsive behavior, undoing, rationalization									
Repression. Selective inattention									
Reaction formation									
Displacement. Conversion symptoms, phobias									

Dissociation. Neurotic denial
Detachment

4. Mature mechanisms (common in healthy adults)
   - Sublimation
   - Altruism
   - Suppression
   - Anticipation
   - Humor
   - Curiosity
   - Work
   - Play
   - Love
5. Other mechanisms (can include combinations of multiple defenses and behaviors)
   - Rites, rituals, myths, procedures, pastimes, hobbies, avocations, culture
   - Games[a]
   - Frigid woman/Impotent man, Let's you and him/her fight, addict, Why don't you—Yes but, psychiatry, lawyer, debtor, polysurgery, Rapo, Schlemiel, Why does this have to happen to me?, There I go again, If it weren't for you
   - Cognitive distortions. Beck, Burns, and others
   - Twisted thinking. All or nothing, overgeneralization, mental filters, discounting the positive, jumping to conclusions, magnification/catastrophizing, minimization, emotional reasoning, shouldering, labeling, personalization and blame

[a]Berne, E. (1964). *Games People Play: The Basic Handbook of Transactional Analysis.* New York: Guilford.

Note: From *Adaptation to Life*, by G. E. Valliant, 1977, Boston: Little, Brown. Copyright 1997 by Little, Brown. Adapted by permission.

Continuing with the third element of this part of the model, Table 2.8 presents an overview of the organization and types of human emotion following the work of Tomkins (1962–1963) and Lazarus (1991). The matrix incorporates the goal-congruent and goal-incongruent emotional subtypes of Lazarus and most of the major types of emotions identified by these two theoreticians. Anger, fright or anxiety, guilt or shame, sadness, envy or jealousy, disgust, happiness or joy, pride, relief, hope, compassion, aesthetic emotions, and sexual emotions are identified. The table identifies the goals or purposes of these emotions as involved in the tasks of expression or environmental adaptation, helping the person be aware of emotion or to learn, and the work of psychological or behavioral defense. The focus or locus of origin for emotions can be in conflicts, defenses, relationships, wishes, desires, fantasies, behaviors, events, or memories. Although the table represents a severe undervaluation of the complexity and subtlety of how humans experience and express emotion, it allows us to begin to appreciate the range and diversity of how humans operate in this realm.

Table 2.9 presents an overview of the last element in this quadrangle, the organization and types of human cognition. Psychological, social, biological, and organizational research on the various dimensions and types of cognition is deep and offers a wide array of conceptual and operational approaches. Table 2.9 identifies some types of cognitive operations from Piaget's operations through logic, problem solving, decision making, judgment, creativity, and so forth. As with Table 2.8, the matrix identifies the goals of the cognitive type as focused on the tasks of mental expression or environmental adaptation, of helping the person be aware of mental operations or to learn, and as the work of psychological or behavioral defense. The focus or locus of origin for cognition also can be in conflicts, defenses, relationships, wishes, desires, fantasies, behaviors, events, or memories.

The inner world of the person is organized into complex and varied patterns that are expressed in and through the different social relationships engaged in during an average day. Consultants and coaches are primarily concerned with people in their roles and relationships at work, yet we see in the elements of the model that the inner experience of any one of the individuals whom we try to help is characterized by a rich landscape of structures and processes. Awareness of conflicts, defenses, and the emotional and cognitive elements of human experience is vital for consultants and coaches, because the origins of most forms of resistance to change can be found in the internal interaction of these elements of the model. Familiarity with these components and how they interact with the components of organizational systems can help practitioners to fully implement intervention strategies in work with clients. They are also key to successful coaching activities with

TABLE 2.8

Organization and Types of Human Emotion

Type	Goal/ Purpose			Focus/Locus or origin					
	Expression or adaptation	Awareness or learning	Defense	Conflict	Defense	Relationship	Wish/desire/ fantasy	Behavior	Event/ memory
Goal incongruent.									
Experienced as negative.[a]									
Anger									
Fright/anxiety									
Guilt/shame									
Sadness									
Envy/jealousy									
Disgust									
Goal congruent.									
Positive and problematic									
Happy/joy									
Pride									
Relief									
Hope									
Compassion									
Aesthetic emotions									
Sexual emotions									

[a]Lazarus, R. S. (1991). *Emotion and Adaptation.* Oxford, England: Oxford University Press. Tompkins, 1962.

TABLE 2.9

Organization and Types of Human Cognition

Type	Goal/ Purpose			Focus/Locus or origin							
	Expression or adaptation	Awareness or learning	Defense	Conflict	Defense	Relationship	Wish/desire/ goal/need	Behavior	Imagination/ dreams	Event/ memory
Core Elements of Cognition										
Reactions[a]										
Concrete operations[a]										
Formal operations[a]										
Cognitive complexity[b]										
Imagining										
Reflecting										
Wondering										
Ruminating										
Calculating										
Judging										
Hypothesis formation										
Assumptions										
Guesses										
Introspection										
Regarding										
Comprehension										
Insight										
Logic										
Problem solving										
Decision making										

Subsidiary Elements of Cognition

- Images
- Ideas
- Whims
- Notions
- Impressions
- Memories
- Convictions
- Beliefs
- Attitudes
- Principles
- Values
- Opinions
- Goals
- Objectives
- Theories
- Fictions
- Fantasies
- Doctrines
- Policies
- Rules
- Philosophies
- Concepts

---

[a]Piaget, J. (1971). *Biology and Knowledge: An Essay on the Relations Between Organic Regulations and Cognitive Processes*. Chicago: University of Chicago Press.

[b]Jaques, E., & Clement, S. D. (1991). *Executive Leadership: A Practical Guide to Managing Complexity.* Arlington, VA: Cason Hall.

leaders and managers. Just how important they are will become more clear in subsequent chapters.

Figure 2.6 presents this last set of components of the model. In it are summaries of some of Davanloo's (1980) considerations and illustrations of people's interpersonal worlds as being comprised of past and present relationships, along with the particular focal relationships in which a person may be engaged at any time. Table 2.10 presents a summary of types of relationships arrayed against the past, present, and focal categories, which produces a matrix of human relationships by type and time. The matrix also presents adaptive issues; relationships can be organized around these issues, and they can include the conflict, defense, emotional, and cognitive elements described above. These types of relationships transcend those usually found in the workplace such as supervisor, subordinate, colleague, teammate, and competitor and include the types of relationships that people experience as they mature in families, churches, schools, communities, and other organizations. Relationships at work often include aspects of these other relationships, as when a supervisor is experienced by a subordinate as behaving in a parental fashion.

FIGURE 2.6

Types of Relationships: Past, Present, and Focal

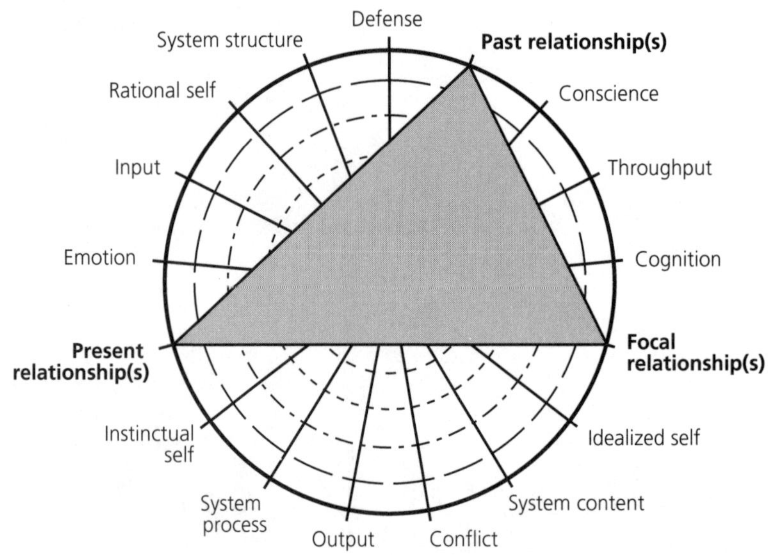

TABLE 2.10

Types and Characteristics of Human Relationships

Type	Adaptive	Past	Present	Focal
Parent				
Child				
Sibling				
Spouse				
Lover				
Other family				
Friend				
Playmate				
Classmate				
Competitor/enemy				
Teammate				
Teacher/mentor/advisor/role models				
Student				
Leader/superior				
Follower/subordinate				
Colleague				
Consultants				
Other helpers. Doctor, lawyer, therapist				
Religious figures. Priest, mullah, rabbi, nun, monk, etc.				
Other professional roles and jobs				

Figure 2.7 presents an interactive diagram of all 17 elements of the model. Each element is shown as capable of interacting with every other element. The purpose of the figure is to demonstrate that consultants or coaches have many variables from which to choose and on which to focus. This model is by no means inclusive of everything of which consultants or coaches should be aware or of the dimensions along which to work. However, the model should illustrate several things. First, the consulting and coaching world is complex and rich in dimensions and meanings that can be useful in helping people and organizations. Second, when choosing dimensions along which to work in an organization or with a particular coaching client, coaches must be aware that we are not choosing other dimensions. This act of choice does not mean that these other dimensions cease to operate in the people and organizations with whom we are working. Third, the types of interventions selected to use in a consulting or coaching assignment will reflect the dimensions chosen to emphasize and our comfort and competence in designing and implementing any one of these techniques or approaches.

Table 2.11 presents an overview of technostructural and human process interventions adapted from Case, Vandenberg, and Meredith

FIGURE 2.7

Dimensional Model Fully Connected

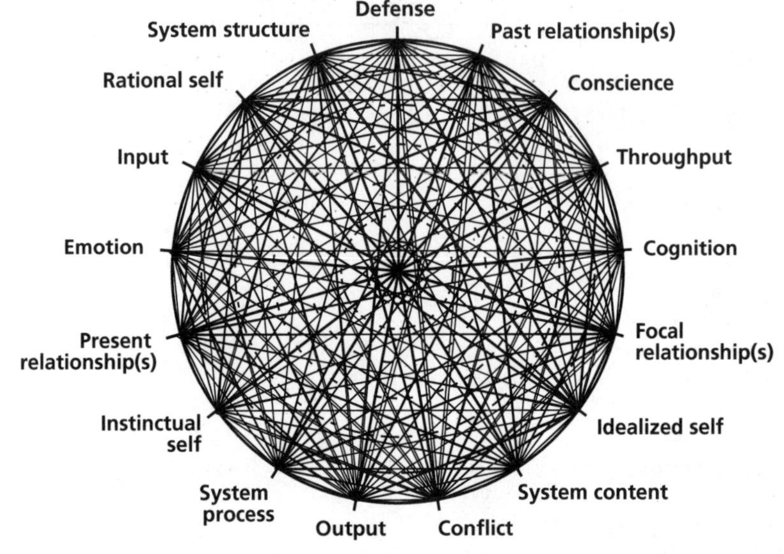

(1990). The matrix demonstrates that technostructural interventions usually are focused either on the whole organization or on its subunits or groups, whereas human process interventions tend to focus on individuals or groups. More information about specific coaching methods will be provided in subsequent chapters, but readers must keep in mind that coaching is evolving as a subdiscipline of organization development, and new techniques and methods are being invented daily. Organizations and their demands continue to press for coaching attention through the needs and problems of individual or group clients. By examining the 17-dimensional model and the intervention matrix, coaches can begin to understand how professionals trained in psychoanalysis, engineering, accounting, psychology, business, economics, sociology, business, organization development, and any number of other disciplines can offer meaningful advice and interventions in the operations of organizations. Coaches can also appreciate the complexity of selecting the right consultant facing any manager who wants to move an organization or an executive into a more effective mode of functioning.

TABLE 2.11

Types of OD Interventions

Technostructural interventions		Human process interventions	
Entire organization	**Subunits/groups**	**Subunits/groups**	**Individuals**
Structural redesign	Structural redesign	Tavistock groups	Counseling
MIS upgrading	MIS upgrading	Organization mirror	Psychotherapy
Planning process changes	Planning process changes	Sensing meetings	Coaching
Accounting systems changes	Accounting systems changes	Process consultation	Behavior modification
Forecasting system changes	Forecasting system changes	Team building/development	Career development planning
Marketing system changes	Marketing system changes	Responsibility charting	Assessment centers
Communication network changes	Communication network changes	Role analysis technique	Sensitivity training
Sociotechnical interventions	Sociotechnical interventions	Role negotiation	Progammed instruction
Technostructural interventions	Technostructural interventions	Team MBO	Job rotation
Job enrichment	Job enrichment	Nominal group technique	Education
Autonomous work groups	Autonomous work groups	Delphi groups	Training
Quality circles (TQM)	Quality circles (TQM)	Brainstorming groups	Mentoring
QWL programs	QWL programs	Conflict management	Junior boards
Confrontational meetings	Confrontational meetings	Arbitration	Communication
Human resources policies/procedures	Human resources policies/procedures	Focus groups	Questions
Human resources accounting	Human resources accounting	Sensitivity training	Clarifications
Human resources planning	Human resources planning	Communication	Confrontations
Training and education	Training and education	Questions	Interpretations
Job analysis	Job analysis	Clarifications	Reconstructions
Performance management systems	Performance management systems	Confrontations	Supportive interventions
Survey/feedback	Survey/feedback	Interpretations	
Compensation plans	Compensation plans	Reconstructions	
Individual incentive plans	Individual incentive plans	Supportive interventions	
Cafeteria benefit plans	Cafeteria benefit plans		
Group incentive plans	Group incentive plans		
Scanlon/gainsharing plans	Scanlon/gainsharing plans		
Grid OD	Grid OD		

Note: MIS = Management Information Systems; TQM = Total Quality Management; MBO = Management By Objectives; QWC = Quality of Worklife.
Adapted from "Internal and External Change Agents," by T. L. Case, R. L. Vandenberg, and P. H. Meredith, 1990, *Leadership and Organization Development Journal*, 11, pp. 4–15.

Both general systems and psychodynamic theory have strengths and weaknesses. However, in my view, they are complementary. Systems theory is useful for its abstractness, general utility and applicability, assistance in organizational and large system assessments, and allowance for prediction and control in some situations. It is not particularly useful in helping people with the content of what is happening internally, or when they find themselves in conflicted or problematic interpersonal situations. In my experience, psychodynamic theory picks up where systems theory leaves off. It is useful in explaining and guiding individuals' behavior, both internally and interpersonally. It provides useful information about the human side of organizational behavior, but it is not inclusive enough to assist a consultant or a coach with the thorough assessment and diagnosis of organizational operations or human behavior. It also lacks specificity in helping clients develop and implement new and innovative behaviors for themselves, their groups, or their organizations.

The description of the 17-dimensional model improves the understanding of why so many types of interventions have been created and are demonstrating some usefulness in the field of organizational consulting and coaching. Given the vast diversity in the variables that affect human organizational life, it is easy to see the impossibility of the average consultant or coach understanding everything that is happening in any reasonably sized organization. As a result, this complexity forces a narrowing of focus to those elements that are considered crucial to organizational or, in the case of a coaching assignment, to individual or team improvement. Thus, a consultant's or coach's knowledge, skill, and comfort with different conceptual and intervention approaches will influence the focusing process and the final selection of strategies. The difficulty arises when consultants or coaches mistakenly assess and diagnose organizations or clients based on our preferences and strengths, thereby intervening in the wrong place and in the wrong way. Consultants and coaches must know our own limits and biases, be willing and able to recognize when we are in situations that demand services that we cannot render, and help clients make proper arrangements for the assistance they need. The model shows how someone specializing in a particular area of organizational structure, process, or content can have a useful impact, but it also shows that a "one approach fits all situations" attitude will not be useful to organizations or individual clients over the long term. The following is an illustration of the model in three case studies.

Case Studies

CASE 1: THE TROUBLED MIDDLE MANAGER

A program manager whose area comprised about 20 staff members located in a larger organizational unit solicited consultation during the final phase of a leadership transition in which the head of the larger unit was stepping down after many years of service. The manager complained about the tension, dysfunction, and criticism of his operations from the members of a major task force that was helping redesign aspects of his organizational unit's operations. A new director of the parent unit, who promised to be a challenge to everyone in the organization, had been selected. The manager who solicited our consultation had been promoted repeatedly by the exiting leader to whom he professed strong loyalty. He did not know how the work would get done by his staff or whether he could handle the pressure. Further discussion led to the disclosure of a major health problem that had compromised him psychologically during the past year. He described symptoms of depression and a significant level of anxiety about the transition to new leadership.

The coach-consultant helped clarify the manager's emotional responses to the leadership transition, the reorganization and reengineering of major aspects of the program's operations, and the psychological response to a chronic physical problem. The individual was referred to the organization's employee assistance program (EAP) for a thorough assessment of psychological functioning, which led to consultation with his physician and the initiation of supportive psychotherapy. The consultant, already engaged in working with the larger unit, helped design an educational intervention for the middle managers that focused on the adjustment processes and expectations required in a leadership transition. The individual's mental status significantly improved, and the new leader of the organization assumed control. To date, no major loss of productivity has been reported. Figure 2.8 displays the major dimensions of the model operating in this case. Systems elements included structure, process, input, and throughput components involved in leadership and followership; structural redesign, communication, and decision making; the specific tasks of the program and of the larger unit; group dynamics; and developmental cycles for systems and leadership. Psychodynamic elements involved included conflicts, defenses, emotion,

FIGURE 2.8

Case 1, Troubled Middle Manager, Dimensional Connections

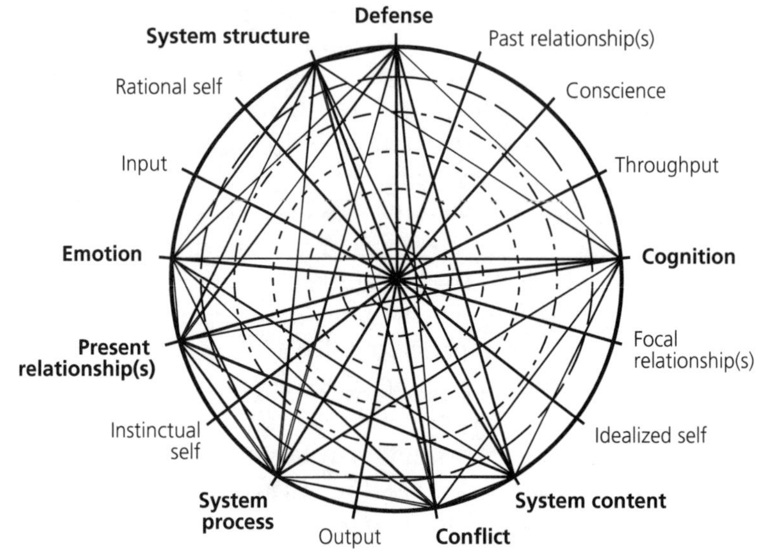

and cognition; present and focal relationships (with emphasis on self-esteem); attachment and loss; and achievement in a group context. The coach-consultant selected both technostructural and human process interventions to address the issues in this situation.

CASE 2: THE CONFLICTED MANAGEMENT TEAM

The consultant was approached by the director of a large organizational unit comprised of nine subunits and a small central office. The subunits were grouped in two areas, each having its own focus of activity. The director and central office supported both operational groups. The director expressed concern that one group had fallen into a pattern of conflicting exchanges, poor morale, indirect and triangulated communications, and inability to follow through on commitments that had begun to affect productivity. An organizational assessment was designed to focus on the management group and agreed to by the members of that group. The assessment revealed many difficulties in the communication and problem-solving operations of the group, difficulties with maintaining proper role boundaries by both the director and the managers, a lack of follow-through on commitments to group norms and values, and ongoing problems in the relationship between the management group and the rest of the organization.

The consultant negotiated a process consultation agreement with the group after an initial, highly charged feedback session. Follow-up sessions revealed layers of conflict among the members of the group and between the group and the director. Unconscious fears of retaliation, anger and envy over mistreatment and special privileges, acting-out behavior, cognitive distortions, and unexpressed grief were explored in a series of meetings. Managerial roles and relationships were renegotiated between the director and the group. An intensive retreat explored leadership and conflict management styles, and it led to an assessment of the participants' lack of compliance with their espoused values and group norms. The group recommitted itself to better implementation and several group projects and has reported more effective functioning.

Figure 2.9 highlights the dimensions of the model in operation during this consultation. Systems structure, process, and content elements were of special concern in the areas of leader and follower behavior, communication, decision making, and conflict management processes, and in the general management of the unit. The psychodynamic quadrangle of conflict, defense, emotion, and cognition was used extensively, with an emphasis on present relationships and the teammate and leader–follower roles. Organizational mission; key values; and the redefinition of roles, norms, and relationships provided a foundation on which the group rebuilt its interpersonal processes.

FIGURE 2.9

Case 2, Conflicted Management Team, Dimensional Connections

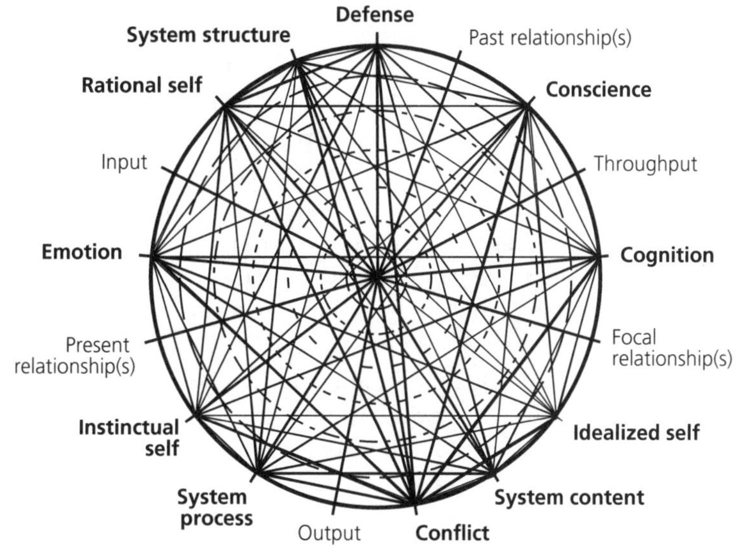

CASE 3: THE MUTINOUS CREW

The consultant was contacted by the new director of a small office whose staff had complained to human resources about managerial mistreatment. The human resources office tried several times to help solve the situation but was requested by the director to stay out of the problem. A process consultation was started with the director and the members of the office staff. Discussions revealed a multiyear history of poor leadership on the unit that had culminated in the previous director's termination. During those years, the staff had coalesced into a cohesive force that worked hard to maintain their own personal and professional integrity, as well as to do the tasks of the unit. The leadership of the organization used them to make the case for dismissal against the previous ineffective director, and they had learned how to function without a formal leader. When the new director arrived, there were major problems in the administration's communication of roles and responsibilities to the staff as well as to the new person. The well-established pattern where the staff bypassed the director and communicated directly to the leadership of the organization continued, with a consequent rise in mistrust and anger from all unit members. The process consultation revealed this mutinous history and continuing pattern and helped to clarify roles and boundaries. Anger, guilt, shame, anxiety, conflicts over control, achievement, attachment, and a set of distorted ideas about the intentions of the organizational leadership were explored. The group made an effort to establish new norms for its communication processes, and two of the staff members moved to new assignments in other organizations. The overall level of daily conflict was significantly reduced, and the group accepted the new director, even though the duties and responsibilities of this person in relation to the rest of the staff are still in flux.

Figure 2.10 indicates the dimensions of the model in focus in this case. Once again, the psychodynamic quadrangle of conflict, defense, emotion, and cognition was used to help identify what unknown dynamic of senior leadership inspired and supported staff mutiny. The emotional aftereffects of poor leadership by the previous director were explored, and the process led to a significant reduction of the tension in the unit. The new director received some coaching on managing the leadership succession process. A new set of operating roles was defined. The systems dimensions of structure and process in the input and throughput dimensions were in evidence in this leadership transition process and in the newly emerging role, behavior, and value structures.

FIGURE 2.10

Case 3, Mutinous Crew, Dimensional Connections

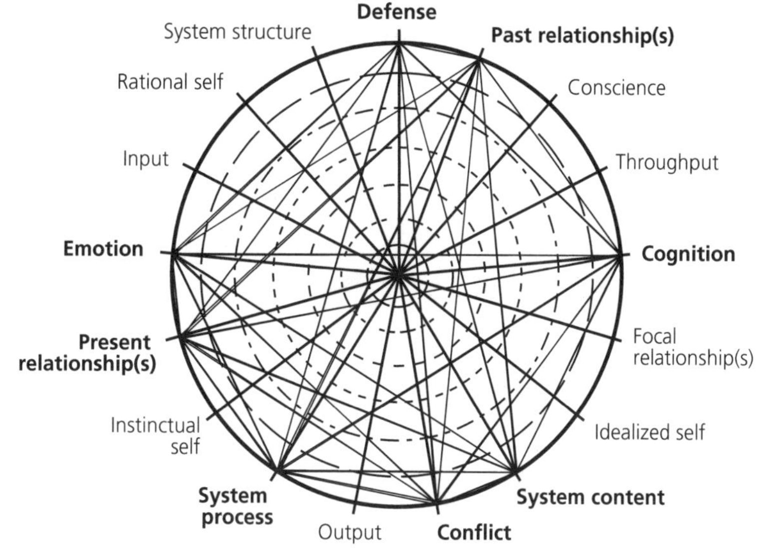

Conclusion

These short case examples demonstrate the usefulness of working from both a traditional systems framework and a psychodynamic set of concepts when consulting and coaching in organizations. They also illustrate that many types of interventions can be used to constructively influence an organization in need of assistance. Careful examination of the complexity of these models and approaches clarifies why practitioners can be successful in organizations, although they may come from a diverse set of professional backgrounds and may use a variety of conceptual models and intervention approaches. As long as consultants and coaches are clear about the dimensions being addressed in interventions, the competency to perform the work assigned, the reliability and validity of the approaches, and the willingness to call on colleagues for assistance when our expertise and approach are inappropriate or inadequate, we will continue to provide meaningful assistance to organizations whether we practice from a psychodynamic, systems, or some other conceptual model. Consultation and coaching practice will continue to place a premium on the individual professional's ability to make these assessments.

3 A Conceptual Understanding and Definition of Executive Coaching

During the past decade, consultation activities that focus on managers and senior leaders in organizations have increasingly been referred to as "executive coaching." As I briefly suggested in chapter 2, this term has taken on a technical meaning within the broad field of organization development, yet the area of practice has suffered significantly from a lack of attention in the professional literature. In this chapter, I provide an explanation of why coaching activities are becoming more welcome, popular, and necessary in the lives of successful managers and aspiring executives. I also review some of the literature available on the topic, summarize a way of conceptually understanding the practice of executive coaching, and introduce a preliminary definition of the term as a way to begin to clarify this practice within the field of consultation and to encourage additional empirical research on the subject.

Organizational and Executive Life in the New Millennium

In the past century, therapists and practitioners developed, refined, and exploited a conceptual and operational model of management that proved enormously successful. We have taught our managers and leaders how to plan, organize, staff, lead, and control organizations in an open systems framework that incorporated core ideas about homeostasis, intentional, and controlled change, and the management of poor individual performance. These concepts and the skills based on them emerged from the experience of the 19th century and the necessity to organize large numbers of people for its wars. One of the unintended but nonetheless understandable outcomes of the wars of the European nation-states was that they created both the need and capacity for large-scale social and commercial organizations to support their aims and activities. In a sense then, nearly all modern organizations were conceived in and forged by the fire and steel of combat.

The requirements of leaders and followers in those times of war were crystal clear. The kings, politicians, and generals decided strategy, including the objectives of the war, where battles would be fought, what forces would be employed, and how the combat should be conducted. Leaders in the chain of command tried to execute their own piece of the plan with the resources at their disposal. Everyone was taught to obey their superior in the chain on pain of death. Plans, orders, rules, boundaries, limits, command and control, communications, discipline, and training became the defining elements in every army and, by osmosis, in nearly every organization associated with the conduct of war. Everyone was taught the value of dependency and the dangers of autonomy. The theory and methods worked then, and they still do. Even as we enter the next millennium, most organizations still deliberately operate within these designs and principles.

Throughout the same time period, other theoretical, conceptual, and operational experiments and developments occurred that challenged the dominant model. Humanism; systems theory; non-Euclidian geometry; instantaneous communications; computers; modern transportation systems; flexible manufacturing; guerilla warfare; terrorism; and the rise of the educated, liberated, independent, or interdependent human being have so transformed the world that the traditional command-and-control model for organization of war, commerce, and human enterprise is under severe strain. Stacey (1992, 1996), Wheatley (1992), and Wheatley and Kellner-Rogers (1996) have written about these changes and the challenges they bring to leaders in modern organizations. Our daily experience in organizations confirms their observations and the difficulties the average leader in an organization currently has in reconciling his or her socialization, training, experience, and psychology—most of which has been in the old models and methodologies of the 18th , 19th, and 20th centuries—with the demands of a world and organizations that—whether or not they want to—are crossing into the 21st century and a new millennium. The results are observable daily in our enterprises and in the personal and professional lives of the people in these organizations.

In this bold, challenging, and dangerous emerging world, the age of the commanding general and the obedient, dependent, and loyal soldier is passing. We remain uncertain and at times nearly in a panic about what will replace the embedded wisdom of our lives. The clients I serve often look up, down, out, in, and all around for answers, direction, and support. They criticize leaders and followers alike and often find themselves painfully lacking in knowledge and skill; paralyzed with shame, guilt, anxiety, sadness, or rage; and unable to devise a strategy and set of behaviors that will work in these complicated times of transition.

Fortunately for us, humanity has simultaneously conducted ingenious experiments with concepts, skills, and methods to address these problems and issues. Careful reading of a diverse, scattered, and nearly incoherent literature, coupled with observations, learning, and reports from various experiences, has convinced me that we have unintentionally evolved most of what the average person and organization need to help unlock the complexities and mysteries of life in modern organizations.

In the 21st century, the evolutionary biopsychosocial framework of human history will remain rooted in its hunter–gatherer and agricultural foundations (Caporael & Brewer, 1991; Nicholson, 1998) with its emphasis on division of labor, hierarchy, emotion before reason, aversion to loss when threatened, pair bonding, tribalism, confidence before realism, classification before calculation, gossip, empathy and mind reading, contest and display, organizational design, and leadership and followership. However, to succeed in the chaotically changing, constantly transitioning, and forever challenging world of the next millennium, leaders, managers, and players at every level in any organization will need to formulate and implement different strategies for survival. These strategies and implementation methods will be based on the fundamental idea that individuals and any sized collective of them increasingly will be self-organizing, self-directing, and self-regulating (Kilburg, 1991; Stacey 1992, 1996; Tsui & Ashford, 1994; Valliant, 1993). Everyone working in organizations will gain mastery of the concepts and skill of reflective self-awareness (Argyris, 1993; Barron, 1993; Ferrari & Sternberg, 1998; Kilburg, 1997; Schon, 1987; Schunk & Zimmerman, 1998). As they do so, they will be more productive and display the features of self-efficacy described by Bandura (1977, 1982) as individuals' "sense of personal efficacy to produce and to regulate events in their lives" (p. 122). Leaders and players at every level in an organization who engage in reflective self-awareness and display self-efficacy will be more resilient as individuals and as teams (Cowen & Work, 1988; Garmezy & Masten, 1986; Luthar, Doernberger, & Zigler, 1993), and therefore, avoid or mitigate the deleterious effects of stress, burnout, and impairment (Hemfelt, Minirth, & Meier, 1991; Kilburg et al., 1986; Roskies, 1987) and their corrosive effects on organizational performance. I believe that executive, managerial, and performance coaching will play an increasingly central role in enabling individuals, teams, and organizations to develop these capacities, and as they do so, organizations will increasingly see human wisdom being created and practiced by larger numbers of individuals and groups of people.

Literature Review

Accessing the current psychological and management literature on the topic of coaching yields hundreds of articles and dozens of books. The majority of the material focuses on coaching activities and techniques as applied to various types and levels of athletic performance. Douge (1993) reviewed the recent literature on coaching effectiveness in athletics, and Howe (1993) focused on the application of psychological techniques in sports. Pratt and Eitzen's (1989) review of the leadership styles and effectiveness of high school athletic coaches and Lacy's (1994) empirical study of various coaching behaviors in collegiate women's basketball are examples of the diverse array of articles in this field.

A second and surprisingly large number of articles cover the application of coaching techniques to changing the problem behaviors of various populations. Morgan (1994) applied peer coaching methods with low-performing, young, preservice teacher trainees and demonstrated improved instruction effectiveness. Murphy (1994) reported on a study in which socially rejected fifth graders were successfully coached on improving skills to increase their ability to be liked by peers. Goldberg (1994) applied coaching techniques to improve card-sorting test scores of people diagnosed with schizophrenia. Hekelman (1994) summarized an effort to use peer coaching to improve the performance of residents in family medicine. Most recently, Maurer, Solamon, and Troxel (1998) reported significant improvements in job applicant performance on employment interviews after receiving approximately 2 hours of coaching. Birdi, Allan, and Warr (1997) also reported significant increases in job satisfaction and organizational commitment when employees participated in development activity. A final example of this type of literature is in Darling's (1994) article describing the use of coaching methods by human resources professionals to help employees with difficult, work-related problems. Scanning through these articles was reassuring in that they demonstrate that if these concepts and methods can be successful with early adolescents who have been socially rejected, people diagnosed with schizophrenia, high school and college athletes, and a variety of other troubled and untroubled people who aspire to improve their performance, they can be equally successful with managers and senior executives in for-profit and nonprofit enterprises.

The recent literature on coaching in the field of management and consultation can be clustered in three related areas: research studies; articles emphasizing methods, techniques, or applications in specific situations; and efforts to modify or expand the role repertoire of managers to include coaching activities. A thorough review of this material is well beyond the scope of this book, but a succinct summary will be provided to the reader as a gateway to the growing body of knowledge in this field.

Most of the formal research being published on coaching in management comes in the form of graduate dissertations on various aspects of the subject. One series of studies focused on managers or leaders as coaches (Coggins, 1991; Dougherty, 1993; Hein, 1990; Spinner, 1988; Stowell, 1987), and Duffy (1984), Peterson (1993), and Thompson (1987) conducted research demonstrating management skill improvements as a function of specific coaching programs. D. J. Miller (1990) and Sawczuk (1991) reported on coaching studies that enhance transfer of management and skill training into the work environment.

A variety of nondissertation research studies of coaching in organizations have also been produced. Morgan (1989) published a factor analytic study of leadership behavior incorporating a scale of coaching and mentoring others. Graham, Wedman, and Garvin-Kester (1993) reported on a program that successfully improved the performance of sales representatives whose supervisors became better coaches. Acosta-Amad (1992) demonstrated improved note-taking and charting by hospital staff members who had been coached effectively. Decker (1982) showed that supervisors who were trained in coaching and handling employee complaints improved employee retention in formal programs. Scandura (1992) demonstrated from a survey of managers that career coaching was positively related to promotion rate.

Although none of these empirical studies reported on the effects of consultants working directly with managers, they are broadly suggestive of the fact that coaching is in general successful in improving aspects of the performance of individuals in administrative positions. The research available and reviewed also highlights the significant, ongoing problem identified in chapter 1—a lack of empirical research on the actual work of senior practitioners in the field.

By far the largest body of literature available consists of articles and books devoted to exhorting managers to use coaching to empower subordinates, solve organizational problems, and push their enterprises toward peak performance. Brown (1990); Evered and Selman (1989); Good (1993); Keeys (1994); Kiechel (1991); W. C. Miller (1984); Orth, Wilkinson, and Benfari (1987); Stowell (1988); Tyson (1983); Wolff (1993); and the Woodlands Group (1980) all provide ideas, advice, encouragement, and warnings that strongly suggest that the executive who does not know how to coach effectively will suffer from poor organizational performance and stunted career opportunities. Cunningham (1991) and Knippen (1990) described the use of coaching methods in the accounting and utility industries. Himes (1984) provided a case study focusing on coaching a group toward being an effective team. Barratt (1985); Leibowitz, Kaye, and Farren (1986); and Shore (1986) specifically defined the manager's role in subordinates' career development as *coaching* them toward increased effectiveness.

A related series of articles in a variety of journals and magazines focus on the subject of coaching subordinates for high performance. Allenbaugh (1983), Aurelio and Kennedy (1991), Bell (1987), Bielous (1994), Chiaramonte (1993), Cohen and Cabot (1982), Herring (1989), Lucas (1994), Rancourt (1995), and Wallach (1983) all explicitly identify one of the key roles of leaders as helping their subordinates to modify their behavior to improve productivity, to contribute more to the growth of a company, and to become the well-known "peak performers" in their organizations. These articles offer a combination of how-to tips, conceptual approaches, minicase studies, exhortations, and rationalizations for the emphasis on coaching. Tichy and Charan (1995) interviewed the CEO of a major corporation and provided a first-hand example of how ideas about coaching have increasingly become part of the way senior leaders think about their roles.

A series of books on executive coaching also appeared recently. Deepose (1995), Ericsson (1996), Gilley and Boughton (1996), Hargrove (1995), Martin (1996), Maxwell (1995), J. B. Miller and Brown (1993), Minor (1995), Peterson and Hicks (1996), Robinson (1996), Shula and Blanchard (1995), Voss (1997), Whitmore (1994), and Witherspoon and White (1997) have all provided in-depth coverage of the topic of managers in their roles as coaches. However, readers should keep in mind that all of this literature is based on little over a dozen recent empirical studies that explore the role of managers as coaches.

An even smaller number of articles has appeared that discuss executive coaching from the vantage point of a consultant working with client managers. Popper and Lipshitz (1992) described coaching as containing two components, improving performance at the skill level and a relationship that enhances executives' psychological development.

They also provide summaries of several types of coaching techniques. Levinson (1991) explored some issues and nuances of coaching and counseling top leaders in corporations. Sperry (1993) explored the relationship between consulting, counseling, and coaching with executives, pointing out the increased stresses with which these individuals live and the need for practitioners to be in tune with the inner psychological worlds of their clients. Lukaszewski (1988) and Kelly (1985) both provided some concrete examples and specific problems that consultants may face in coaching assignments with managers. O'Connell (1990) emphasized process consultation with senior managers on corporate strategy using Socratic[1] techniques in four types of interventions including coaching. Ferguson (1986) covered 10 types of problems occurring in organizations that organization development techniques such as coaching help resolve. I edited a special issue of the *Consulting Psychology Journal* in 1996 that compiled the most comprehensive set of articles that has appeared to date on the practice of executive coaching (Kilburg, 1996a), in which the strength, sophistication, and variety of approaches currently being used in the field was demonstrated. Finally, Hall, Otazo, and Hollenbeck (1999) offered an inside look at part of the process and content of coaching, currently practiced as a result of a study they completed.

This brief review of the literature on coaching demonstrates an extensive history and broad empirical base on the general topic, especially in athletics and dealing with the problems of populations with special needs. The application of coaching as a concept and set of techniques to the art and practice of management has been growing rapidly through the 1980s and 1990s. However, the scientific basis for these applications is limited at this time. This is even more true for the practice of coaching in the context of consultation. Only two of the research studies covered by this review can be said to be even tangentially related to what is now being extensively marketed and practiced in the field. This lack of an empirical foundation has not inhibited practitioners or authors from advocating their approaches or from publishing their views. This review also raises a question as to whether executive coaching is simply the newest label practitioners are putting on a specific focus of consultation and set of techniques that they use in their work with executives. Regardless of what the research suggests, that the practice of executive coaching is racing ahead is very clear.

---

[1]Socratic techniques emphasize the use of questions, logical inference, metaphor, and stories to help clients build their own models and methods with which to address the problems they face.

A Conceptual Approach to Executive Coaching

The 17-factor model of systems and psychodynamics introduced in chapter 2 illustrates how it is possible to navigate in the complex world confronting individuals who do executive coaching. It demonstrates that a consultant working with an individual manager can focus on any of the 17 factors, their subcomponents, or their interactions and still rationally call what he or she is doing "executive coaching." The financial expert helping a client bring a new company forward to a public stock offering, the systems engineer assisting a manager to choose or install a new software product, and the organizational psychologist working with an executive to redesign the competitive structure of an enterprise are all providing consultation—that is, *helping services*—to a client manager. The focus of the effort may be radically different and the processes widely divergent, but the goals are usually to assist the person with authority and responsibility in a given organization to improve his or her performance and that of the enterprise. Within this broad approach, it seems almost impossible to differentiate executive coaching from other forms of consultation, training, and organization development.

Figure 3.1 presents a modified version of the model to help clarify this complexity and perhaps to begin to differentiate executive coaching from these other types of consultation strategies. In this figure, the 17 dimensions of the model are extended and organized into three foci: the executive focus, the system focus, and mediated focus (the relationship and behavioral factors that mediate all interactions and activities between the manager and his or her organization). A consultant working with a client executive can provide assistance to an individual inside of or crossing over any of the foci. However, I suggest that a more rigorous conceptual approach to executive coaching as a specific consultation service would choose the executive focus presented in the figure as the primary target of the consultation. These coaching activities would flow over into the other foci primarily as a way of helping the individual learn how to better function as a person and as a leader in a given organization and for a specific set of environmental circumstances.

Table 3.1, based on Weinberger (1995), outlines five major components of executive coaching interventions. In his work Weinberger tries to identify the common factors in approaches to psychotherapy. Most of these apply equally well to most relationships in which someone is playing a helping role with an individual identified as a client. These five components—establishing an agreement, building a relationship, creating and maintaining expectations of success, providing experiences of mastery and cognitive control, and evaluating and attributing coaching success and failure—provide a road map of the process and content of executive coaching relationships. By the implementation of these five processes, the true work of coaching takes place.

The first of these components can be further elaborated by an examination of Table 3.2, which presents a summary of the typical goals built into coaching contracts. These statements follow the emphasis of Figure 3.1 in that the first six are targeted on improving the functioning of the individual executive as both a person and a manager. The goals use the 17 dimensions of the systems and psychodynamics model as a base from which to operate in a coaching relationship, simultaneously acknowledging and using the organizational environment in which the manager operates, selecting various aspects of the individual's behavior for tutorials, and always pushing the individual to improved levels of professional performance.

Table 3.3 presents an abbreviated list of various coaching methods and techniques. The consultant will use these techniques during the implementation of each of the five components of a coaching intervention. Some of these methods will be described and illustrated more fully in subsequent chapters. A consultant working in a coaching relationship has a wide array of methods available to assist the executive.

FIGURE 3.1

Foci for Executive Coaching

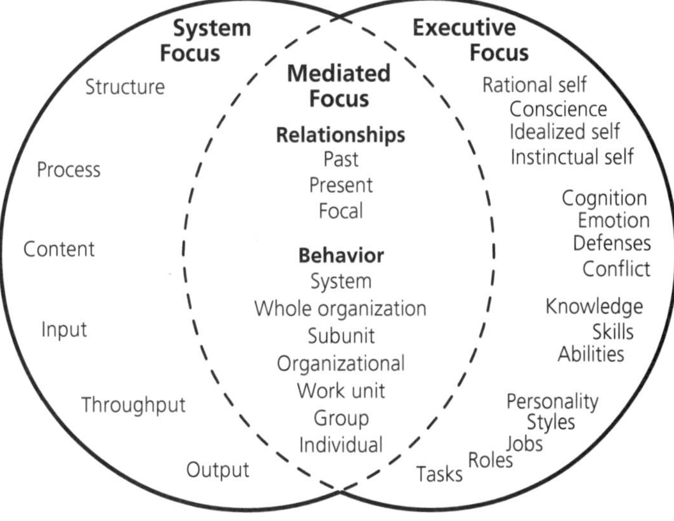

TABLE 3.1

Components of Executive Coaching Interventions

1. Developing an intervention agreement
   - Establishing a focus and goals for the coaching effort
   - Making a commitment of time
   - Committing other resources
   - Identifying and agreeing on methods
   - Setting confidentiality constraints and agreement
   - Establishing amounts and methods of payment—if appropriate
2. Building a coaching relationship
   - Establishing the working alliance
   - Identifying and managing transferences
   - Initiating and preserving containment
3. Creating and managing expectations of coaching success
4. Providing an experience of behavioral mastery or cognitive control over the problems and issues
   - Assessing, confronting, and solving problems and issues
   - Identifying and working with emotions
   - Identifying and managing resistance, defenses, and operating problems
   - Identifying and managing conflicts in the organization, in the working relationship, and in the unconscious life of the client
   - Using techniques and methods flexibly and effectively
   - Making the unsaid said and the unknown known—getting the issues on the table
   - Using feedback, disclosure, and other communication techniques to maximum effect
   - Emphasizing the reality principle—what will work most effectively with the best long-term outcomes
   - Being prepared to confront acting out, moral issues, or ethical lapses in a tactful way
   - Trying to use and engaging in yourself and your client the highest level defensive operations—sublimation, learning/problem solving, communication, curiosity, humor, creativity
5. Evaluating and attributing coaching success or failure—assessing each of your coaching sessions together; periodically looking back over what has been accomplished

Traditional test-and-tell approaches, such as using a 360° performance review instrument, help the manager become familiar with various dimensions of his or her behavior and provide the coach and the client with a language and a set of concepts with which to conduct their sessions. Education, training, role modeling, simulations, and several other methods identified in the table foster growth of knowledge and stimulate the client to try new behaviors in the context of the coaching relationship. Traditional clinical methods of communication, clarification, confrontation, interpretation, and reconstruction can be extremely helpful when clients are struggling with significant emotional responses to and conflicts in their learning, jobs, relationships, or personal lives. Care and caution must be exercised when using these

TABLE 3.2

Typical Goals of Executive Coaching

1. Increase the range, flexibility, and effectiveness of the client's behavioral repertoire.
2. Increase the client's capacity to manage an organization—planning, organizing, staffing, leading, controlling, cognitive complexity, decision making, tasks, jobs, roles, etc.
3. Improve client's psychological and social competencies.
   Increase psychological and social awareness and understanding (see the 17 dimensions of Figure 2.1).
   Increase tolerance of ambiguity.
   Increase tolerance and range of emotional responses.
   Increase flexibility in and ability to develop and maintain effective interpersonal relationships within a diverse workforce .
   Increase the client's awareness and knowledge of motivation, learning, group dynamics, organizational behavior, and other components of the psychosocial and organizational domains of human behavior.
   Decrease acting out of emotions, unconscious conflicts, and other psychodynamic patterns.
   Improve the client's capacity to learn and grow.
   Improve the client's stress management skills and stress hardiness.
4. Increase the client's ability to manage self and others in conditions of environmental and organizational turbulence, crisis, and conflict.
5. Improve the client's ability to manage his or her career and to advance professionally.
6. Improve the client's ability to manage the tensions between organizational, family, community, industry, and personal needs and demands.
7. Improve the effectiveness of the organization/team.

clinical techniques. The client must know and agree that such methods may be used and that such emotional issues may be addressed. The coach must also have the appropriate levels of training and experience to use these techniques wisely and professionally. Finally, methods such as crisis management, behavioral analysis, group process interventions, and relationship interventions with key subordinates or superiors also may be used to assist the manager in surmounting problems encountered on the job. Choosing from this diverse array of techniques is one of the constant challenges of the coaching consultant.

At a minimum, the client gains some knowledge about himself or herself in most coaching situations. Some experimentation with new behaviors may be attempted or resistance to change worked through. In other cases, the client may improve working relationships, adaptation to marital or family life, or career satisfaction. In many situations, the coach provides significant assistance in helping the manager change the organization and improve its performance. The final component of coaching interventions calls for the client and the coach to evaluate

TABLE 3.3

Abbreviated List of Coaching Methods and Techniques

Assessment and feedback
- intelligence, leadership style, personality dimensions, interpersonal style and preferences, conflict and crisis management approaches, knowledge, ability, skills

Education

Training

Skill development
- description, modeling, demonstration, rehearsal, practice, evaluation of life experience

Simulations

Role playing

Organizational assessment and diagnosis

Brainstorming
- strategies, methods, approaches, diagnostics, problem solving, intervention plans, evaluation approaches, hypothesis testing, worst-case analysis

Conflict and crisis management

Communication
- active–empathic listening/silence, "free association," open and closed questions, memory, translation, interpretation, analysis, synthesis, and evaluation questions

Clarification
- restatement of client's communications; explanation of coaching communications

Confrontation
- verbal interventions to direct the client's attention to issues, behaviors, problems, thoughts, or emotions that are evident to both the client and the coach

Interpretation
- verbal interventions to direct the client's attention in a meaningful way to issues, behaviors, problems, thoughts, or emotions that are evident to the coach but are out of the conscious awareness of the client

Reconstruction
- attempts based on what is present in and missing from the client's communications, memories, etc., to fill in an apparently important gap in recollection of some life event along with its actual emotional and reality repercussions

Empathy/encouragement

Tact

Limit setting

Boundary maintenance

Depreciation and devaluation of maladaptive behaviors, defenses, attitudes, values, emotions, fantasies

Punishment and extinction of maladaptive behaviors

Establishment of consequences for behaviors

Behavioral analysis
- gathering and assessing information

Group process interventions

Working relationship interventions
- key subordinates or superiors

Project- and/or process-focused work on structure, process, and content issues in the organization or on input, throughput, or output problems/issues

Journaling, reading assignments, conferences, and workshops

Other interventions using organization development or training technologies the process and assess the dimensions of success or failure. In my experience, the client's attributions of success usually focus on the degree to which the coach provided a supportive relationship; stimulation to think, feel, and explore new ideas and behaviors; and assistance in working through resistance to change. Recognition of the catalytic role of the coaching relationship is common. Most often, clients suggest that one of the most helpful components of coaching is that it forces them to take time to reflect on aspects of their performance and the performance of the organization. The value of pushing a busy manager to be more reflective on a regular basis should not be underestimated. Still, in some coaching relationships, the client or the coach will judge that the interventions had little or no positive impact.

Table 3.4 presents a series of hypothesized factors in both the client and the coach that may contribute to negative coaching outcomes. These factors are modified from Mohr (1995), who provided a succinct summary of the literature on negative outcomes in psychotherapy. I would like to suggest that executive coaching shares some but not all of the characteristics of psychotherapeutic interventions and, consequently, some factors that have been demonstrated to contribute to negative outcomes in psychotherapy may cross over and generalize to coaching situations. These factors range from severe psychopathology and resistance to change in the client to poor technique, lack of empathy, and lack of ability to clarify the coaching contract in the consultant. Individuals who wish to do executive coaching should keep these factors in mind as interventions are planned, and, in particular, to consult the lists when and if coaching sessions do not appear to be accomplishing much for the individual or the organization.

Working Definition of Executive Coaching

Having reviewed some basic concepts integral to the process of conducting a coaching intervention with a client, I propose a working definition of executive coaching in the field of consultation. Such a definition may be helpful for both practitioners and scholars alike as the field continues to evolve, in that it serves to clarify theory and technique and encourages the conduct of research on these types of interventions. In the context of the concepts provided above, *executive coaching* is defined as a helping relationship formed between a client who has managerial authority and responsibility in an organization and

TABLE 3.4

Hypothesized Factors Contributing to Negative Coaching Outcomes

In clients

Severe psychopathology
  psychotic symptoms, major character problems, obsessive–compulsive disorder, etc., with client refusal to obtain treatment

Severe interpersonal problems
  client unwilling or unable to develop or maintain working relationships; significant or protracted negative transference

Lack of motivation
  client experiences little pressure from self or others to change

Unrealistic expectations of coach or coaching process
  client expects coach or the process itself to substitute for or do the work of the executive; major or repeated violations of the coaching agreement

Lack of follow through on homework or intervention suggestions

In coaches

Insufficient empathy for the client
  coach does not truly care about the well-being or future of the client

Lack of interest or expertise in the client's problems or issues

Underestimating the severity of the client's problems or overestimating the coach's ability to influence the client

Significant or protracted negative countertransference
  coach overreacts to the client emotionally; has echoes of past significant, problematic relationships that cannot be managed appropriately

Poor technique—inaccurate assessment, lack of clarity on coaching contract, poor choice or poor implementation of methods

Major or prolonged disagreements with the client about the coaching process
  coach believes that client's views of the agreement, problems, methods, implementation, or evaluation of the coaching efforts are flawed in major ways that become unmanageable

Note: For more details, see Mohr (1995).

a consultant who uses a wide variety of behavioral techniques and methods to assist the client to achieve a mutually identified set of goals to improve his or her professional performance and personal satisfaction and consequently to improve the effectiveness of the client's organization within a formally defined coaching agreement.

4 Creating and Using a Reflective Containment: The Core Method of Coaching

The Case of a Dream Turned Sour

"I got your name from a consultant we're about to use to help us with some strategic planning," Ken said to me with a distinct southern accent. Over the telephone, he sounded intense and frustrated, like a man looking for answers. As a way of establishing an initial, personal connection and to start my assessment of the situation, I asked him to describe his current situation. Ken rapidly filled in the details of the leadership dilemma that he faced:

> Three years ago, my partner and I left an academic department to establish a commercial business customizing software applications for small- and medium-sized companies. We won a major contract that required us to grow rapidly in a very short time. We took the business away from a local vendor who had established good working relationships with some of the people in the customer company.
>
> My partner and I had a vision of the kind of organization that we wanted to create. We were both fed up with large bureaucracies, professional infighting, and a true lack of recognition and appropriate compensation. We wanted to create a work environment for professionals in computer science and information technology that would reflect both our values and interests. Because of our rapid growth, we've recruited a number of our

> personal friends and colleagues from around the country. In addition, we took on several of the senior professionals from the vendor who held the previous contract with our major customer. My partner and I dreamed of creating an egalitarian professional society that would be responsive to customer needs and truly support our personal and professional lives.
>
> After 3 years of open warfare with our competitors and some of our customers, we have successfully built our business, but both my partner and I are ready to quit. Getting a decision made by our [other] partners has been nearly impossible. I stopped trying to lead the organization 9 months ago, and my partner has just taken a medical leave of absence because of a life-threatening stress disorder. I need to decide in the next 3 weeks whether I'm going to continue with this company and respond to our major customer's request for a new and exclusive contract with them.

Ken went on to give me a clear description of the nature of their software applications business, the key interpersonal and group dynamics issues that he saw operating with his partnership group, and his own internal emotional reaction to the complex situation he faced.

"How would you describe the goals that you would have for your work with me?" I asked him. Ken's response was specific:

> I've learned enough to know that I need a safe place to reflect on the situation that I'm in with my colleagues and this business. I need to look carefully at my options, try to understand more clearly what my emotional responses are to the situation, and figure out how I'm interacting with my colleagues. I don't think I need therapy, but I do need to understand the complex interactions of the organization, the group that I have put together, and my own contribution to the whole mess.

I successfully negotiated a coaching agreement with Ken that took us through the 4-week time that he indicated was critical for him. We worked successfully together to explore the complex situation that had evolved in this entrepreneurial, start-up company. Through it all, Ken demonstrated a remarkable degree of insight into his own character structure and the way in which he interacted with the other business partners and with his customers. He came to understand many more dimensions of his motivation to be in the business, the strengths and weaknesses of the approach that he had taken in building the organization, how he preferred to work with other professionals, and how the situation had evolved to the point where he felt depressed and ready to walk away from his dream. This chapter explores Ken's case in more detail.

Islands of Reflection

Ken's response to my question concerning his goals demonstrated a remarkable grasp of the core component of an executive coaching relationship. I have come to believe strongly that the most effective thing that coaches do with their very able and largely successful clients is to provide a safe environment and a process that forces both parties to be reflective about the situation facing the leader. The life of the modern executive has become so packed with activity, information, and pressure that there is virtually no time available to examine the work being done; the performance of the organization being led; or the individual's cognitive, emotional, and physical responses to life on the leadership racetrack. As a result, people in leadership positions often feel extraordinarily pressured and often either misdirected or ineffective in their activities. A properly executed coaching agreement and process creates a structure through which the coaching client can safely explore as many dimensions of his or her life as time, motivation, and other resources permit. I often feel when approaching a client's office that I am rowing out to an island to meet a colleague as far away from the daily pressures of executive life as possible. Most often, I am both amazed and pleased at how refreshed, renewed, and relieved my clients become as a result of spending as little as an hour thinking, feeling, and talking about what they are doing and how they are reacting to their experiences.

Table 4.1 identifies many of the core components of the reflective containment that good coaches build with and for their clients. Stacey (1996) and Kilburg (1997) emphasized the importance that such reflective zones can have for leaders and their colleagues as they cope with the increasing pressures and unpredictability of their unstable and often chaotic organizational worlds. Successful executive coaching begins with the creation of an island for temporary retreats to sanity.

The first step in creating such a containment consists of establishing a formal agreement with the coaching client. The major components of the agreement are fairly straightforward (see the Appendix for a model of such an agreement). I have found it important to be as clear as possible about the issues of time, fees, confidentiality, goals, and follow-through on suggested activities. Without an initial agreement, it becomes nearly impossible to clarify problems and controversies as they arise. Through the agreement, a baseline of understanding can be established that gives both parties a set of boundaries and mutual understandings from which any additional negotiations for desired changes can be conducted.

TABLE 4.1

Core Components of the Successful Coaching Containment

The relationship is predictable and reliable for the client.

The issues of time, fees, meeting place, confidentiality, self-report requirements, participation, practice, follow-through and homework, cancellation policies, information exchange, and goals are made clear in a formal agreement (see Kilburg, 1996b).

The coach consistently displays the following behaviors toward the client:
- Respects the client as a person, a learning manager, and a striving performer in the organization.
- Displays consideration and understanding for the complexities of the client's life at work, at home, and in his or her inner world.
- Maintains courtesy in managing the various technical and interpersonal issues that arise.
- Possesses accurate empathy for the client and his or her struggles.
- Provides an experience of nonpossessive positive regard, of friendly and, when possible and desirable, tender feelings that can approximate the early learning acquired with nurturing; contacts parents or teaching others in the client's life.
- Consistently and, at times, playfully challenges the client to change, grow, explore, reflect, be curious, and ultimately be responsible for participating fully in the coaching process.
- Engages in tactful exchanges with the client.
- Provides assistance for the regulation and direction of attention.
- Interacts with the client in a nondefensive, authentic, and genuine fashion.
- Provides knowledge, skill, and technical assistance on the client's organizational systems; behavioral interfaces; working relationships; and psychological components of institutional, managerial and, at times, personal lives.
- Uses coaching interventions in an appropriate, timely, and effective fashion.

Emotions such as shame, anxiety, sadness, anger, and sexual arousal are monitored, identified appropriately, and regulated in such a way that the client can use them productively in the work of personal and professional growth.

The client and consultant constantly and consistently reflect on and explore issues and methods that either impede or improve the executive's or the organization's performance, especially the manifestations of defensive operations, resistance, and conflict.

For consultants working inside medium- to large-scale organizations in which they may have multiple clients, it is also critical to establish who is the coaching client. Often, when clients are being referred for professional development or derailment prevention, the initial agreement may need to include other parties, such as the vice president for human resources, and the executive's manager or manager once removed as part of the negotiations and for accountability for outcomes and payment. These types of agreements are more complex to negotiate and implement, but with careful attention to the various components of goal setting, confidentiality, report requirements, evaluation of progress, and activity plans, worst-case scenarios leading to misunderstanding, coaching failures, or loss of client business can be avoided.

Once the relationship has become predictable and reliable for the client by virtue of implementing the coaching agreement, the level of trust and rapport can be deepened by establishing a behavioral framework for the coach-consultant that includes the items identified in Table 4.1. Displaying respect, consideration, understanding, courtesy, empathy, and the traditional attitudes associated with all helping relationships creates a working space in which most clients feel free to express themselves openly and honestly. As the coach and the client constantly and consistently reflect together, pay attention to the regulation of emotions, and focus on the work at hand, significant change usually occurs.

Figure 4.1 presents the circle of awareness, a 6-stage process that effective coaches can use repeatedly during a coaching session. Once the containment has been initiated, the coach should specifically and respectfully invite the client to expand his or her ability to reflect on the current organizational environment, the leadership situation, and his or her experiences with it. It may be useful at this time to review Schon's (1987) three levels of reflection to assist the client to understand the nature of the task:

1. *Learning in action.* The ability to be self-aware as one performs a task. For example, when riding a bike into a complex and dangerous intersection, the rider needs a sense of the traffic around him or her, the strategy to pursue to get through the pattern safely, and anticipation of the potential dangers.
2. *Reflection on learning in action.* The ability to be aware of the ways an approach to a task could be modified as the task is being performed. In the bike example, the rider checks his or her progress through the intersection against the original plan; responds to unanticipated changes in traffic and weather conditions; and monitors the status of the bike and his or her physical responses to the situation, and then is able to smoothly make the changes needed to complete the task.
3. *Reflection on reflection on learning in action.* The ability to be aware of the multiple levels of complexity, paradoxes, and polarities in the situation or experience and the ability to review the initial conditions, environmental variables, personal responses, strategies, tactics, and behaviors that were used and their results or outcomes with the intent of learning how to better perform in similar circumstances in the future. In the biking example, this might involve reviewing how the rider negotiated the intersection after the ride. He or she might note the time of the day and the traffic conditions; the lanes in which he or she chose to ride; safe places to stop; particularly tricky moments in the passage;

FIGURE 4.1

Circle of Awareness
Components of a reflective coaching process.

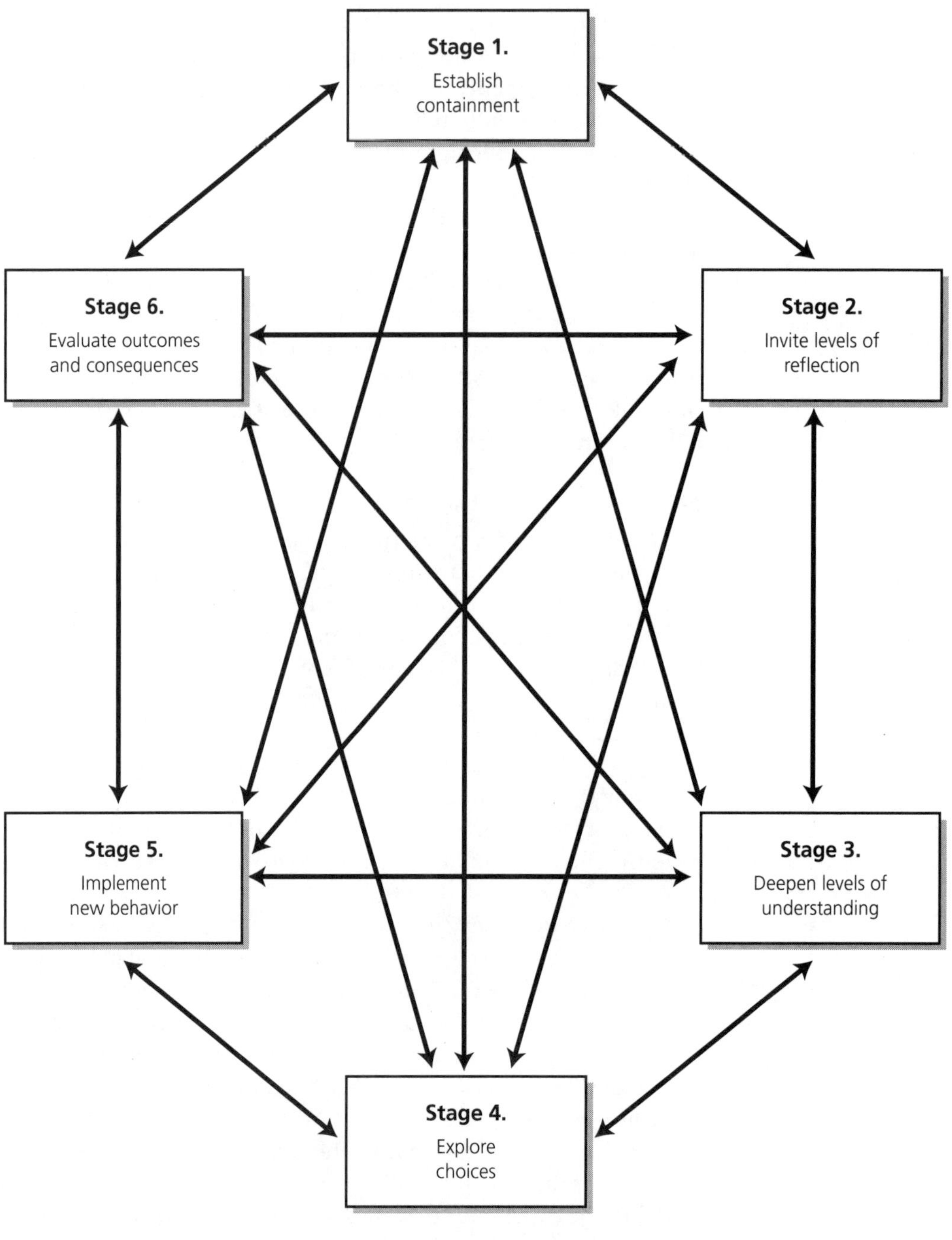

> his or her feelings throughout the intersection; and what he or she might do the next time, including whether to try it at all. By conducting such a review, the rider can permanently alter the way that he or she approaches that section of a bike ride and prevent future problems. In other words, the rider can learn, and the next time he or she will be wiser and better at the task.

Hargrove (1995) described this reflective process as *triple-loop learning,* a slight modification of Argyris's (1993) double-loop learning. Figure 4.2 presents a graphic illustration of Hargrove's suggestion. In it, an environmental context presents tasks of external adaptation and internal integration that interacts with our own identities as people and with the culture of the enterprise in any organizational learning situation. We construct an understanding of the situation for ourselves that invokes both organizational learning and defensive routines, and then from this constructed understanding or meaning we invent and implement strategies for action. These strategies lead to consequences, costs, and benefits. In single-loop learning or incremental improvement, we use the feedback from the consequences to change the specific actions we used to implement the strategies. For example, the bike rider might select a different lane to approach the intersection next time. In double-loop learning or reframing, we use the feedback to alter the constructed framework that we use to understand ourselves and the strategies that we select to address the situation. Thus, the rider might choose to alter the time of day the intersection was approached or the clothes worn to ensure better visibility. Finally, in triple-loop learning or transformation, the feedback might lead to a change in the context, in how our individual identities are constructed, or in the culture of the organization. In the example, a traumatic experience in the intersection might lead the rider to avoid that situation in the future or to quit riding in urban settings. A truly transformative experience might lead the rider to stop riding altogether or to create a lobbying organization to garner support to alter the intersection to make it safer for bikers.

These levels of reflection and types of learning loops can be applied to a client's external environment; the circumstances, structures, processes, and contents of the current organization; relevant current relationships; and the client's inner psychological and physical worlds both past and present. Coaches need to be alert simultaneously for the types of reflection and learning that are needed in a situation to help our clients shift their attention from level to level. Most often, I share these definitions and descriptions early and openly with my clients and, if a situation calls for it, I suggest that we reflect together at different levels. At times, coaches can use sports, performing arts, or other relevant metaphors to help a client understand what he or she is trying to do. Using terms such as *developing a game plan, huddling up, time outs, half-time reviews* and *adjustments,* and *watching the postgame films* can assist many people to understand what a coaching session can be about. Similarly, terms such as *rehearsals, backstage discussions,* and *post-performance reviews* or *critiques* are helpful. If a client begins to use the language—requesting some time to "reflect," "huddle," or "rehearse," the coach can be reasonably sure that the client has begun to understand the importance of reflection and how it can aid in improving performance.

Once the containment is established for a client, each session begins with an effort by both the client and the coach to reconnect and create this island of reflection. It may be as simple as an informal "Hello, how's it going?" At times I start by asking, "What do you want to reflect or work on today?" Often, sessions start simply with reports of professional or personal events. Everyone who coaches will need to address the issue of boundaries around how much of his or her personal life can be safely shared with the client. Some coaches may be comfortable with a large measure of sharing and others may be cautious. There are implications regardless of which boundary a coach chooses. I have become fairly comfortable telling clients about my life in general terms. I use examples from my experience if I think they are relevant, while remaining alert for the possible impact on the client. I am cautious about sharing intense emotional reactions in the moment

FIGURE 4.2

Organization, Group, and Individual Learning

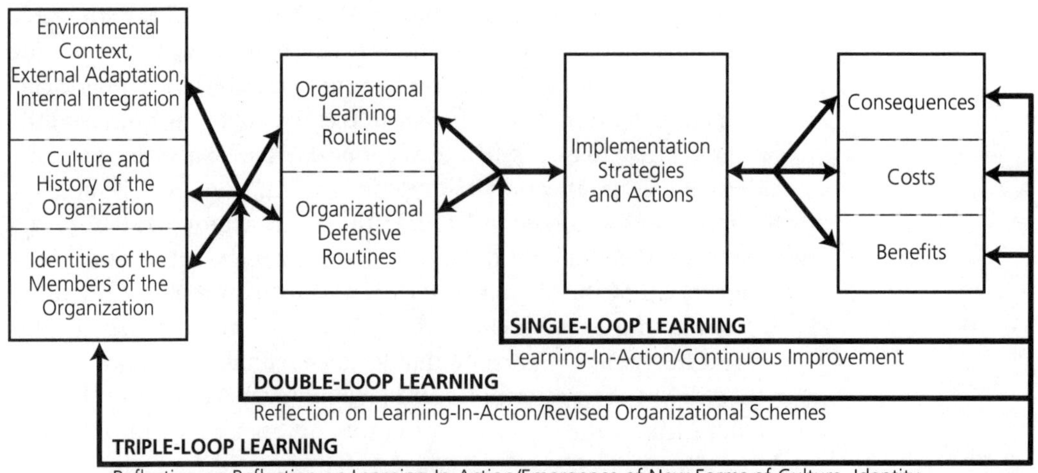

because of the potential for acting out on my part, so I prefer to take time to reflect privately on these situations before I talk about them with a client. I answer reasonable questions such as "What are you doing for the holidays, vacation, the weekend?" I talk about personally challenging situations in the past and about some aspects of my family life. I do not delve into my personal problems or difficult challenges because of the tendency for role reversal.

Clients do invest in their relationships with coaches. They come to respect and need them, and they may be excellent caretakers and coaches in their own right. However, unless an explicit contract for mutual coaching has been negotiated, clients deserve to have their coaches' full attention on *their* issues, and use of a client's time to address a coach's problems usually abuses the coaching relationship and can cause disruption in the client's level of trust and rapport. By now, I've been in enough of these situations to know what I am comfortable revealing and when to keep firm boundaries. Everyone who coaches will need to address this issue as part of establishing and maintaining the containment.

COACHING, CONSULTING, AND COUNSELING

I have been asked many times about the differences among coaching, consulting, and counseling. I have come to believe that there are no sharp lines between each one. The distinction between coaching and consultation is blurred when I work with a client on the direct problems of the organization and its systems, but I tend to think of this more as consulting. Similarly, I tend to think of the work on the client's behaviorally mediated interactions with the organization's systems and people as well as his or her adaptation to the role of manager or executive as coaching. When the inner psychological world of the executive opens up as part of an assignment, coaches need to proceed carefully, especially if the client has no previous experience with counseling. I have become conscientious about negotiating clearly with clients about entering into their inner psychological experience because of the slippery and complex situations that can arise quickly, without warning. I am always prepared to help a client frame a difficult set of circumstances or inner problems as a set of issues that would be better and more safely dealt with in a therapeutic situation and am quick to refer people who I think might be helped. I try to frame such referrals in the context of a manager or executive adding another professional to his or her supporting network. I often share that I see my therapist several times a year to check up on myself or to work at a deeper level on problems that I might encounter. I usually ask the client if he or she has a physician, dentist, lawyer, priest, rabbi, imam, minister, accountant, contractor, electrician, and so forth. I then suggest that it is good to have an experienced therapist who knows us well to whom we can turn if we need help in a particularly tough time. This approach often meets with less resistance than more traditional forms of making a referral.

Figure 4.3 graphically shows how I think about the distinctions among these various forms of helping relationships. As I have said, I do not believe that there is a formal line that a coach crosses between consulting, coaching, and counseling, either in a particular session or during an engagement with a client. Rather, I believe that a helping relationship can have a number of zones and characteristics. The figure shows that we move from being involved at all times in a human

FIGURE 4.3

Types of Helping Relationships From Friendship to Counseling

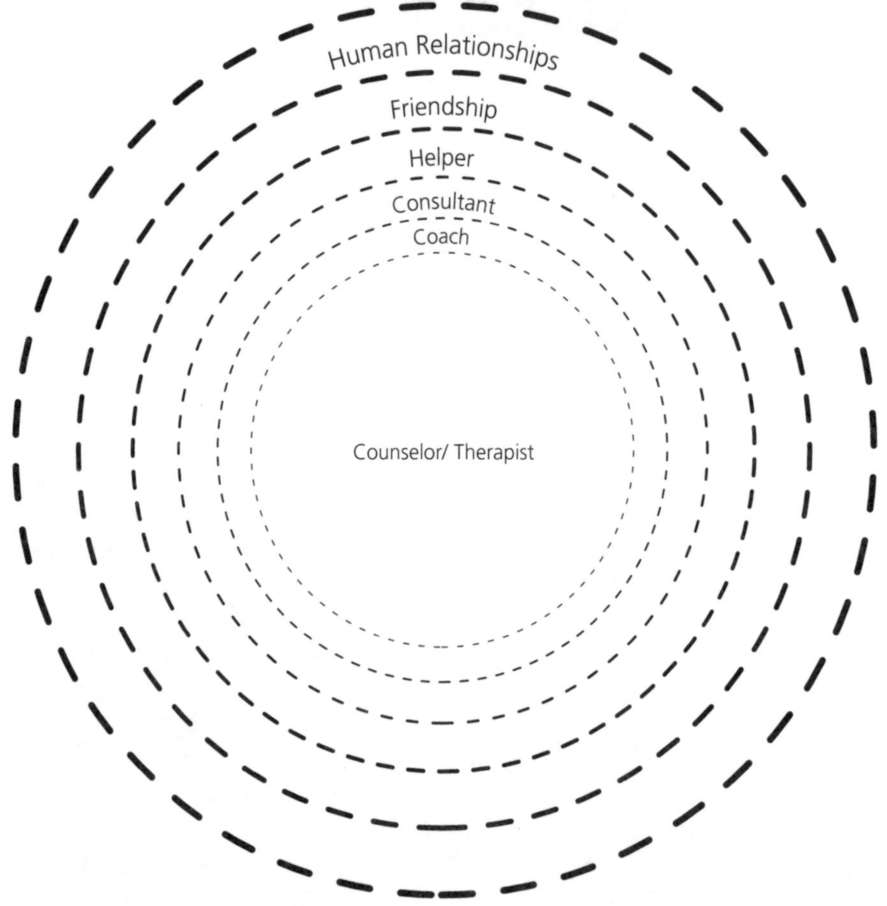

relationship with a client to progress into some elements of friendship and then to helping, consultation, coaching, and counseling or psychotherapy. The boundaries between these forms are not fixed but rather are fluid so that the self-disclosures of a client in a coaching session can be as candid and self-revealing as those that are experienced in psychotherapy. Coaches who are trained in counseling and therapy will be more comfortable entering into this zone, but again, great caution is indicated here for those with this background and even more for those without it.

In coaching a client, the relationship is not that of a patient and therapist. The social, ethical, moral, and legal expectations and boundaries are still evolving for coaches, but for therapists, there are a hundred years of practical experience, research, laws, and regulations to provide guidance. Currently, a coaching failure carries many fewer potential consequences than a therapeutic failure. However, as coaching increases in popularity and use, I believe that we can fully expect to see attempts at regulation and efforts to bring greater accountability to the field. I also believe that there will be malpractice and negligence liability. Coaches who feel the material in a session has brought them into the therapeutic zone should clearly state that the issue seems like a significant one and that the client might benefit from spending some time working privately with a therapist. I am usually happy to try to facilitate such a referral. However, I have been told by several colleagues with whom I have conducted joint coaching sessions that my own therapeutic training enables me to move more deeply and safely into that zone than they would feel comfortable. I have come to see that this is in fact the case, but I believe that every person who coaches will need to spend some time pondering these boundary issues for themselves. Some personal distinctions I have drawn between coaching and therapy boundaries include the following:

- It is usually safe to have a meal with a coaching client. The more informal setting can deepen the sense of trust, lead to greater and more meaningful self-disclosure and feedback, and open up previously unexplored material.
- Although I am cautious about it, a coach may on occasion visit the homes of long-term coaching clients, have meals with clients and their spouses, and even meet their children. I have talked briefly with a spouse, who can provide insightful information about how a client is truly doing and what seem to be key issues. I am careful about taking his or her advice because of the danger of being inappropriately triangulated in a marital conflict.
- The presentation of gifts in a business setting must be negotiated carefully. Often, clients express their gratitude in ways that would

be inappropriate in a therapeutic relationship but are the norm for their business.

- When working in a particular corporate culture, a coach may need to alter his or her appearance or manner of dress to fit the norms of the company. Many organizations are now moving to more informal dress codes, and clients may well expect a coach to honor and respect their norms while visiting their facilities. I have found these opportunities a refreshing change and that a willingness on my part to become visibly integrated into the clients' worlds speeds my acceptance and ability to coach.
- The management of fees and contracts is also set in the company culture, processes, and procedures. Most of my clients have been comfortable with a request for a retainer and periodic reports of the time and activities logged on the agreement. I have never asked a patient for a retainer for work to be accomplished in the future.
- Some coaches and consultants are now requesting and receiving parts of their compensation in the form of stock options and grants. I have not read or heard much discussed in the consulting field about this trend, and I believe that it has many pros and cons that should be explored carefully. Of particular importance is the potential loss of neutrality if an executive is performing certain activities that may well increase the price of a stock in the short term at the long-term expense of the company and its people. A coach's ability to discuss these issues could be compromised if he or she stands to benefit significantly from a "shady" or corrupt practice.
- Finally, I try in every way that I can to communicate to clients and their companies that I am truly interested in their advancement and development. I want them to feel safe with me and to know that I will not exploit them.

THE COACHING SESSION

Figure 4.4 depicts the stages and flow of a coaching session. The six-stage model begins in Stage 1 with establishing contact, recreating the interpersonal connection, and extending an invitation to do the coaching work together. Often, a client says how he or she is doing, reports on personal or family matters, and asks me how I have been. If it has been a long time between sessions, this kind of catching up can take a while. However, I think it is worth the investment because the client must see a coach as a multidimensional human being. As this evolves naturally through the history of a coaching relationship, more and more of our selves as people can be incorporated into our work with

Stages and Directional flow of a Coaching Session

Stage 1.
Establish contact

Stage 2.
Present
current situation

Stage 3.
Explore
current situation

Stage 4.
Choose foci

Stage 5.
Implement the
working dialogue

Disclosure/
feedback loops
single-, double- &
triple-loop learning

Disclosure/
feedback loops
single-, double- &
triple-loop learning

Disclosure/
feedback loops
single-, double- &
triple-loop learning

Stage 6.
Closure. Review,
evaluation, & follow-up

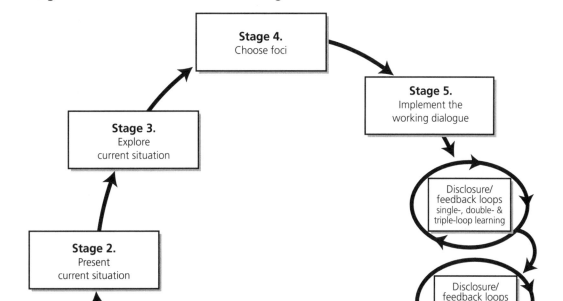

clients. Some of my coaching relationships now extend over 7 or 8 years; I have annual retainers with several organizations and may talk with clients once a month or once every 3 months. In these circumstances, it can take a little time to warm up to the topic.

Stage 2 involves the client telling a story about his or her present situation. As I come to know the client and the home organization, I often feel as if I am reading the latest installment in a complex historical novel. The characters, events, situations, conflicts, pressures, relationships, and goals are constantly moving. I find it fascinating to reengage the strains of the narrative and to listen to "what happened next." During this phase of the session, the more I can feel and display the attitude and emotion of "and then? ... what then?"—in other words the excitement of being inside their unique and heroic story—the better the connection becomes with the client, the security of the containment increases, and it is more likely that I can be influential in ways that the client needs.

In Stage 3, I usually delve deeper into the present situation, following the clients' leads. Over time, they learn to go to where the trouble, puzzlement, or pain burns brightly. I am alert for defensive efforts to keep things on the surface or undiscussable, but this tends to be more of an issue early in a coaching relationship when trust and rapport are lower. At some point during Stage 3, it usually becomes clear that the client both wants and needs to focus on a particular issue or set of issues. I may help to clearly denote this by saying something like "it sounds like we need to spend some time exploring or reflecting on ..." or by issuing an invitation to explore the situation. Often my experienced clients will begin a session with a list of items to explore. This makes the choice of foci easy, and thus Stage 4 tends to pass the most quickly of all. Sometimes, the shift is not clear, and we just progressively deepen the discussion about a particular topic. As this unfolds, I become aware that we have moved into Stage 5, a working dialogue.

Depending on the length of the session, which can range from 5 to 10 minutes, to 8 to 10 hours, these cycles of disclosure and feedback loops can flow repeatedly. During the dialogues, a variety of coaching and consulting methods from traditional counseling approaches can be used. These may include active listening, client-centered reflections, interpretations and confrontations, goal setting, behavioral rehearsals, role modeling, planning, and brainstorming. During Stage 5 a coach truly earns his or her fee from the client. In subsequent chapters of this book, approaches and events that occur during the working dialogue, especially managing conflict, defense, emotion, and cognition will be discussed.

As the session winds down, we move into Stage 6, the final stage, in which the coach and client come to closure. Often this is facilitated by a formal time limit to a session. When an hour is set aside, it is easy to keep time and point out when it is appropriate to review what has been dealt with or discussed. Usually, I ask clients if the session has been helpful and if anything in particular was notable. I also pay attention to nonverbal cues, because some clients can have difficulty telling coaches that something that was said or done was not helpful or was even injurious. These can be some of the most critical moments in coaching and the ones that often move a client forward. If any follow-up or homework is indicated, it is good to review and identify deadlines. Promises to provide references or materials, make calls, practice skills, or confront situations are easy to review at this point, and this makes the following sessions easier to structure.

I do quite a bit of my coaching on the telephone and in the evenings, and the boundaries around time can be very fluid during these sessions. I am usually careful to monitor the time and try to avoid moving past an hour. However, for clients with whom I am in less frequent contact, these longer sessions can be extremely useful and productive. I have deliberately tried not to stick to therapeutic norms and boundaries because I have come to believe that a coaching relationship must be much more fluid and flexible to be successful.

The circle of awareness and the process of a coaching session can be demonstrated through an example. In the situation that opened the chapter, Ken faced a major decision about whether he would stay with the company that he started. After approximately 6 hours of coaching, he called me on the evening before a retreat for the partners of the business to determine their strategy and next steps in pursuing a renewal of the contract with their major client. During a brief, 30-minute session, we went through both the circle of awareness and the stages of coaching.

I opened the telephone exchange with him by asking, "How are you doing?"

Ken answered, "I put the whole thing on hold last weekend to focus on spiritual matters. I am intensely involved in my church, and I spent the weekend with my family and fellow church members. Many of my friends there kept asking me a lot of questions about what was happening. They said things like, 'You don't look exhausted all the time, or you look a lot better, what's been happening?' "

Ken then launched into his assessment of the role that he needed to play in the retreat the next day. He saw himself as the visionary for the organization and expressed the difficulty that he faced in pulling back into the ownership group. He felt a wide separation between himself and the other members of the group. During the preceding week, he had spent a great deal of time performing an economic analysis about the future of the business and was very concerned about the narrow operating margins within which the company functioned. He felt that he could sit in the meeting but worried that he would be overreactive if the atmosphere turned critical. We discussed the role of the facilitator that the organization had hired to help them with the retreat.

We decided to focus on Ken's role during the retreat process. As we explored this, Ken came to see that he could effectively interact with the group by expressing his current vision and technical understanding about the business. We also worked on trying to clarify the distinction among the organization, himself, and the role of organizational leadership. We hypothesized that the group might be very defensive and that his own responses to them might elicit the traditionally vicious circle of attack and withdrawal that they were all accustomed to enact. During our discussion, he decided to try to focus on the key decisions that they faced as a group about going forward with a new bid on the contract and to be as nonreactive to personal attacks as possible. I reinforced his commitment by highlighting how defenses can operate in groups and the strong tendency for humans to move into familiar if viciously ineffective patterns of behavior.

I asked him to reflect on his emotional responses as he anticipated going into the retreat the next day. He quickly stated that he felt a good bit of anxiety about being attacked by the other members of the group. We probed this together, and he came to see that the anxiety was in anticipation of being humiliated by his colleagues and his likely overreaction by getting angry at them. Because he tended to dominate the group interpersonally, he worried that if he got angry, it would destroy any chance that the partners would have to work through the problems that they faced together. He also worried that if he were not willing to stay involved with the company, the organization would fail. I encouraged him to think of the emotions elicited during the heat of the conversation as normal by-products of human interaction rather than as personal attacks and in terms of negotiating a shift in his role in which he would have a more limited engagement with the organization. We discussed the possibility of developing a new arrangement with the ownership group and being able to close out the obligations from his initial roles as founding partner, supervisor, and visionary leader. I also encouraged him to consider if there were any responsibilities he had not met or accomplished well for the organization and what he needed to say to the group about that. We ended the brief session with me asking him if he felt ready for the retreat.

"I feel calmer," he replied. "What I will decide personally will be tied to the results of the retreat. I would like to get the organization to go forward, but I don't know if it's possible."

I then asked him how he felt about the session.

"This helped me think through what I need to do tomorrow. I know what the challenges will be, but I'm not sure what I'll do if the situation turns ugly."

I encouraged Ken to try to stay focused on both his goals and his role. I expressed confidence that he would be able to handle the challenges from his colleagues. I suggested that he try to use his ability to be reflective during the retreat, particularly at moments that he felt might be emotionally challenging. We ended the session with me wishing him good luck.

During this brief telephone session, we can see the circle of awareness in operation through the first five stages. After 6 previous hours of coaching, containment is quickly established in the initial exchange of greetings. If the client is secure in the holding environment, he or she takes it for granted, and the issues immediately fade unnoticed into the background. Coaches know the containment is secure when it does not arise as an issue. When it does, a coach can look to the basics such as the nature of the agreement, the goals, confidentiality, the manner in which an issue was approached, or major resistance or defenses in either the client or coach as areas to explore.

Similarly, the mature, coaching-savvy client typically moves almost immediately into the reflective zone of Stage 2. In this example, Ken dove into the material concerning the retreat, his role, and emotional reactions with almost no invitation on my part. Again, a coach knows how ready a client is to explore by how difficult it seems to start a reflective process.

Ken obviously did a lot of homework before the telephone session, so that he was well prepared to discuss his expectations of the retreat; his thoughts about his participation; and some of the problems that he anticipated, such as his ability to tolerate criticism and the group being ineffective. I pushed him further in both, exploring his likely emotional responses to the hypothesized events—a form of behavioral rehearsal—and in becoming more aware of how he could work with the retreat facilitator. We explored his choices for behavior in the meeting by playing a little "what if?" and "if then?" We discussed how he could frame what would likely be his strong emotional responses. And finally, he was able to experiment at least mentally with implementation as he thought about being able to sit, listen, and watch reflectively as the facilitator worked with the group, and he accepted the criticisms and strong emotions that he knew he would have. He thought about what his presentation would look and sound like and what goals he needed to accomplish in presenting the data that he had accumulated. We did not evaluate consequences, because he had not formally implemented anything.

Obviously, we moved quickly through the first three stages of the session: establishing contact and presenting and exploring the current situation. Ken stated his explicit desire to focus on the retreat, his role, and his likely reactions. Again, these are all indications of a mature client at work. Ken clearly saw the coaching session as a resource for himself, did not experience a great deal of emotional conflict about doing the reflection, and had worked through his defenses sufficiently to be immediately available for deep and sophisticated work. We quickly focused on the retreat and moved rapidly from topic to topic. We covered the facilitator's role, the likely responses of other key members of the group's participants, his anticipation of both events and process, and his emotional state in our session and as he anticipated it might be in the retreat. We also explored alternatives and options and mentally rehearsed him in his role and reactions. This took place in approximately 30 minutes, an amazing amount of work in that time but not atypical in my experience with hardworking clients. We closed the session with me wishing him good luck and good humor, to which he responded with a slight laugh and a statement of determination to do his best.

During sessions, a coach is only aware of the circle of awareness or the coaching process if things are going poorly, if he or she feels a need to make a transition to a different stage of the session or topical area, or if a process issue arises. The containment and holding environment usually provide a consistent and nurturing framework for the interactions to continue and for the consultant to coach creatively and spontaneously. When everything works well, it feels both seamless and nearly effortless for both client and coach. However, coaches should always keep in mind that our structures, processes, methods, and expertise make these effortless miracles of reflection possible.

Coaching and Chaos

Vaill (1991), Stacey (1992, 1996), and Wheatley (1992) have described the world of the modern leader as being unpredictable, complex, and very stressful and point the way to using complexity theory and other concepts and methods as anchors in the daily hurricane of managerial life. I understand and agree with their formulations, and I see that some aspects of chaos theory can be used to deepen the understanding of coaching theory and to strengthen skills and methods. In this section, I briefly describe how coaches can translate these very intriguing concepts into effective coaching practices.

In addition to the Stacey and Wheatley references given above, the following description relies on the pioneering work and analyses of Zeeman (1976), who applied the theory of nonlinear dynamics and geometry to human behavior, and a host of others who have followed him. Excellent gateways to these concepts and applications in the literature are provided by Butz (1997), Finke and Bettle (1996), Gleick (1987), and Masterpasqua and Perna (1997). There is also a growing empirical literature as exemplified by the work of Bosserman (1982); Flay (1978); Guastello (1987); Guastello and Guastello (1998); Zeeman, Hall, Harrison, Marriage, and Shapland (1976); and a host of others. No effort will be made here to review the fundamentals or details of this useful and exciting set of concepts, but I will try to demonstrate how several of the basic ideas can greatly inform and enrich efforts to provide executive coaching services to clients. For other ideas about applications in behavioral contexts, see the recent books by Butz (1997) and Masterpasqua and Perna (1997).

Chaos and catastrophe theory were developed in response to the need to identify and predict patterns in naturally occurring systems that are seemingly random in nature. The dripping of a faucet, traffic patterns on an interstate highway, or the arrival and departure of a tornado within a thunderstorm are the types of natural systems that invited such studies. Individual and organizational behavior share many of these general characteristics in that they are naturally occurring systems with many interacting variables that are difficult—if not impossible—to control or predict. Chaos theory also deals with that most troubling aspect of behavior within systems, namely, their propensity to change radically and often without any warning. An individual suddenly changes his or her mind about accepting a job offer, a group of executives suddenly turns on their leader and attacks a poor decision, an organization with a track record of excellent financial performance suddenly experiences six successive quarters of red ink—these are all examples of catastrophic change in human systems. To apply chaos theory to executive coaching, we need to begin with a brief description of several of the major principles used in more detail in subsequent chapters.

First, change in a behavioral system can be either continuous or discontinuous. Figure 4.5 depicts a classic case of change within what is called the *cusp catastrophe*. Pursuing the example of the group turning on its leader, the diagram's lower level represents the group as functioning in its normal cooperative mode. As alienation or disaffection; frustration, anger, or aggression; and tension (depicted on axes ABC) increase within the group and are not managed well by the leader or the members, the team begins to move closer to the catastrophic zone (depicted by the shaded fold). At a certain point in time, shown on the bottom part of the diagram as point *T* on a continuum, the tension, anger, and alienation pass a critical zone where the disorder within the group jumps catastrophically into an open attack on the leader. To the untrained eye, the behavior is unpredictable, unforeseen, and unmanageable. In reality in this example, the moderating or splitting factor in the catastrophic change consists of the diagnostic and conflict management skills of the leader. In this situation, an unperceptive manager or one whose behavioral skills are insufficient to manage a very tense moment will enable the catastrophic shift to occur. An external observer may be able to see nonverbal signals that suggest that the tension within the group seems to be increasing gradually at point *S*

FIGURE 4.5

Schematic of a Cusp Catastrophe in a Group

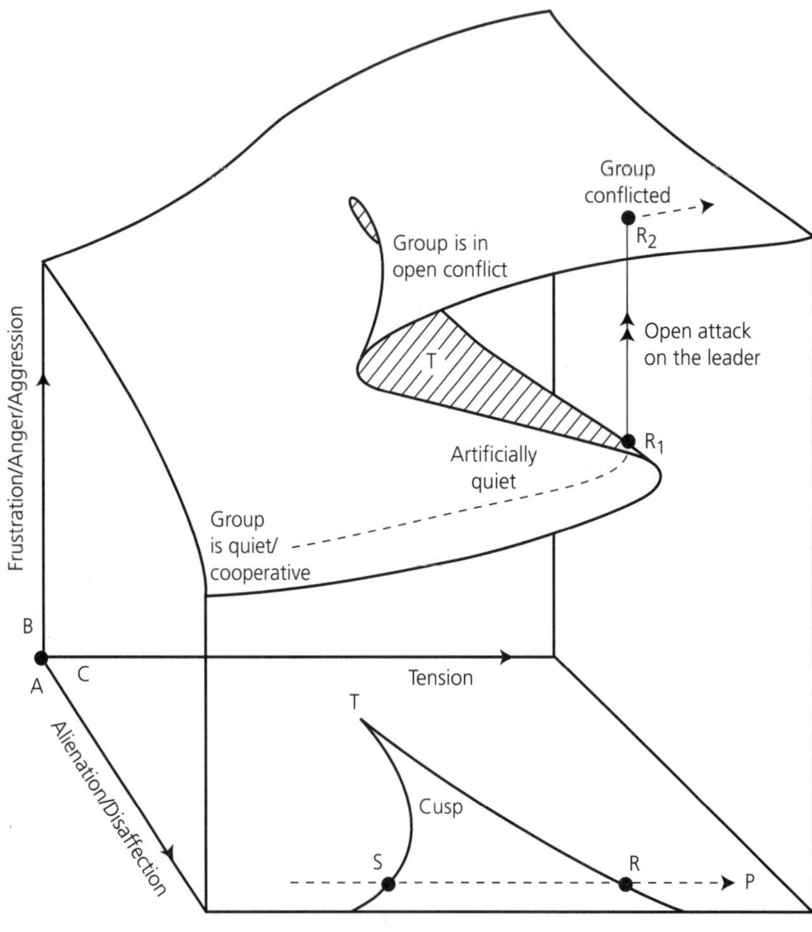

on the continuum; however, once the attack is under way at point *R*, the entire behavior pattern of the group shifts to the upper zone shown in Figure 4.5. This is shown as the change from point *R*1 to point *R*2. The new behavior patterns can remain there at point *P* for a short time or be prolonged, depending on the conditions within the group and what the leader chooses or is able to do in the circumstances. Chaotic attractors or repulsors can exist on the lower and upper planes of the drawing. Attractors are virtuous or vicious patterns of behavior that individuals or groups use readily and usually have no or lower barriers to enter them. Repulsors are the opposite, namely, virtuous or vicious patterns of behavior that individuals or groups do not use readily and usually have moderate to high barriers to enter them. If the group is uncomfortable and unskilled at open conflict, the attack probably will be short lived because the behavior pattern can be thought of as a repulsor. The opposite is equally true. Namely, if the group is experienced and reasonably comfortable with open conflict, the shift at point *R* will be into another chaotic attractor and may be difficult to change. Executives and their coaches are often faced by these disconcerting and discontinuous shifts in individual, group, organizational, or market behavior.

Second, these concepts show that behavior can be understood in geometric or spatial terms. Although we are familiar with the graphical outputs of computer programs and statistical analyses, Figure 4.5 allows us to penetrate to a deeper understanding of these multidimensional systems. The cusp catastrophe is the simplest of an entire subfield of non-Euclidian geometry described by Thom (1972). In his pioneering work, Thom pointed a way to understanding these types of changes in systems from the standard three to an infinite number of geometric dimensions. Most of the theoretical and empirical work done to date with these mathematical forms in human behavior has concentrated on applications of the simpler types of catastrophes. The research base will be enriched greatly during the next decade with the application of these more complex mathematical forms, and those geometric studies will help unravel some of the real phenomena witnessed in the spaces of human behavior.

Third, in open, interconnected systems, small, repeated changes in one part of an organism or organization can often produce huge and catastrophic changes in other parts. A staff member who unwittingly mistreats a crucial customer, an executive who sexually harasses his subordinate who in turn sues the company, or a research scientist who attends a conference and learns a new approach to a problem that leads to a new line of products for a company are examples of this principle. Increasingly, as I coach managers, I have tried to keep this principle in mind as I encourage clients to take multiple, small steps as they learn new concepts and skills; I try to encourage them with the idea that such small steps can create unforeseen, enormous, positive changes for them and their organizations.

Fourth, as described before, the various regions of geometric, behavioral space contain "strange attractors" and "strange repulsors." Figure 4.6 depicts a way that these attractors and repulsors can be visualized. They may have structure, contents, and processes much like any other system of behavior. We can also hypothesize that attractors and repulsors can possess such characteristics as intensity, frequency, duration, depth, width, height, and slope. Thus, Attractor A in the figure can be seen as a fairly large, shallow, and narrow shape without much

FIGURE 4.6

Visual Representations of Chaotic Attractors and Repulsors

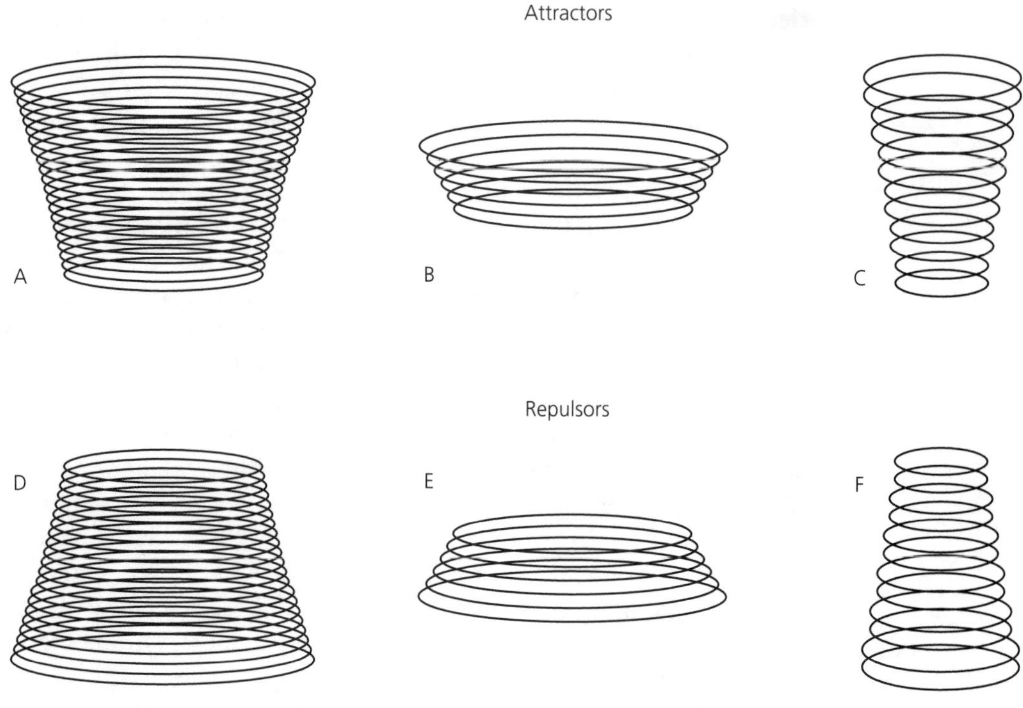

slope. Its frequency of occurrence, intensity, and duration can all be hypothesized as part of the example. Perhaps the best example of an attractor in operation is a vicious circle of nonfunctional behavior on the part of a manager.

In the case example featuring Ken, we see a good example of a vicious, anger dominated attractor. During one of our coaching sessions, he described a frequent pattern of his behavior in his interactions with fellow leaders. When faced with a complex and difficult set of external challenges to the business, Ken often turned to his colleagues and requested assistance. The majority of his colleagues were slow to respond to his requests because of a lack of skill and experience on their parts and their anxiety about interacting with Ken, who was an intense, brilliant, and energetic businessman. Their indecision and lack of responsiveness infuriated Ken to the point where he would explode at them with visible displays of anger and verbal criticism. He would then proceed to solve the problem by himself, which led him to be more resentful of his colleagues, more fatigued with his role in leadership within the organization, and feeling more hopeless about whether the business would succeed as in his dream. His behavior, in turn, added additional depth to the furor and misunderstanding his colleagues brought to their reporting relationships with Ken. He found it easy to move himself out of this pattern by decreasing his requests for assistance, staying busy with his own interests and role within the organization, and using his key confidants to vent some of the emotion these situations generated. Ken could not predict when he would fall into this vicious pattern of behavior, with the exception of when he felt he needed help from someone in the ownership group.

Attractor C in Figure 4.6 is illustrated as having steeper slopes. These types of attractors would probably be experienced as more intense patterns that generate either problems or solutions. As stated above, the frequency and duration characteristics displayed by an attractor for someone can also vary widely. In Ken's case, the attractor that I have described occurred often for him but did not last for a long time. The emotional and behavioral intensity of the episode in which he entered the attractor varied widely and often in accordance with his own emotional resilience, the scope of the problems that he was seeking support to solve, and the degree to which he was rebuffed by his colleagues.

There are several general types of attractors and repulsors. They can be virtuous and creative as they operate for a person, group, or organization. They also can be vicious and regressive, as we have seen in the example of Ken. Finally, they can be homeostatic, maintaining virtuous, vicious, or neutral patterns of behavior. In Ken's case, virtuous attractors were demonstrated in his application of analytic skills, an excellent work ethic, intense curiosity, and a powerful drive to achieve and succeed whenever confronted by an external problem. Ken most often chaotically popped out of his vicious circle or attractor and into his virtuous circle or attractor with little effort. However, he was unable to change the way in which he interacted with his colleagues before the initiation of coaching activities. Relating to his colleagues constructively appeared as a repulsor for Ken. He found it difficult to modify his behavior toward them in any significant way. Any effort to change his behavior pattern before coaching led to regression into the vicious circle or attractor.

Figure 4.6 also depicts three forms of repulsors, which are shown as mounds or the reverse geometric forms. While attractors pull people into and hold them in, repulsors do the opposite. A repulsor operating in a particular region of behavior will usually elicit avoidance behavior or a pattern of defensive operations that will be difficult to describe or explain. Often, a coach will watch a client approach a new and virtuous pattern of behavior only to see him or her seemingly bounce off the better pattern. This produces a great deal of consternation and concern for both the coach and the client. In other instances, some clients seem to instinctively avoid vicious circles, knowing when to exhibit tact, patience, diplomacy, self-awareness, and self-efficacy. These clients are easy to coach. Again, using Ken's case, a virtuous pattern of being able to create a constructive dialogue with his colleagues to achieve a higher level of understanding about the threats or problems facing the business and to elicit their cooperation and assistance in addressing these types of issues remained out of reach for him and his partners. Whenever he attempted to change himself, Ken would experience some response or change from his colleagues that short-circuited the improved pattern and led to the vicious one. These types of virtuous and creative repulsors appear as E and F in Figure 4.6. Before coaching, any effort to climb into this steep and virtuous pattern of behavior had nearly always ended in failure for Ken and his colleagues.

When I am coaching a client, I introduce the idea of virtuous or vicious circles or cycles of behavior as an exercise in self-awareness. I then make an effort to chart the structure, process, and contents of the circle that we are exploring. If I think it will help a client, I also describe some relevant concepts such as discontinuous change, attractors, and repulsors. I may also suggest that the client do a homework assignment of either mapping an existing attractor or repulsor or describing a new pattern or cycle that might be different and more effective than the one currently in use. The creation and use of a reflective containment greatly aids the activities of the coach and the client because it produces a safe arena in which to explore, experiment, and potentially change what a client is doing.

Within the containment, the executive coach behaves much like a scout or guide. Dangerous places and things to avoid are pointed out, as well as how to behave safely in a strange environment. The ability to anticipate and modify an approach based on information that is acquired before action is required is demonstrated to clients. Together, the coach and client explore the current approach being used to create meaning in the executive's life. Positive and negative feedback are provided by the coach to assist the client in creating, modifying, and even destroying attractors and repulsors, those virtuous and vicious circles of behavior. The coach constantly pushes the client away from vicious and regressive patterns and toward homeostatic, virtuous, and creative alternatives. When clients succeed, they have usually improved the ability to manage themselves in a wide variety of circumstances and therefore have created new and more functional meaning in their lives.

Developing Executive Wisdom

A well-designed and effective coaching process facilitates the emergence of wisdom in the executive client. Sternberg (1990) and a group of colleagues published a set of papers focusing on the characteristics and development of human wisdom. Kitchener and Brenner (1990) described *wisdom* as the development of reflective judgment and identified four major aspects of this capacity:

1. The presence of unavoidably difficult, "thorny" problems inherent in the lives of adults.
2. A comprehensive grasp of knowledge characterized by both breadth and depth.
3. A recognition that knowledge is uncertain and that it is not possible for truth to be absolutely knowable at any given time.
4. A willingness and exceptional ability to formulate sound, executable judgments in the face of this uncertainty. (p. 213)

Arlin (1990) described *wisdom* in general terms as the "art of problem finding." She went on to suggest that wisdom and problem finding share several of the following characteristics:

- preoccupation with questions rather than with answers
- the search for complementarity among points of view
- the detection of asymmetry in the face of evidence implying symmetry and equilibrium
- openness to change, pushing of the limits, and possible redefinition of those limits
- a taste for problems that are of fundamental importance
- preference for certain conceptual directions.

This is a wonderful description of the normal characteristics of the executive coaching process. The coach and client progressively use the reflective containment to engage in this creative type of problem finding. When coaching is successful, a client ultimately develops a better ability to engage in problem finding when needed. Truly successful clients are also able to coach and assist others in their organizations to become wiser in their own practices and approaches.

Pascual-Leone (1990) identified three principles that all executive coaches would do well to understand and use in their approaches to clients:

1. Wisdom causes the expert counselor to adopt a paradoxical attitude that fosters freedom while stressing the authority of reason and reasonable tradition.
2. Wisdom involves restricting one's interventions on others and on the world to those needed to restore harmonious relations among others and among elements of the world.
3. Wisdom involves dialectical integration of one's soul with one's agency in the world.

What a way to summarize the stance that we should take toward what we are trying to do with clients and toward the nature of the work we are doing. Coaches must recognize that as we help clients build self-awareness, the ability to work reflectively, and to make good decisions in the face of often extreme uncertainty and suffering, we are facilitating the emergence of human wisdom. As we do so, we often have profound influences on clients and on everyone that they influence. For those coaches who are blessed with and challenged by clients who work at the top of huge human organizations, coaching activities can potentially affect thousands of lives. I believe that it is absolutely necessary that anyone doing coaching in organizations must understand this potential for doing good in the world and for having disastrous—if unintended—effects when coaching does not go well.

I close the chapter by returning to Ken. Recall that he engaged a coach because of the major decision that he faced about whether to stay with his business or depart. During our last coaching session, Ken reported on the events that transpired in the retreat with his business partners.

"I got hammered, but I kept my mouth shut," he said with tension in his voice.

I listened carefully to what he said as he described what occurred in the all-day event. Ken reported that the facilitator for the retreat opened the meeting with a review of the information that she had gathered from the leadership team and the business itself. She emphasized both the strong points and the difficult business position that faced the group.

"She was able to get the group talking, but they started to criticize me. One person even asked for my resignation."

"What did you do when that happened?"

"I listened carefully to what he was saying, and I found myself writing a note on my pad that said 'assets = liabilities.' I recognized that many of the things he was describing that were very troubling to him and the other members of the group were precisely the activities that I felt I needed to undertake to preserve the business. However, I also recognized that some of what I did made people upset and quite defensive. I was quite pleased that I was able to take it all in without exploding. That was very different for me."

Ken went on to describe additional details of the meeting. I found his observations of the group, the facilitator's activities, and particular individuals to be very detailed, and his ability to understand what was going on in the group significantly improved from when we started our work together.

"After we spent about 6 hours, the facilitator left. I then presented my assessment of the status of the business. I tried to be as neutral and professional as possible. One of the other members of the group then stepped up and did a good job leading the discussion of my presentation. I was quite surprised by how well he did and the response of the group. It was exciting watching the group respond in a constructive fashion."

Ken and I then discussed what might have been occurring during the first 6 hours of the retreat. I pointed out that the members of the group may have felt much more comfortable as a result of their ability to discuss difficult material with him because he did not explode when confronted by one of his colleagues.

"I felt frustrated, though. After the discussion, the group decided to set up three task forces. All of them requested that I help them with the activities with which they were charged. Part of me wanted to tell them to 'go to hell' after all of the negative stuff that they said about me."

I pointed out to Ken that the group was acknowledging his expertise, energy, and commitment to the future of the business. I also suggested that the group was asking him to play a different role in his work with them. I encouraged him to think of himself as a consultant or coach to these three work groups. He went on to complain that he would need to do much of the work himself because of the primitive nature of the business skills of his colleagues.

"Think of it as though you were being asked to coach a Little League team that was just starting. What would your expectations be for the team's performance?" I asked.

"They would be lousy."

"Why?"

"Because they wouldn't know anything."

"And what would a good coach do in that situation?"

"I guess he would have to teach them."

I could hear Ken ponder this new way of thinking about his relationship to his colleagues. We went on from this conversation to consider what would have to be done to preserve the immediate future of the business. I suggested that he could attempt to negotiate a contract extension under the present arrangements and buy some time to let his business partners further develop their skills and motivation. I also suggested that the meeting was a significant success because they ended in a constructive place with virtually everyone agreeing to work harder as team members to preserve the business. I also pointed out that at the end, they were in fact all asking him to stay in the business and work with them using his skill and energy. They volunteered to be better leaders and stewards of the business. He acknowledged that he did not see the outcome quite so constructively before our session. We both discussed the strong emotions that he experienced during and after the session and how such feelings can shape perception, engage non-productive defensiveness, and lead to acting-out behavior.

"I'll be interested to see what happens next," Ken said.

Ken went on to thank me for our work together. "I never could have sat through that meeting and listened as well as I did without your coaching. I am very grateful for your help. I think I will try to negotiate a contract extension and see if our group can learn to work better together."

We finished our coaching session with a brief discussion of other consultants that the business might engage to help improve the group's collective performance.

This final excerpt of the case study illustrates all of the principal points discussed in this chapter. Having already established the containment within which it had become safe to explore and expose what was going on in his life, Ken willingly and effectively described what had happened to him. We used the circle of awareness and the process of coaching sessions to examine the details of the meeting and his reaction to it. He described his improved ability to avoid the vicious, regressive circle of becoming defensive, angry, and attacking his colleagues. He was able to avoid this catastrophic shift in his behavior during the retreat. Instead, he was able to enter a more virtuous and creative attractor and pattern of behavior. His accepting silence, willingness to listen, and refusal to become defensive enabled the group to better hear what he had to say later in the meeting. New leadership emerged during the latter part of the meeting and demonstrated a much higher level of maturity, wisdom, and professionalism. His colleagues then turned to him and asked him in a respectful way to play a new role in relationship to them. Through the containment provided by the coaching process and the work that he had done in it, Ken sustained a much more productive approach to this stressful set of interactions. He was also able to begin to conceptualize a new way of providing leadership to the organization without being trapped by the original dynamics of the start-up process. The net result of his coaching was to enable Ken to behave in a much wiser fashion. He made better choices for his behavior in conditions of extreme uncertainty, finding specific problems that he had previously ignored such as the lack of leadership skill and business training in his colleagues. He handled his own emotions with greater maturity. And, he felt proud of what he accomplished in a short period of time. When coaching works effectively, these are the outcomes that coaches hope to achieve.

5 Coaching and the Psychodynamics of Executive Character and Organizations

The Case of a Prickly Person

Susan, a senior staff member and programmer in the management information systems unit of the computing department, sought an appointment with me after she had witnessed significant, positive changes that her supervisor had made in his approach to the management of their department after approximately 3 months of executive coaching. I was already somewhat familiar with Susan from my work with her supervisor, who was struggling to make sense of a leadership succession process while working for an interim director. He supported her decision to solicit coaching assistance.

Susan had a reputation for technical excellence in her position. She worked very hard, completed her assignments on time, and expected her colleagues and clients to do the same. Many of her projects crossed multiple administrative lines within the organization, which required her to rely on others, work as part of multidisciplinary teams, and juggle many tasks with few resources under her control. She had two assistants who possessed reasonable competence, but she believed strongly that she had to watch their work carefully because of ongoing problems with lapses in quality.

Susan described her history of conflict with subordinates, peers, clients, and her supervisor. She complained bitterly of difficulties in obtaining the resources she knew she needed to do her job well. Her clients often complained about jobs being late, customized software that developed or was delivered with operating bugs, and problems in communicating with her staff. Susan maintained an attitude of unflagging support and diplomacy with clients in the organization, but she had a reputation as a picky perfectionist who would explode verbally with subordinates, colleagues, and managers in other departments on whom she sometimes depended for resources and administrative support. Her staff repeatedly went to her supervisor behind her back with complaints about her, and they also discussed the unit's problems with staff members in other departments.

In our first session, Susan described her frustrations with an administration that refused to supply the resources that she repeatedly and, as she saw it, tactfully requested. This situation forced her and her subordinates into untenable situations with clients in which they were often unable to deliver high-quality systems within the time frames expected. On many occasions in team meetings and administrative forums, her colleagues and others complained about the difficulties in quality and delivery they experienced from the products and services of her unit. These confrontations often resulted in harsh and sometimes nasty exchanges. Her supervisor had been approaching these issues by triangulating himself between Susan, her staff, and the others with whom conflict emerged. He often left Susan out of the loop, choosing whether to communicate about one of his discussions based on how much energy he had for dealing with her interpersonally, as well as how he evaluated the degree of political risk in a particular situation. This history made Susan resentful, suspicious, and often combative with him. During our session she said that she was very impressed by the way her supervisor had changed his behavior toward her and that their relationship was now one that she felt she could count on for support. We agreed to work together to assist her in refining her administrative and interpersonal style and to create a different approach to her professional relationships.

After several months and four or five sessions and telephone conversations in which we explored many of the troublesome aspects of her current situation and behavior and during which I constantly and tactfully pushed her toward an increased awareness of the complexities involved, Susan came in for a regular appointment bringing a copy of an e-mail note that she sent to her boss. It was an effort to educate him about a problem in one of her projects and about the effects that resource shortages and lack of cooperation from other departments had created for her and her staff. She wanted feedback from me about the content and tone in the note, observing that she had labored over the two paragraphs to try to ensure that it contained a constructive and problem-solving tone. As I read through the note, I discovered a typographical error in which she referred to the "moral" (meaning *morale*) of the unit staff. This typo was embedded in two paragraphs that described the various ways in which she and her staff were being forced to fail by the problems and difficulties in their department. To be sure, she had used constructive language and had certainly attempted to identify real problems.

I asked her what she thought the typo meant, and initially she simply laughed it off. She said that she was proud of the message and that she often had misspellings in her e-mail notes. I said that I could find only the one mistake in the note and wondered out loud if she might be making a statement about how she believed her superiors were managing the situation. She laughed again and said "not consciously." I agreed with her and asked if she wanted some feedback on the note. She said certainly. I proceeded to point out that the approximately 10 sentences all identified some form of failure. Although she had used tactful language, the note was actually one long complaint in which, between the lines, she repeatedly told her supervisor how he was failing her and their clients. I suggested that the typo actually might represent her true thoughts, namely, that she believed that her supervisor and many of his colleagues in the department had a problem behaving "morally" with regard to resource allocation, decision making, and interpersonal relations.

Susan was stunned by this suggestion. She claimed that this was not her intent. I asked her if that was what she thought, and she replied immediately "of course" and smiled broadly. This led to a discussion of the organizational and political constraints of her supervisor and their department and to an exploration of her tendency to demand perfection from both herself and the others close to her. We explored several major dimensions of emotion as they affected job performance, including anger, sadness, shame, and anxiety. Susan admitted that she was chronically angry with those with whom she worked. During the session, she also disclosed that her mother had been orphaned during the Holocaust and that both of her parents were demanding, preoccupied with doing what they considered right, and angry and depressed most of the time. At the end of this discussion, Susan acknowledged that these were real problems that she must solve if she wanted to make professional progress. She promised to take up these issues with her outside psychotherapist, who had never really questioned her about her job difficulties. She stated that she would make a series of additional appointments with me to explore further these issues.

In our next appointment, Susan and I made progress on her anger, clarifying some of the stimulus conditions and typical response modes that characterized many of her interpersonal exchanges. We identified several techniques that she could use when she felt herself "losing it" with someone. We also spent a little time further exploring her expectations of others in light of her own developmental experiences and those of her parents. She described the emotional burden that many children in Holocaust families feel to challenge what is wrong in the world and to succeed in all things. She stated that she had never seen or experienced this largely unconscious pattern as causing any trouble for her, but she now understood that her high standards; tendencies to demand, overgeneralize, and think categorically; and willingness to fight overtly and sometimes with unrelenting negativity made her a target for rumors, gave her a reputation for being hard to get along with, and had probably caused her to lose several promotional opportunities.

A week after this session, Susan called me and described a series of meetings that made her furious. However, she retained control of her temper and used several of the techniques that we had discussed, including timing herself out, making notes rather than knee-jerk responses, and being careful to stay problem focused and assertive rather than trying to correctly apportion the blame on her colleagues. She was pleased with what she had accomplished but complained that it was draining and difficult for her to do. She also said that her superiors had announced that they would be getting a new department director.

Several days later, one of my colleagues in the human resources department stopped into my office. She wanted to let me know that Susan had been terminated and offered a generous severance package. She said that Susan had asked if I could continue to coach her as she made her transition. Surprised and concerned, I agreed to do so.

At our next session, Susan and I discussed her derailment. She was remarkably composed and not overly concerned about finding another job in a full employment economy. She said she could see how she had contributed to the situation that led to the decision to release her. She was concerned with some of the formal language in the termination letter, stating her belief that it potentially placed most of the blame for the situation on her. Despite a promise by the organization that the letter would never be shown to anyone but her, we discussed her approach for negotiating changes in the letter and her plan for outplacement, and we scheduled a series of follow-up meetings.

At the next meeting, Susan came dressed in jeans and a T-shirt. She reported that she was able to negotiate successfully for the removal of the offensive language from the termination letter by using her sense of humor; excellent history of working relationships with key colleagues; and tactful, diplomatic assertiveness and by staying out of the attractor of angry, blaming, and threatening behavior to which she felt constantly drawn. She had been to see her outplacement consultant and already had an informational interview with her previous employer from whom she expected a job offer. She said that she was feeling tired from the emotional strain of the changes, but she was happy about how things seemed to be working out for her. She said that she wanted to focus our work on how she could ensure that she would not repeat the negative pattern of behavior in a new position.

This example illustrates many of the typical issues that coaching practitioners face with clients who are in deep trouble in their organizations and careers and may not even know it. The complex interactions between organizational systems, group and organizational behavior, and the conscious and unconscious components of the patterns and dynamics of behavior in individual clients and organizational units present some of the greatest challenges and problems to coaches. This chapter briefly describes three core problems in coaching executives on psychodynamic and performance issues and identifies conceptual and technical approaches to manage these problems: executive character as a complex self-organizing, adaptive system that influences the unconscious aspects of organizational life, unconscious and conscious psychological conflict as key motivating factors in individual and organizational behavior, and the challenges of changing executive character and behavior to improve organizational performance.

Executive Character as a Complex Self-Organizing Adaptive System

Within the approach described in chapters 2–4, it can be seen that individual, group, and organizational behavior arise from the interaction of 6 system and 11 psychodynamic dimensions. Many other authors have described both system and psychodynamic issues as they interact in human organizations (Baum, 1987; Czander, 1993; Diamond, 1993; Fineman, 1993; Kets deVries, 1984; Kets deVries & Miller, 1987; Levinson, 1981; Lowman, 1993; Obholzer & Roberts, 1994; O'Neil, 1993; Schwartz, 1990). As stated in previous chapters, Stacey (1996) examined the interaction between complexity theory and psychodynamics as they operate in human organizations. He emphasized that the future of any institution and its people depended on the ability to move individuals, groups, and organizations into a phase state in which compulsive and largely defensive behavioral routines can be transcended without regressing into emotionally pressured, pathological symptoms and disorders. In these paradoxical phase states, Stacey believed that creativity and growth become possible. He also maintained that the self-organizing, adaptive success of any human system, including that of individual executives, depends on the ability to enter into and benefit from the new ideas and pattern-breaking behaviors that become possible when anxiety and human resistances can be contained and managed. In chapter 4, I examined some of these ideas through the application of chaos concepts and showed that successful coaching can enable a client to do complex and difficult executive work with a greater degree of human wisdom.

Figure 3.1 depicted the foci for executive coaching as initially described by Kilburg (1996b) in which the systems dimensions become one routine focus for coaching sessions. All of the psychodynamic dimensions along with the issues of job requirements, roles, tasks, and knowledge, skills, and abilities become the second major focus for coaching. In this second zone the traditional issues of leadership style, personality, and character are usually addressed. In organizations, human relationships serve as the place in which both of these foci tend to play out as work is conducted by the people engaged in the enterprise.

The opening case study presented a typical illustration of these various dimensions in real-time operation in an organization. Susan, the manager responsible for designing and delivering high-quality outputs and software products to demanding internal customers, had to mobilize herself and her subordinates and the structures, processes, and contents of the organization's systems to do her job. Although she had been successful at creating and delivering the products and at managing her unit's resources, various components of her conscious and unconscious behavior, as manifested through and mediated by her working relationships with subordinates, colleagues, and superiors, led to the derailment of her career in the organization. Susan did everything that she could think of to prevent this from happening, but her adaptive efforts clearly failed, and our coaching activities obviously began too late in the process.

Susan understood a lot about herself; she had worked for years with a private psychotherapist. She had direct access to her emotions and could identify and tolerate them sufficiently to discuss them with me. She quickly made the connection between her inability to constructively channel her anger and the difficulties that she was encountering on the job. However, the contribution of the dynamics of her family-of-origin to the creation and functioning of a demanding and perfectionistic conscience was completely unconscious until she brought in the e-mail message for discussion. Once this issue surfaced,

Susan demonstrated a remarkable ability to use the material consciously, and she quickly began to change her approach to her superiors and subordinates. The knowledge that part of the source of her anger and the extent of her demanding and desire for perfect performance from others came from inside of her, and that it had evolved partially from her family's transgenerational experience helped her move in a different direction.

Unfortunately, her superiors and colleagues had already decided that they were unwilling to grant her any additional time to change her behavior. The combination of the leadership succession process and an absence of leadership support for Susan led to the preparation and delivery of an "eviction notice" from which there was no appeal and within which there was little room to negotiate. The collective action of the connected group of colleagues to reject and expel her was done as a surprise *fait accompli*. Comments by the human resources manager led me to understand that the leadership team in the unit was frustrated and angry at Susan for her approach to situations, her constant battles with those around her, and her "negativity." From the consultant's perspective, I felt that Susan was scapegoated by the group for the many flaws and problems in operating systems, historic inadequacies in management and supervision, and real resource shortages. No person in the administrative system was willing to sit down with Susan and review the history and problems with her or specify that changes in her behavior must be made. Instead, the group eliminated her position in a "reorganization" that would give the new director a free hand in redesigning and shaping the unit. This is a fairly typical outcome in many of these situations in that organizations and their leaders act in a way consistent with their own patterns of conflicts, defenses, and emotions. The outcomes of these actions are not always in the best interests of the organization and certainly not of individuals.

Within these models and this example, it can be seen that executive character is both complex and adaptive. It has many dimensions, both conscious and unconscious, and its influence on organizations and individuals can be profound. The example also demonstrates how difficult these complexities can be for executives and their organizations. Mismatches between an individual's character and the culture, relationship matrix, and psychodynamic patterns of an organization can lead to failure of the executive, the team or subunit, or the entire organization. Similarly, failures by consultants or coaches to consider the complex, adaptive nature of executive character and these psychodynamic patterns of behavior in enterprises in their work often lead to major resistance to organization development interventions (Stacey, 1996).

Unconscious Psychological Conflict in Individual and Organizational Behavior

We might ask why individuals, who consciously desire to succeed and do an excellent job, who bring energy and passion to their work, who put in long hours and "sweat the details," and who possess superb educational foundations and technical backgrounds for their jobs, manage to fail so often? Hogan et al. (1994) suggested that up to 50% of executives will "derail" or fail in their efforts to advance in their careers. To me, this figure is staggeringly high, and it indicates that organizations are woefully underprepared to help managers perform well in their jobs and succeed in their careers. The case of Susan demonstrates some of the complexities in this arena, because conventional approaches to professional development failed in her situation.

Susan routinely attended professional conferences to keep her knowledge and skills sharp. She had also taken advantage of some of the internal course offerings on management and supervision in her organization's training department. Susan also had obtained the services of an outside psychotherapist, whom she said was very helpful to her. In spite of these efforts and the availability of the resources and administrative support in her organization, Susan's behavior on the job never changed until she began working explicitly to do so in a coaching relationship. As she started this work, she could identify many of the problem behaviors and contributing factors. She could describe these issues and complexities in insightful detail. However, she had been unable to change her behavior. Only after manifesting and exploring aspects of the unconscious components of the behavior was she able to mobilize herself and begin to make creative efforts at doing something different. I believe that this example amply demonstrates the second major problem of coaching executive character, namely, that unconscious psychological conflict in individuals, work groups, and organizations often impedes executive and organizational performance.

Figure 5.1 presents a flowchart of the structure and process of psychodynamic conflict and adaptation; it represents a pictorial summary of the detailed work of theorists such as Brenner (1976), Conte and Plutchik (1995), Anna Freud (1966), Sigmund Freud (1916, 1923, 1933), Gray (1994), Greenspan (1989), Langs (1973, 1974), and O'Neil (1993). The chart begins with stimuli of two major types, external reality, such as challenges and trauma, and internal states, such as wishes and drives. These stimuli are informed and influenced by the person's

FIGURE 5.1

Structure and Process of Psychodynamic Conflict and Adaptation
The unconscious or shadow system of behavior.

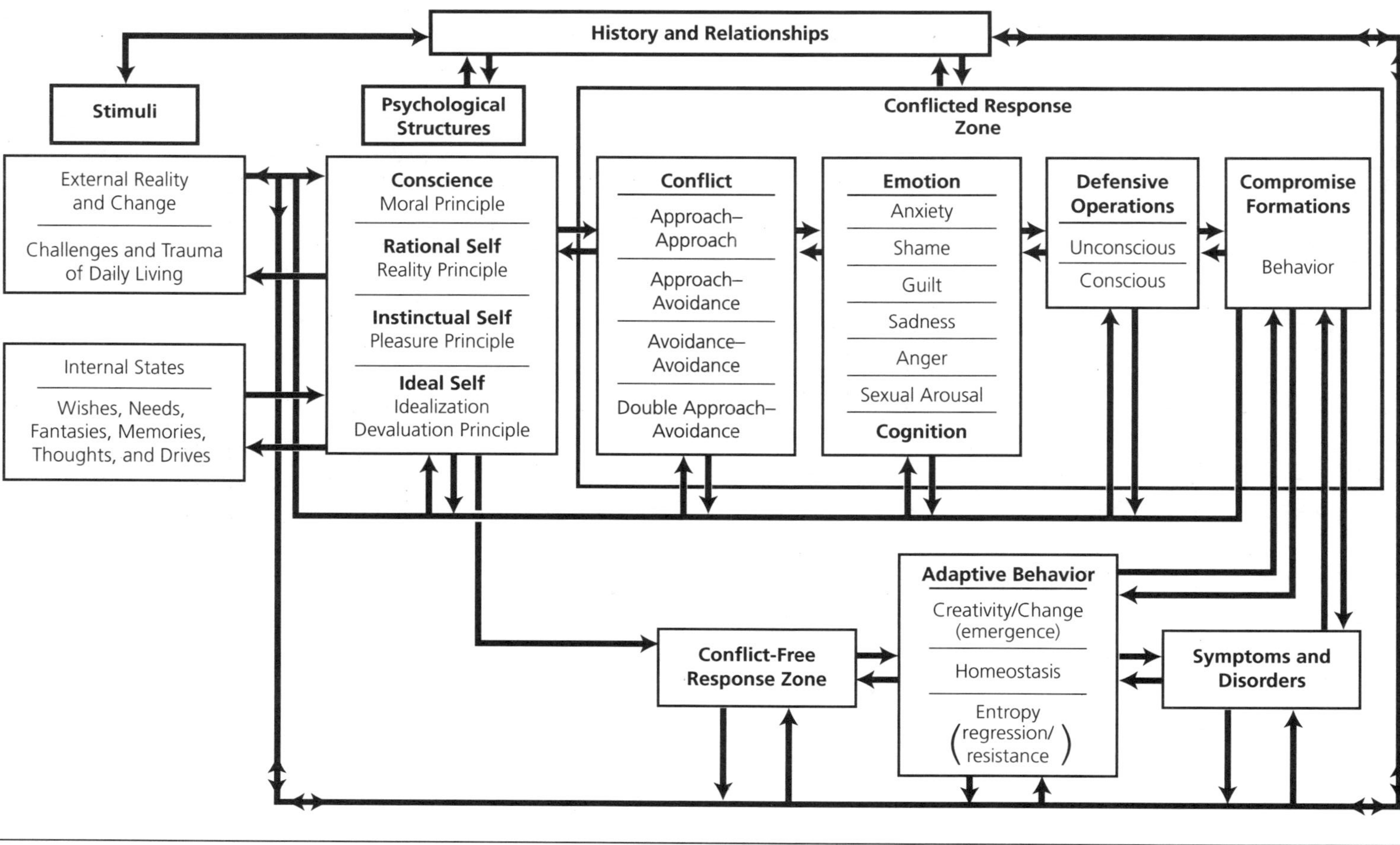

history and relationships and push the major psychological structures of conscience, rational self, instinctual self, and ideal self to respond from each of their major organizing principles. If these structures are not in conflict about what is occurring and the responses that are required to meet the stimulus demand, the result is behavior that can be said to exist in a "conflict-free zone" and that can produce adaptive efforts that can have homeostatic, entropic, or emergent properties. In other words, the adaptive behavior can lead to maintaining the status quo; creating change; or causing decaying, regressive behavior.

However, if the psychological structures are in conflict over the stimulus, the feelings generated by the stimulus, or the response that should be made, the resulting behavior enters into the conflicted-response zone. As described in chapter 2, conflicts of various types (approach–approach, approach–avoidance, avoidance–avoidance, and double approach–avoidance) are mediated by and interact with emotional and cognitive systems. The emotions of anxiety, shame, guilt, sadness, anger, and sexual arousal play particularly important roles. Defensive operations such as splitting, denial, projection, rationalization, intellectualization, detachment, isolation, humor, creativity, and others are then brought into play, and the result is a behavioral response to the stimulus called a *compromise formation*. These compromise behaviors represent the best that a person can do under the circumstances of inner unconscious or external conflict.

These behaviors can be thought of in two major categories. The first comprises the adaptive efforts described above. I suggest that most compromise formations, even as they represent the results of unconscious conflict, do lead to adaptive efforts. History and clinical material are replete with examples of major creative or destructive acts performed by individuals as a result of their inner conflicts. The second, and more problematic, category is behavior that produces symptoms and disorders for the individual (American Psychiatric Association, *Diagnostic and Statistical Manual of Mental Disorders*, 4th ed; *DSM–IV*, 1994). Table 5.1 provides example compromise formations that are often seen in executive behavior. These examples are summarized from Horney's (1937, 1942) celebrated exposition of neurotic trends in human behavior. Several of these compromise formations are at work in the character and behavior of Susan in the case study. Her drive for perfection, need to dominate others, and need for affection and recognition all contributed significantly to her professional derailment. It is important to note that consultants can, in fact, encounter almost any symptomatic behavior or psychological disorder in their work in organizations. The *DSM–IV* (1994) formally recognizes 10 types of personality disorder, the worst forms of character disturbances. No effort will be made here to describe them despite the fact that these disorders can

TABLE 5.1

Examples of Compromise Formations

1. Need for affection and approval
    - indiscriminant desire to please others and live up to their expectations
    - strict conformity; fear of self-assertion; fear of conflict or hostility in self or others
2. Need for a partner who takes over life
    - love solving all of the problems in the world
    - fear of abandonment; fear of being alone
3. Need to restrict one's life within narrow borders
    - reduced ambition, necessity to remain in second place
    - modesty as the supreme value
    - fear of self-expression or making demands
4. Need for power
    - seeking dominance in all things and relationships
    - combativeness; basic disrespect for others' feelings and dignity
    - adoration of strength and contempt for weakness of any kind
    - fear of loss of control or helplessness
    - belief in the omnipotence of intelligence and reason
    - fear of mistakes, errors, and bad judgment
    - belief in the omnipotence of will
    - hyperresponsive to any frustration of wishes
    - fear of recognition of any limitations
5. Need to exploit others
    - pride in exploitation of others, bargaining, possession
    - fears of being exploited and possessed
6. Need for social recognition or prestige
    - self-image and esteem based entirely on social acceptance
    - fears of public humiliation or shame
7. Need for personal admiration
    - narcissism, entitlement
    - need to be admired for one's fantasy image of self
    - fears of public humiliation or shame
8. Need for personal achievement above all else
    - self-esteem dependent on being recognized as "the best"; constant striving to compete and defeat others; workaholism
    - relentless anxiety-ridden drive for success
    - fears of failure
9. Need for self-sufficiency and independence
    - fears of attachment, love, needing others
    - detachment as the major source of security; difficulty in belonging to a team or group
10. Need for perfection
    - fear of errors, mistakes, flaws, criticism
    - fears of public humiliation or shame

Adapted from *The Neurotic Personality of Our Time* and *Self Analysis* by K. Horney, 1937 and 1942, respectively. New York: W. W. Norton. Copyrights 1937 and 1942 by W. W. Norton.

have major negative effects on organizations. If the destructive effects of character problems are to be minimized, these disorders and the unconscious patterns of conflict and behavior that contribute to or result from them must be addressed directly by consultants when they are encountered.

I have come to believe that when these compromise formations are shaped into repetitive responses to social or psychological stimuli, chaotic attractors emerge as described in chapter 4. Thus, patterns identified in Table 5.1 can represent chaotic attractors for individuals who find themselves repeatedly and somewhat uncontrollably falling into or engaging the compromise formation. Depending on the strength and viciousness of the particular compromise, the extent of its negative or positive effects on the person and the organization, and the motivation for changing what may be acknowledged as a problem or seen as a strength for the client, the coach will have an easier or harder time in an assignment. It is clear that individuals have varying degrees of psychological self-awareness with regard to what these patterns are in their own lives or in the lives of their work groups. One of the major tasks of coaching involves being able to recognize these patterns and determine how they function for individuals or the teams with which they may be working. It will be critical for coaches to recognize that such patterns or attractors often are experienced as strengths by the client and can be difficult to challenge because they often serve to protect and advance the client's interests—at least for the short term.

The flowchart also indicates that each component of this complex system can interact with any and all of the other components. Defenses can affect psychological structure, emotion, cognition, the nature of a conflict itself, the original stimulus, and the individual's relationships and history. Adaptive behavior, particularly creative change, clearly can affect all of these components as well. Indeed, coaching efforts systematically try to push clients into this creative and adaptive zone, what Stacey (1996) called a *paradoxical phase state,* in which new learning that makes fundamental changes in the way in which an individual operates can occur.

Bion (1961) and Kernberg (1998) demonstrated that groups themselves can have organized defensive operations in response to conflicts such as fight–flight, dependency, and pairing. These patterns also act as vicious circles or chaotic attractors for groups and organizations. Chapter 8 provides additional information and observations about group and organizational defenses. Many of the authors identified earlier in this chapter have described the operation of similar unconscious processes and structures in organizations themselves. These levels of conflict and adaptive or symptomatic behavior frequently are influenced by or are causally related to the inner lives of the members of the organization, including components of their characters or personalities.

The structure and process of psychodynamic conflict comes into focus whenever consultants are called on to help an individual or organizational client address a problem that relates to character issues. These patterns often exert major influence on organizational performance. Susan was broadly known in the organization as a "prickly character." Some of her behaviors routinely caused problems for her colleagues and superiors, leading to major conflict between organizational units and individuals. Nothing that they tried to do had any impact on the behavior. Susan herself suffered greatly from being such a character, and she clearly wanted to change. She even had external psychotherapeutic assistance, but the patterns persisted until she was forced out of the organization. After she was able to identify and explore some of the levels of unconscious conflict directly tied to the daily experience of her work life in her coaching sessions, she began to make steady progress in changing the way she related to her colleagues. Her interactions around standards of performance and errors became less infused with anger, and deliberate efforts to make people feel guilty and ashamed or to control them decreased. She became somewhat more realistic about her role in the organization and the degree to which she was responsible for problems that arose. As her awareness of her levels of anger increased, she proved more creative and flexible in managing the emotions in the moment. She started to talk to her therapist actively about the degree to which the unstated values, assumptions, wishes, beliefs, and largely unexplored traumatic history of her family might be affecting her behavior at work through the processes and various compromise formations that have been discussed. Most of this progress was made after she brought in the e-mail for a brief review. A single slip, the deletion of an "e" from a critical word, and the way in which I was able to work with that material freed Susan to enter into a more creative and constructive effort to change her behavior.

Many consultants who do coaching do not subscribe to a psychodynamic perspective and, therefore, would be unwilling and even unable to work with clients in this fashion. Many of their efforts can still be successful, and Figure 5.2 suggests why. Keep in mind that a great deal of behavior for any individual can be said to operate in the conflict-free zone. If an individual has a need to learn something new or to change some behavior that has been or become a problem, and there is little or no conflict about what must be done, the person and the consultant will usually be able to work together successfully to address the issue. Similarly, in a group or organization that is motivated to examine what must be changed and to move forward, there is often

FIGURE 5.2

Multidimensional Components of Executive Character

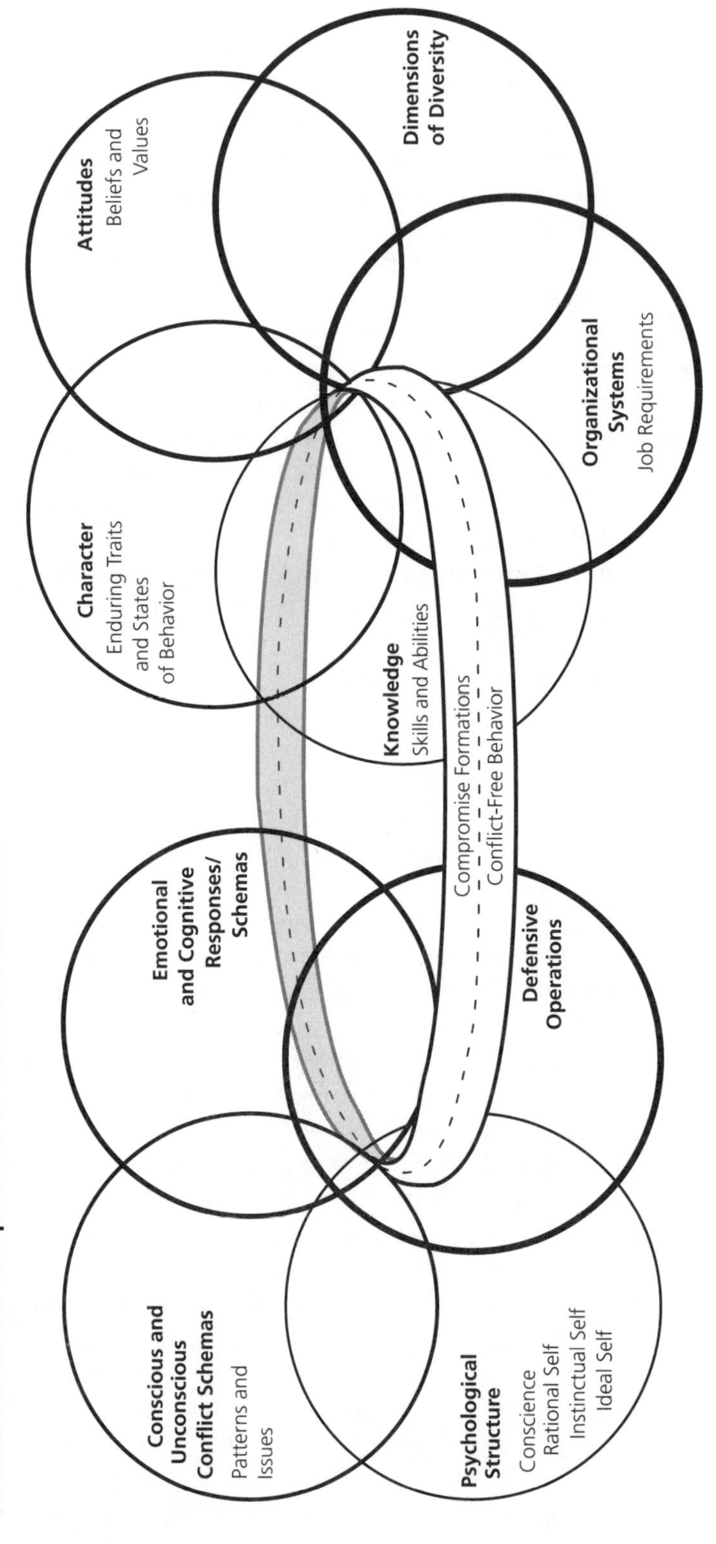

no true need to explore the shadow or unconscious side of its functioning. However, when conflict does appear, when behavior does not change despite overt assurances that the motivation to do so is high, where major resistance is encountered, and when clients say everything they have tried has failed, coaches should be alerted to the possibility that psychodynamic conflict may be present and will need to be managed effectively for progress to be made.

Figure 5.2 further illustrates this complexity by presenting the multidimensional components of executive character in a somewhat different view. The major components of the 17-dimensional model from Figure 2.1 are arrayed in a series of interlocking Venn diagrams. At the center of each of the diagrams is a zone of behavior depicted as a band that can range from conflict free and adaptive to symptomatic and disordered. This behavior zone links the three major psychodynamic dimensions, including the psychological structures of conflict, defense, emotion, cognition, and the various forms of relationships. In addition, the diagram extends Figure 5.1 by illustrating that these psychodynamic dimensions are also linked through behavior, structure, and process to what is called *character*, or "the sum of a person's relatively fixed personality traits and habitual modes of response" (American Psychiatric Association, 1980; p. 31), a person's attitudes, beliefs, and values; the individual's dimensions of diversity, including age, race, ethnicity, gender, sexual orientation, marital status, managerial style, and so forth; the organizational systems and job requirements of the present position; and the person's knowledge, skills, and abilities. This figure illustrates that character is thus intimately interconnected with all other psychological, behavioral, and organization dimensions and that this linkage is most often seen in either conflict-free behavior or compromise formations. A consultant's coaching efforts can and may need to enter any or all of these domains to help an individual client develop. Coaches and consultants will be more successful with a wider range of clients and in more conflicted situations if they can keep these psychodynamic principles in mind, and if they can help clients find meaningful ways to address unconscious issues that may be uncovered.

Changing Executive Character and Behavior

I have demonstrated that coaching with executives can be a complex phenomenon involving dynamic systems and requiring an understanding of unconscious conflict. However, most of the material presented thus far concentrates on the issues of why this work is so difficult and on where to look when major problems arise. The case study suggests part of the third and final problem, namely, how coaches work with executives to help them change themselves and their behaviors. At conferences, in workshops, in the hallways of consulting organizations, and in supervision sessions, that issue dominates many of the conversations. This is one of the most challenging issues facing consultants and coaches. I would like to suggest that it is possible to construct a systematic approach to the issue that borrows liberally from the century of empirical and clinical work of our psychotherapeutic colleagues but that retains the unique components of working with so-called "normal" people, usually in their work settings. What, then, are the components to this systematic approach?

First, as explored in chapter 4, the major principle underlying the provision of effective executive coaching services is to improve the self-awareness of the client. Recent empirical research has demonstrated a significant positive relationship between managerial self-awareness and managerial performance (Church, 1997; Wohlers & London, 1989; Yammarino & Atwater, 1993). These studies have suggested that as managers become more insightful about various aspects and requirements for the execution of their jobs by way of participation in 360° reviews, ratings of their managerial performance by subordinates, peers, and supervisors improve. The empirical nature of these findings is reassuring, but in reality these studies represent an extension of what practicing clinicians and clinical researchers have demonstrated repeatedly with vast numbers of people and a huge array of problems. As human beings improve their ability to be self-aware, they become more able to change things for the better in their lives. Although self-awareness itself is no guarantee of improvement, as people change things for the better, their mental and physical health and their performance in chosen spheres of activity get better. This principle, then, provides solid and strong guidance for executive coaches. Any activity, structure, or process that increases a client's ability to be self-aware ultimately can positively affect his or her management and leadership skills.

Self-awareness can be improved through a variety of mechanisms. As stated above, formal 360° review instruments have demonstrated a positive impact on executive growth. These reviews are now routinely included in many organizations' formal approaches to executive coaching (Peterson, 1996; Saporito, 1996). Some consultants also are using other psychological tests, family interviews, and behavioral observations to provide additional data to clients (Kiel, Rimmer, Williams, & Doyle, 1996). These approaches extend the traditional uses of the assessment center (Howard & Bray, 1988) to provide information and ongoing efforts to change the behavior of specific clients and not just to select them for positions or promotions. As described in previous chapters, psychotherapy can be useful for many clients in increasing access to their emotional lives, understanding family-of-origin dynamics, working through the toxic effects of various traumas, and improving clients' ability to voluntarily direct their flows of attention. Barron (1993), S. Freud (1937), Goldberg (1993), Gray (1994), and Horney (1942) have described the uses and many of the techniques of self-analysis, an effective and traditional approach based on psychodynamic theory and psychoanalytic technique. Thus, a wide variety of human activities can be useful in pushing and supporting an individual's quest to improve self-awareness.

Keeping this fundamental principle in mind, a consultant can then orient him- or herself in virtually any situation with a client. One of the major goals is to improve the client's self-awareness, and, because the steps to such improvement also increase managerial and leadership performance, the consultant acts in a tactful and sensitive way with individuals or groups to

- Always try to get problems "on the table," where they can be approached consciously and explored actively.
- Make the unsaid said. Keep in mind that organizations and their people often know or perceive precisely what the problems are with individuals or systems, but they often collude to keep silent or to use nonproductive and at times symptomatic compromise formations instead of describing what is happening and engaging in constructive problem finding and solving—that is, engaging human wisdom.
- Make the unconscious conscious. As described in the case study and previous material, this can be an extremely useful and productive approach. However, not everyone is equipped to do the work. A coach who believes that unconscious aspects of behavior are at work in a client and who does not feel comfortable addressing these issues can look for a partner to help or someone to whom to refer this aspect of the coaching project.

Second, as explored in detail in chapter 4, creating a safe containment for the coach and client in which reflection, creative exploration, and self-examination are encouraged and supported is a necessary first step. Table 4.1 identified some characteristics of the coaching relationship that will help coaches build and maintain that safety zone with clients. It borrowed from the work of Langs (1974), Meissner (1996), Stacey (1996), and Winnicott (1965). As Stacey described in his recent book, the goal is to create a phase state between the controlled, homeostatically balanced, and defensive behaviors of everyday life and the destructive potential of a psychotic regression. In a safe, holding environment that has the characteristics described in Table 4.1, it becomes possible to explore, experiment, think, feel, and do what seemed impossible, and to grow as a human being and as a manager.

Third, and finally, coaches should always try to approach the client from the side of the rational self. Keep in mind that coaching activities and the coaching relationship themselves can become stimuli that move a client into the zone of unconscious conflict. Consultants must work hard to keep their own work with clients as clear of this zone as possible. Table 5.2 provides an array of methods and techniques that can facilitate growth and minimize resistance. These approaches can be combined with many of the other organization development interventions identified in Table 2.11 to create complex change strategies for clients.

Virtually any coaching intervention that overtly or covertly judges behavior has the potential for siding with the client's conscience and eliciting a great deal of historical material related to moral development, episodes of public embarrassment and shame, relationships in which struggles for control and autonomy were significant, and events and activities about which there may still be a great deal of unresolved guilt. A coach acting as an agent of moral development, enforcement, or social control takes significant risks with the future of the consulting work because characteristics of the client's past relationships, some of which may be extremely dysfunctional, may be brought into the ongoing coaching relationship. There is currently no real guidance on or technique for managing these types of transference relationships outside of psychodynamic psychotherapy and psychoanalysis. I believe that it is highly doubtful that the techniques that have proved effective and safe in the therapeutic environment will be entirely or easily applicable to coaching relationships. However, moral and ethical issues can be addressed forthrightly by coming at them from the side of reality. Inviting a client to consider consequences, providing suggestions or data points that a client might want to consider before acting or in making reparations, or telling someone the kinds of issues that would readily come to mind if the coach were placed in a similar position are techniques that can maintain the quality of the relationship. They can also stimulate the client to explore thoroughly a difficult matter and consider actively choosing a different course of action, without evoking compromise formations or chaotic and dysfunctional attractors that lead to maladaptive behavior, symptoms, or disorders.

Similarly, siding with the instinctual self of a client can be a risky tactic. Encouraging a client to act on events that have produced strong emotions such as anger, fear, shame, or sadness or to take a course of action that seems logical but perhaps impulsive invites the client to "act out" with permission. If the action taken proves ill-advised, the client might blame the coach for not stopping him or her from doing something harmful. In addition, in those cases in which there is an internal history of conflict between the client's instinctual self and the conscience or rational self, a coach runs the risk of being "judged" by these other structures and found to be not helpful, professional, effective, moral, and so forth. Here again, responding to the client from the rational side, which encourages reflection, consideration of consequences, and alternative and creative courses of action, but also empathizing with the desire for quick action in response to strong emotion, will ultimately prove more consistently helpful. This does not speak to the case in which there may be a crisis that demands rapid and rational responses. In those situations, a coach does his or her best to help clients determine how they feel, what may be reality-based or emotional consequences, and to scan rapidly through the range of acceptable and effective responses.

Situations in which a coach feels drawn to idealize or devalue a client or some aspect of his or her behavior or performance also must be handled with caution. Clients are human in every way. They want to be admired, and they try to avoid being devalued at all costs. Providing the basic containment for the coaching relationship addresses most of these issues (see Table 4.1). Communicating basic respect for a person and for their efforts to improve themselves and their organizations, encouraging exploration, and tolerating frustration and anxiety that comes with risk-taking are all appropriate parts of the basic coaching relationship. Unnecessary compliments, encouragements, flattery, or courting favor will usually lead to trouble in coaching relationships. When circumstances call for a coach to provide "bad news"; "negative feedback"; or simply to challenge or discourage attitudes, values, beliefs, assumptions, or behavior that the coach thinks will lead a client to a poor outcome, extreme caution rules the session. Coaches must gauge the extent to which a client is ready to receive such information or engage in a real dialogue. I usually try to prepare a client by setting up a "good news–bad news" format to a feedback session, or by asking the client if it is a good time to move to some difficult material. It has been my experience that clients can be remarkably courageous in exploring and reflecting, if the relationship is sound, the information is presented in the spirit of enabling the client to explore and consider safely, and the coach is prepared to reduce pressure if the situation seems to call for it. In addition, humor, metaphors, reframing, and personal examples in these situations can be extremely useful if a coach is sensitive to when a comment, story, or example is the best way to make a point and not simply put the client in a one-down, defensive posture.

TABLE 5.2

Coaching Methods to Facilitate Growth and Minimize Resistance

Use of appreciative inquiry (Cooperrider, 1996) and Socratic method (Overholser, 1993) to establish a reflective, dialectic dialogue.

Exercising great care in the choice of language:
- Nonnormative, descriptive statements.
- Permissive statements (using *could* instead of *should*, and making suggestions or providing ideas that "might be considered, explored, reflected on, or thought about").
- Skillful and tactful maneuvering when the consultant believes that he or she made an error of omission or commission (including apologies and amends when necessary).
- Use of metaphors, symbols, stories, and examples to which the client can easily relate.

Requesting permission to ask questions, explore issues, challenge or push the client.

Issuing invitations to explore issues and events; receive feedback; consider other options, choices, ideas, data, opinions; be curious; experiment with new concepts and behaviors; and play creatively.

Asking for assistance and help in learning about the client's world, history, relationships, experiences, and ways in which the person thinks, perceives, feels, responds, solves problems, learns best, defends, manages conflict, and generally behaves.

Working together to create and play "what if" games, build scenarios, create simulations, explore future considerations, and anticipate potential developments or outcomes.

Encouraging the client to develop and use empathy and to employ it to reflect the positions, behaviors, attitudes, and values expressed by the other important people in the environment.

Encouraging the use of higher order psychological defenses including sublimation, reality testing, problem solving, creativity, humor, constructive play, curiosity, communication skills, and accurate empathy.

Exploring the overt and covert meanings of statements, behaviors, and positions.

Clarifying values and assumptions that underlie statements, behaviors, and positions.

Listening actively and carefully at all times for indications that other dimensions of behavior and reality may be active in a situation, especially when there may be conflicts and contradictions in what is said, implied, or described by the client, and when there may be multiple motives, unstated wishes and needs, situations in which behavior or performance is being judged overtly or covertly, and circumstances that may be repeating historical patterns of behavior or conflicting client expectations based on the client's history or dimensions of diversity.

Being aware of the client's dimensions of diversity and being prepared to explore any that may be relevant to the problem or issue being discussed.

Being judicious in the use of self-disclosure.

Providing assistance in properly "framing" and/or "reframing" an issue, event, or problem.

Working carefully to identify and manage defensive behaviors and resistance to exploration, growth, and change when they occur.

Using your skills to assist the client to choose the appropriate focus for the coaching work and the correct zone and mode for his or her attention:

- Adaptive problems of external reality at work or in the client's personal or professional life.
- Internal states involving wishes, needs, fantasies, memories, thoughts, and drives.
- Actions, responses, predispositions and expectations of the inner psychological structures of conscience, rational self, instinctual self, and idealized self.
- Conscious and unconscious psychological, interpersonal, and reality-based conflicts.
- Emotions, especially anxiety, anger, shame, sadness, or sexual arousal, and thoughts.
- Compromise formations that express the outcomes of the processes of conscious and unconscious conflict and result in various forms of adaptive behavior or that can lead to the formation of symptomatic behavior and mental and physical disorders.
- Conscious and unconscious defensive operations and resistance to learning, change, and self-awareness.
- Knowledge, skill, and ability strengths or deficits.

Providing new information, ideas, concepts, methods, skills, and material that can stimulate learning.

Providing emotional support for the processes of exploration and change, including hope, encouragement and, when appropriate, confrontation.

Practicing or rehearsing new or altered skills and behaviors.

Using other techniques and tools of organization development, psychotherapy, behavior modification, and education.

In every session with a client, the coach's helping skills are tested and on display. Coaches listen; empathize; provide feedback; give information; create scenarios; challenge; symbolize; and explore the wonderful, often wacky, and sometimes traumatic worlds of executives and work teams. At each turn, the client watches and listens to the coach very carefully for how he or she conducts the session. Clients judge their coaches realistically and at times harshly. In the end, the client must determine whether the time, energy, and financial investment is worthwhile.

Finally, coaches must recognize that one of their most essential skills is how they help a client direct his or her attention. Each component in Figure 5.2 becomes a potential world for the client to explore with coaching assistance. The coach uses his or her judgment constantly to assist a client to determine on which of these issues a particular session or segment of a session should concentrate. The growth of a client and the success of a coaching agreement are concrete indications that the consultant has selected strategies wisely and helped to direct the client's attention effectively.

Figure 5.3 presents a final Venn diagram that follows on Stacey's (1996) concept of the need to build a space or phase state for creativity in individuals, groups, and organizations. It depicts three zones, one for adaptive behavior, one for symptoms and disorders, and one for creativity and growth. This figure builds on the material presented in Figures 5.1 and 5.2. In the zone of adaptive behavior, homeostatic control remains the primary feature of behavior and, in some situations, can also be a phase state in itself, particularly when a consultant is trying to help a client move from symptomatic behavior into equilibrium. Individuals work to keep themselves well regulated. In most situations, coaching clients may be unaware of any need to move out of this zone because the behaviors are mostly functional, not typically challenged from either inside or out, or are so well protected by psychological defenses that they are nearly impervious to change. This zone overlaps with the zone of creativity and emergence, and where that occurs, change becomes possible.

In the zone of symptoms and disorders, behavior can be rigorously structured, heavily defended, and extraordinarily regressed. In the worst cases, the client can demonstrate major psychopathology up to and including psychotic states, and these types of regression can also be considered as phase states with sometimes severe negative consequences. In my experience, psychosis is rare in organizations. However, some forms of symptomatic behavior such as workaholism, alcohol abuse, perfectionism, and features of narcissistic preoccupation with the self are fairly common. Where this zone overlaps with the zone of adaptive behavior, consultants are likely to see high levels of resis-

FIGURE 5.3

Zones of Behavior and Coaching Goals

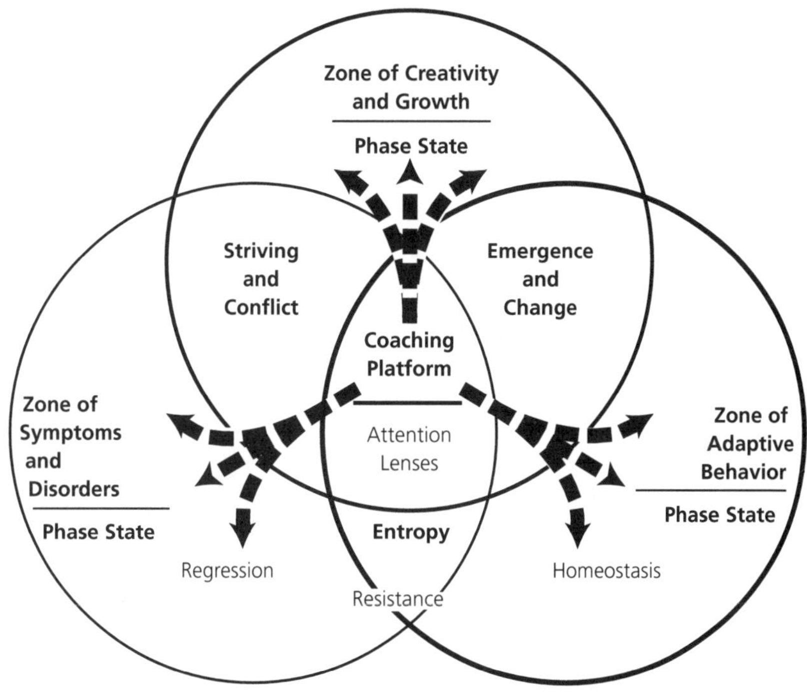

tance to change, major regressions (especially in times of high stress), and a general state of entropy in which it will be hard to motivate or mobilize the client.

In the zone and phase state of creativity, growth and experiments with new behaviors are possible. In this zone, coaches often experience themselves making the biggest difference and having the most impact on clients as they witness the wonderful and amazing process of emotional and behavioral change. In the middle of all three zones, we see the coaching platform from which the consultant deploys his or her attention and that of the client. Regardless of which zone a session focuses on, the coach consistently encourages and directs the client toward increased self-awareness, and through that baseline strategy, supports the steady growth that is possible in a well-managed process of individual change.

Each zone can be understood within the framework of complexity and chaos theory discussed in chapter 4. Individual and organizational clients can perceive and experience these zones as either attractors or repulsors. Often coaches are trying hard to help a client identify and move out of vicious, regressive attractors that may ultimately ruin a career. However, it may also be difficult in these circumstances for the client to leap into a virtuous, creative circle. These new patterns of behavior may be experienced as repulsors with high costs of admission. Making a compromise formation conscious can induce high levels of uncomfortable emotions such as anxiety, shame, sadness, and anger. Similarly, encouraging a client to try new behaviors that feel awkward or risky can elicit similar emotions and incredibly creative defenses. Often coaches are left with no alternative except to reach for the less satisfying but nonetheless effective homeostatic pattern that merely helps the client not engage the destructive responses that have been prevalent.

In Susan's case, the first step in helping her change did not consist in developing sophisticated communication and problem-solving skills in the face of extreme internal emotions. With my encouragement, she tried to contain her anger and tendency to blame others for their inadequate performance in her interactions with colleagues. This had a salutary effect for her and her peers in that the situations stopped deteriorating into shouting matches. In the few opportunities she had before she left the organization, she was sometimes able to do problem solving where once it had been impossible. Within our conceptual framework, Susan was able to move out of the regressive, vicious circle with which both she and her colleagues were familiar and into a more functional if only homeostatic attractor that featured the absence of the worst features of the regressive one. At times, these changes are merely temporary way stations on the path to much more creative and adaptive patterns. At other times, the achievement of a new homeostasis without the more negative features represents the best that a client can achieve in a given time period. Although coaches can always hope for more, it is important to recognize our own needs and values in these situations. What we want for a client is not uniformly what they desire or need, and coaches can be trapped by their own expectations and demands.

When these concepts, methods, and techniques are applied systematically by coaches to the problems encountered with and created by the personalities and character structures of executives, it becomes possible to stay on task, to create a sense of security that enables the client to do some of the most difficult work possible for a human being, and to facilitate true change where no one believed it to be possible. This is not to say that this represents a sure-fire recipe for success. Executive coaching is one of the most challenging assignments for a consultant, and it is difficult at best. However, the creative merger of evaluation methods, organizational and managerial knowledge and skill, and approaches and techniques pioneered by mental health practitioners provides a working coach with a flexible and strong structure within which coaching executive character can be accomplished despite the difficulties and problems involved.

6 Chaos and Its Role in Organizational and Individual Regression

Many models of organizational change and performance have been developed during the past 50 years, and there is now a vast literature that offers consultants a variety of points of reference concerning the issues and processes faced in work with organizations. This literature defies any effort at a succinct summary. Although many of these approaches are useful in general terms, to the consulting or coaching practitioner they often lack specificity in helping to diagnose where an organization is in its ability to perform and to define activities that should or could be undertaken to help the organization achieve a higher level of effectiveness.

New texts that provide overviews and descriptions of conceptual approaches and intervention experiences arrive regularly (Argyris, 1993; Collins & Porras, 1994; French & Bell, 1990; Goodman & Associates, 1982; Hamel & Prahalad, 1994; Hammer & Champy, 1993; Harvey & Brown, 1992; Parsons & Meyers, 1991; Stacey, 1992, 1996; Wheatley, 1992; Wheatley & Kellner-Rogers, 1996). Recent reviews of developments in research on organizational behavior by O'Reilly (1991) and Rousseau (1997) have summarized most of the experimental findings and theoretical changes in the field. In addition, Barnett and Carroll (1995) have integrated the recent conceptual approaches and empirical findings in their review of adaptive and selective mechanisms

---

This chapter has been adapted from Kilburg, Stokes, and Kuruvilla's (1998) description of their model of organizational regression and applied to the context of executive coaching.

of organizational change. They provide succinct overviews of life-cycle approaches (Cafferata, 1982; Child & Kieser, 1981; Greiner, 1972; Kimberly & Miles, 1980), population ecology, and structural inertia theory (Hannan & Freeman, 1977, 1984; Peli, Masuch, Bruggerman, & Nuallain, 1994).

A related but somewhat detached body of research and theory grew significantly in the sixties and seventies and focused on organizational effectiveness and performance. Cameron (1978), Kirchhoff (1977), and Steers (1975, 1977) provided overviews of the approaches, models, empirical findings, and methodological flaws in the struggle to define what enables organizations to succeed over time. Kirchhoff defined *organizational effectiveness* as a property that "emerges as the ultimate outcomes of a combination of managerial effectiveness and factors not under organizational control" (p. 348). Univariate and multivariate models of effectiveness have been built. Thorndike (1949) described the earlier univariate models that focused on defining one major criterion of performance such as profit margin, growth, stability, productivity, or goal accomplishment. These simpler approaches were succeeded by multivariate paradigms, most of which are summarized by Steers (1977), and they try to incorporate routinely such criteria as adaptability–flexibility, productivity, satisfaction, profitability, resource acquisition, absence of strain, control over environment, development, efficiency, growth, integration, and open communication.

As described in earlier chapters, Stacey (1992, 1996), Wheatley (1992), and Wheatley and Kellner-Rogers (1996), among others, have made systematic efforts to apply complexity, chaos, and catastrophe theories to analyses of organizational leadership and change. Within these approaches, complex biological, physical, and behavioral systems are described as facing environments and having experiences that are fundamentally unpredictable. Small, unpredictable, and at times imperceptible changes in initial starting conditions for the internal or external environments of enterprises are capable of producing dramatic and even drastic changes that can threaten their very existence. Chaotic change is nonlinear and can occur in a fashion in which at one moment in the organization's life, a radical shift can put the enterprise on a completely different course or in a tremendously altered set of internal or external circumstances. Examples of these kinds of changes include the entry of new and potentially deadly competitors in a market, legal or regulatory shifts, environmental disasters, or losses of key members of the organization. Chaotic change is much more difficult to manage because of its unpredictability and fundamental ability to threaten the future survival of any institution. These theorists have posited that leaders are always managing chaotic conditions, even when their organizations appear to be in more conventional and predictable states, because the exact circumstances and timing of the radical shifts are fundamentally unknowable in any rational way.

All of these models describe and discuss the fact that some organizations consistently demonstrate the ability to outperform others. Structural inertial theory specifically explores some of the major components that lead to organizational death such as organizational rigidity and the liability of newness. Although these conceptual contributions provide useful ideas for the consulting practitioner, they fall short when the realities of a complex organization are confronted alongside the professional imperative to provide immediate, useful advice to a client about what may be wrong in an enterprise and what to do to fix a problem once identified and defined. Kernberg (1978, 1979, 1998) has made a significant contribution to our collective ability to understand and work with this complexity in his application of the psychodynamic concept of regression to the behavior of leaders and organizational units. The essence of his approach consists of the argument that, under certain external, environmental pressures or due to the internal psychological or physical forces present in the leaders and followers in an organization, the behavior of the individuals and of the enterprise as a whole can become dysfunctional and primitive. Within this model, *regression* follows the American Psychiatric Association's (1980) definition as "partial or symbolic return to more infantile patterns of reacting or thinking" and is "manifested in a wide variety of circumstances such as normal sleep, play, physical illness, and in many mental disorders" (p. 118). This chapter attempts to expand and apply the psychodynamic concept of regression to the behavior of organizational units and entire enterprises. The material to be presented will provide the practicing consultant/coach with both a more elaborate and useful approach to assessment, and some concrete ideas about specific actions he or she can recommend to clients that might help them improve the function of individuals or whole institutions when they face either reasonably predictable challenges that follow traditional paths, or chaotic changes that cannot be foreseen and may well ruin the ability of an organization to function.

This chapter provides an overview of a conceptual approach to understanding organizational regression; describes the consequences of regression to an organization from the vantage points of the individual member of the enterprise, the organization, and the host community of the organization; presents several brief case illustrations that use the model to describe the behavior of actual organizational units; and provides several case examples of organizations trying to cope with and ameliorate the effects of a regressive process.

Model of Organizational Regression

This model of regression rests on the 17 dimensions of systems and psychodynamics explored in chapter 2. The knowledge of these dimensions of organizational behavior and the factors involved in creating high levels of organizational effectiveness enable coaches to see that organizations can be differentiated on the basis of how well they perform. As described above, conventional measures of performance always include financial margins, goal attainment, and customer satisfaction, among others. Organizations performing well in these areas are usually seen as functioning more effectively than those that do not. But how can consultants or coaches come to see clearly the structures and processes that enable organizations to continue to do well or, conversely, that lead them to dysfunction or even death?

Table 6.1 summarizes some characteristics and phases of organizational regression. In this model, organizations are seen as potentially occupying or entering into six identifiable phases of regression or development: superresiliency, normal operations, regressive oscillations, visible regressive patterns, chaotic organization, and dying organization. Kilburg, Stokes, and Kuruvilla (1998) recognized that these phases represent a somewhat arbitrary number of steps or grades of functioning, but each corresponded to real organizations worked in or consulted to and has a certain degree of face validity based on those experiences. They also recognized that the movement from one phase to another is not necessarily a crisp or easily observed phenomenon. As described previously, some shifts occur chaotically and unpredictably and are experienced by the members of an organization and consultants alike as world shattering, but they are more often slow and incremental. Table 6.1 also provides seven characteristics that are used to differentiate each of the six phases: organizational problems, behavioral symptoms, coping methods, organizational performance, organizational consequences, restoration or enhancement approaches, and descriptive metaphor. The entries in the table provide abbreviated descriptions of characteristics for each phase.

The Phase 1, superresilient organization represents a theoretical ideal to which it is hoped that all organizations aspire. These enterprises function extraordinarily well, managing growth and both the tasks of internal integration and external adaptation superbly (Schein, 1990). Organizations in this phase use the most advanced aspects of human and organizational behavior, management theory, and other concepts in all of their operations. They are developmentally oriented for both individuals and the entire organization. Performance is terrific on a sustained basis—even in the face of environmental or internal turbulence.

The results consist of healthy financial margins, growth, and organizational and individual effectiveness. The organization uses advanced strategies such as organizational reflection (Argyris, 1993) and learning (Senge, 1990), dialogue and appreciative inquiry (Cooperrider, 1996; Hammond, 1996), visioning (Vaill, 1991; Collins & Porras, 1994), and cognitive complexity (Jaques & Clement, 1991) to both restore itself when needed and to enhance itself on an ongoing basis. These organizations are like radiant stars, providing steady nurturance and growth to their members and beacons of excellence to the human community.

Phase 2 organizations can be thought of as being the normal, productive enterprises that are commonplace. For the most part, they continue to grow and manage their developmental challenges well. Behavioral symptoms are largely confined to transient effects that can be seen as the organizational equivalents of colds. In general, these organizations regulate their development well and cope effectively. They usually achieve their goals and provide a healthy place to work for most of their members. They are viewed as highly effective, producing solid returns, and demonstrating normal stresses and strains. They typically use the same restorative and enhancement methods as superresilient organizations. Metaphorically, they can be seen as normally radiant stars that occasionally produce solar flares.

Phase 3 organizations demonstrate patterns of regressive oscillations. They often appear normal and function as do Phase 2 enterprises much of the time. However, these organizations tend to have recurrent problems that seem difficult to solve as well as the normal adaptive problems faced by Phase 1 and Phase 2 institutions. Whereas some of the symptoms can be transient, these organizations will often have patterns of problems or maladaptive behavior that can appear for periods of time and then disappear. Their coping efforts are systematic, but there are periodic breakdowns that result in recurrent injuries to the organization or its members. These organizations do reach their goals but usually with significant stress and strain. There are real operating problems, and people may be unhappy. Most often the enterprise achieves reasonable financial returns, but that is not assured, and there may be periodic failures in the organization's performance. These organizations use some developmentally oriented restorative and enhancement strategies. However, the presence of the ongoing problems often leads to the need for crisis management and firefighting. These organizations can look like normal stars from a distance, but close observation will reveal sunspots or ongoing performance or behavioral storms that do not spontaneously or easily abate.

Phase 4 organizations demonstrate visible regressive patterns that most people can readily observe. They have adaptive problems that recur despite all of their efforts or that are permanent features of the

TABLE 6.1

Characteristics and Phases of Organizational Regression

Characteristics of the Organization	Phase 1: Superresiliency	Phase 2: Normal operations	Phase 3: Regressive oscillations	Phase 4: Visible regressive patterns	Phase 5: Chaotic organization	Phase 6: Dying organization
Organizational problems	Growth and adaptation; internal integration; external adaptation	Growth; adaptive problems; internal integration; external adaptation	Adaptive problems; some recurrent problems	Adaptive, recurrent, permanent problems	Permanent problems; organizationally threatening	Permanent problems; organizationally threatening
Behavioral symptoms	Problem solving; creativity; communication; trust; humor; curiosity; sublimation; love	Transient effects; behavioral colds	Transient effects, symptoms; patterns of symptoms appear for periods of time, then disappear	Quasipermanent, visibly maladaptive symptoms	Permanent, visibly maladaptive symptoms	Maladaptive symptoms flagrant and out of control
Coping methods	Individual and organization development, enhancement (Fix the problem not the blame)	Internal coping and regulation sufficient; some development, enhancement	Internal coping breakdowns; recurring injuries; equilibrium mostly reestablished	Internal coping failures; permanent injuries; equilibrium; failures in some areas	Regular failures of coping efforts; permanent visible injuries; visible equilibrium failures	Most coping efforts have ceased

Organizational performance	Excellent; goals achieved; a healthy place to work	Goals typically achieved; mostly a healthy place to work	Goals reached with strains and lapses; some real problems; people are unhappy	Goals hard to attain; people ill; low morale; real achievement problems	Chronic underperformance; very low morale; acting out; turnover; organization's future threatened	Goals not attained; high turnover of best people; acting out among those that remain; organization dying
Organizational consequences	Healthy returns; effective organization; normal stresses and strains	Solid returns; effective organization; stresses and strains; no permanent consequences	In the black, but often shaky; periodic failures; periodic identifiable consequences	Periodic deficits; unpredictably predictable failures; permanent identifiable consequences (loss of market share)	Chronic deficits; predictable failures; permanent identifiable consequences (loss of market share, lack of innovation)	Death, dismemberment, liquidation imminent
Restoration/ enhancement approaches	Reflective; dialogue and metalogue; development; strategic vision; cognitive complexity	Reflection; dialogue and metalogue; crisis management; development; vision; cognitive complexity	Crisis management; firefighting; some development and planning efforts; attempts at dialogue	Chronic crisis management, firefighting; episodic flights into health; islands of sanity in organization	Firefighting; infighting; lifeboat behavior; heroic measures	Heroic measures fail; too little, too late
Descriptive metaphor	Radiant sunlight	Solar flares	Sunspots	Jupiter storms	Dying planets and stars	Black holes

organization's existence. Behaviorally, they have quasipermanent and visibly maladaptive symptoms such as poor communications, unclear goals and roles, lack of core values, and difficulties with leadership and followership. Although they attempt to use coping strategies, they often fail, resulting in permanent injuries, disequilibrium, and aspects of organizational ineffectiveness. These organizations find it difficult to attain their goals but will do so often enough to stay in business. Their employees are often ill and have low morale. Individuals and the organization have real achievement problems. The consequences of these patterns consist of periodic financial deficits, unpredictably predictable failures, and permanent identifiable problems such as the loss of market share. Although these organizations may have islands of organizational health in well-run subunits, they do not typically use developmentally oriented restoration and enhancement methodology. Rather, they depend on crisis management and "firefighting" approaches that can restore order and appear to create flights into health for the enterprise, but they are not able to sustain these gains. These institutions are like the planet Jupiter and seem to have permanent, visible, and dangerous storms that often rage out of control.

The Phase 5, chaotic organization usually faces life-threatening, permanent problems. Behavioral symptoms such as leadership and followership difficulties; poor communications; and market, product, and service deficits are permanent and visible to external observers. Efforts to cope with the problems regularly fail. There are consistent, visible, and often dangerous injuries to the enterprise and its people. Periodically and seemingly unpredictably, the equilibrium of the institution completely fails, and this results in chronic underperformance; low morale; high turnover; and often regressive, acting-out behavior by individuals and groups, such as acts of sabotage. These enterprises have compromised futures and face the possibility of organizational death. The organizational consequences are chronic financial deficits and failures in performance that are visible to customers and other stakeholders. These result in permanent difficulties such as losses of market share and lack of innovation. The restorative and enhancement approaches that Phase 5 organizations use concentrate on crisis management and firefighting. Individuals engage in "lifeboat behavior," spending a great deal of time looking for other jobs. Leadership often engages in heroic measures as they try to salvage the enterprise. These organizations function as though they are dying planets or stars.

The final category of organization represented in Table 6.1 is Phase 6, the dying organization. Like Phase 5 organizations, they demonstrate permanent problems that threaten the ongoing existence of the institution. However, behaviorally they have flagrant, maladaptive symptoms that are out of control. They often have open, injurious conflict between members of the leadership team. Goal setting is nearly impossible, and the organization has often stopped measuring results accurately to hide the magnitude of the problems. Communication fails often in these enterprises, and the quality of their products or services suffers significantly. Most of the coping behavior of Phase 6 organizations has ceased to any recognizable degree. They fail to attain their goals and suffer from very high employee turnover. Those employees that remain often engage in severe acting out. Sabotage, theft, and other antisocial behaviors are frequently seen. The organization is perceived both from within and without as dying. Dismemberment and liquidation are imminent. Although management may engage in heroic restoration efforts, these initiatives are usually experienced as too little and too late. These enterprises are the black holes of the organizational universe, sucking resources in, but giving nothing productive back.

Figure 6.1 presents a flowchart of the stages in the management of organizational regression. In Stage 1, we have the superresilient and normal organizations. These enterprises are depicted in Figure 6.2 as possessing leadership–followership, psychosocial, administrative, and change mastery. However, they also can be viewed from the vantage point of the model of organizational regression, and in doing so, a deeper understanding is obtained of some of the dynamics that occur even in the most functional and effective institutions. Figure 6.3 shows a superresilient organization with its normal characteristics. It interacts with its external environment in constructive and creative ways and produces products and services of significant value to the part of the world in which it operates. The organization also faces internal and external regressive forces (IRFs and ERFs) that constantly pressure the entity and its people.

Table 6.2 lists some types of ERFs. These include competitive pressures; resource limitations; demographic, social, environmental, political, and legal changes; economic changes and setbacks; market shifts; and technology changes. Table 6.3 presents many types of IRFs that organizations face or generate for themselves. These forces are even more numerous than the external ERFs and include human needs, individual psychodynamics, the physical and health problems of organizational members, group dynamics, and leadership and followership dynamics. As can be seen in the abbreviated lists of Table 6.3, these IRFs include many of the traditional problems and issues faced by managers and by the consultants who attempt to assist them.

Figure 6.3 also shows that these IRFs and ERFs are balanced or overwhelmed in the superresilient organization by what can be called *balancing and barrier forces* (BBFs). Table 6.4 identifies many of these types of forces, including psychosocial, administrative, leadership, and

FIGURE 6.1

Stages in the Management of Organizational Regression

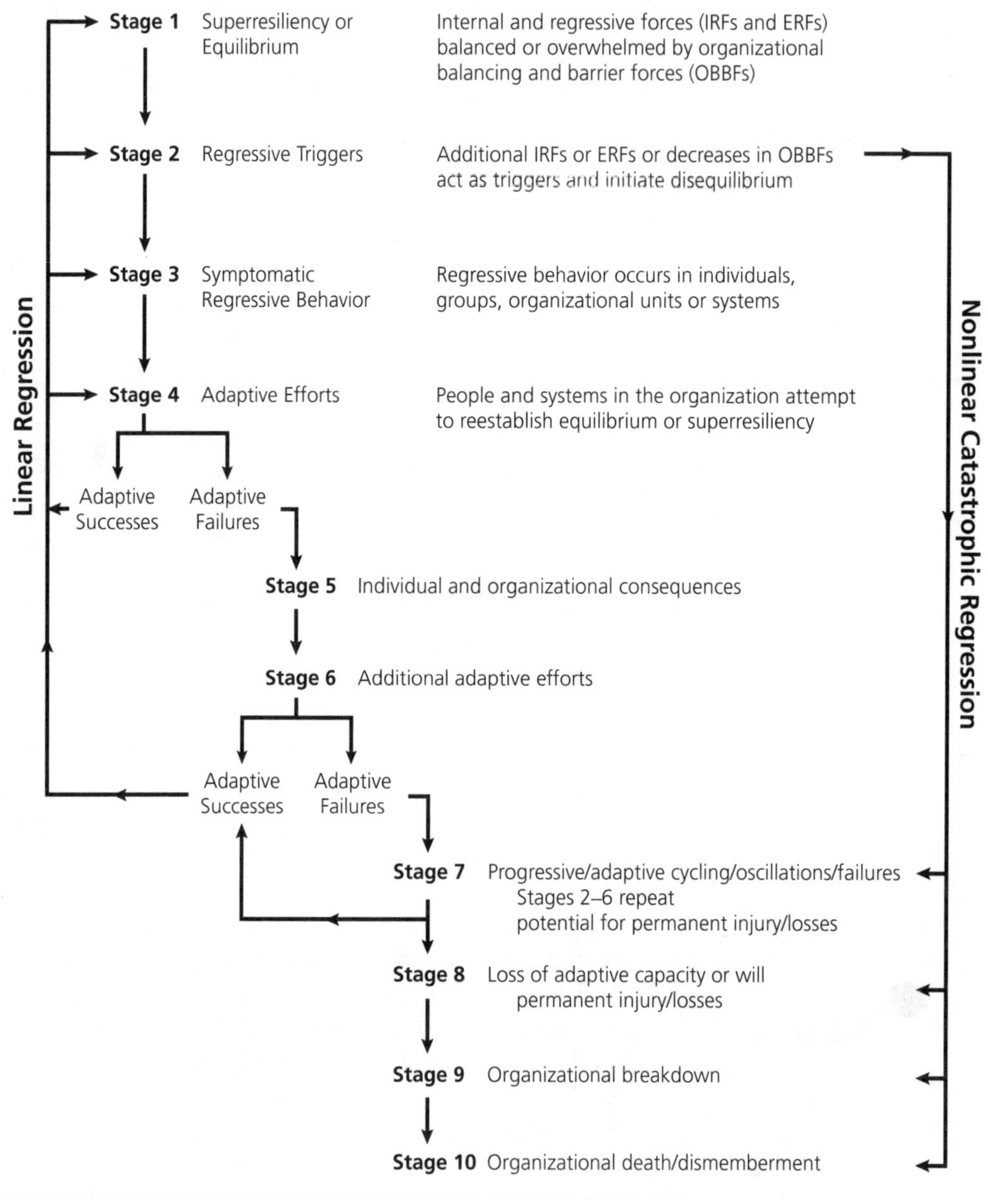

FIGURE 6.2

Mastery Model

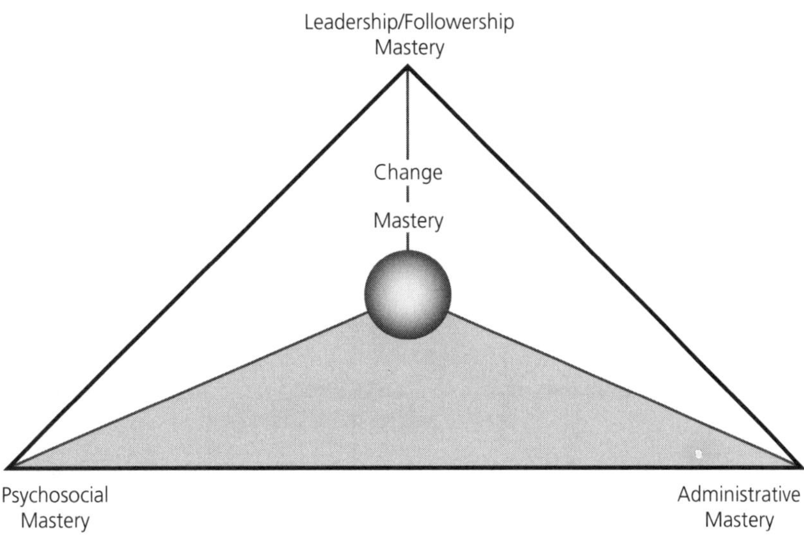

organizational mastery; personal and professional well-being of the members of the organization; organizational attributes such as vision, mission, and identifiable core values; organizational structures; organizational processes; effective leadership and followership dynamics and behaviors; and a functional organizational culture. Many balancing forces can be regulated at least partially by the members and leaders of the organization, as can many of the regressive forces. The ability of the leaders and members of the organization to understand that these forces can be managed potentially provides them with a set of tools through which they can attempt to attain or maintain the state of superresiliency, which I believe can and should be the goal to which organizations and their leaders and stakeholders should aspire. The implications for coaches are obvious in the sense that we are hired to assist leaders with their efforts to guide their organizations toward superresiliency and to build the knowledge, skills, and abilities necessary for them to do so.

In Stage 2 of the management of organizational regression (see Figure 6.1), IRFs or ERFs increase in magnitude, frequency, or intensity, or the organization experiences a decrease in its BBFs. In either case, the organization and its people begin to suffer from organizational stress and compression. Depicted in Figure 6.4, organizations facing stress or compression experience changes in function and can move

FIGURE 6.3

Superresilience, Homeostasis, Containment, and Adaptation
Open systems model of organization.

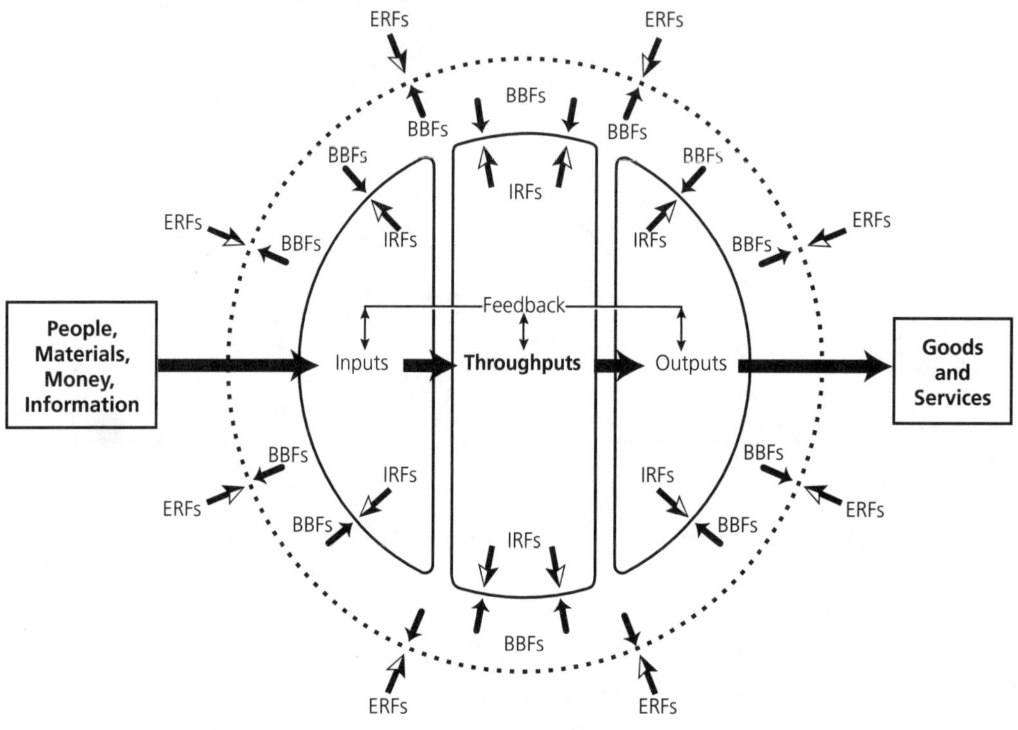

TABLE 6.2

Types of Regressive Forces External to the Organization

Competitive pressure

Resource limitations

Demographic, social, environmental, political, legal, regulatory changes or pressures

Economic changes, setbacks, and disasters (in communities, states, nations, families, psychosocial support groups)

Market shifts

Technology changes

TABLE 6.3

Types of Internal Regressive Forces (IRFs) in the Organization

Human needs
- Maslow's needs. Physiological, safety, social, esteem, self-actualization
- McClelland's needs. Power, affiliation, achievement, transcendence
- Drive states
- Other motivational states

Individual psychodynamics (see Kilburg's 17-dimensional model)
- Rational self, conscience, instinct, ideal self
- Emotion, cognition, defense, conflict
- Past, present, and focal relationships

Physical problems and health issues

Group dynamics
- Human conflict. Fight–flight, pairing, dependency, leadership failure or derailment
- Conformity. Deviance, norms
- Vision, mission, values, or role conflicts or confusion
- Communication problems. Lack of dialogue, metalogue
- Diversity/issues
- Decision-making and problem-solving problems
- Task implementation deficits
- Authority issues
- Subordination and dependency issues
- Power differentials and dynamics
- Affiliations and social networks. Formal and informal
- Evaluation and performance issues
- Stage of development. Forming, storming, norming, performing, adjourning
- Other. Competition, politics, territoriality, socialization, social facilitation or its absence

Leadership dynamics
- Personality characteristics. Neuroticism, extraversion, openness, agreeableness, conscientiousness
- Orientation to task. Mature (organized/flexible); detailed (compulsive/rigid); inattentive (hit or miss/careless); chaotic (impulsive/disorganized)
- Orientation to people. Secure supportive/autonomous); preoccupied (controlling); dismissing (abandoning); unresolved (traumatizing/invasive)
- Knowledge, ability, skills. General management, subdiscipline, industry
- Cognitive complexity
- Intelligence
- Social intelligence
- Political savvy
- Other patterns. Dominance/submission; caretaking/dependency/codependency; competitive; narcissistic (idealizing/devaluing); passive–aggressive; sadomasochistic; judgmental; manipulative (Machiavellian); suspicious/paranoid

Followership dynamics
- Personality characteristics. Neuroticism, extraversion, openness, agreeableness, conscientiousness
- Orientation to task. Mature (organized/flexible); detailed (compulsive/rigid); inattentive (hit or miss/careless); chaotic (impulsive/disorganized)
- Orientation to people. Secure (supportive/autonomous); avoidant (indifferent/ignoring); ambivalent (soliciting then rejecting); disorganized (no visible strategy)
- Knowledge, ability, skills. General management, subdiscipline, industry
- Cognitive complexity
- Intelligence
- Social intelligence
- Political savvy
- Other patterns. Dominance/submission; caretaking/dependency/codependency; competitive; narcissistic (idealizing/devaluing); passive–aggressive; sadomasochistic; judgmental; manipulative (Machiavellian); suspicious/paranoid

Organization dynamics (see Kilburg's 17-dimensional model)
- Process, structure, content
- Input, throughput, output

TABLE 6.4

Organizational Balancing and Barrier Forces (BBFs)

Psychosocial mastery
- Developing individual and group self-awareness
- Managing human communication, motivation, conflict, diversity, learning and problem solving, and relationships

Administrative mastery
- Planning; organizing; staffing; controlling; implementing interpersonal, informational, and decisional managerial roles

Leadership mastery
- Establishing a core vision for the organization
- Identifying the mission for the organization within that vision
- Identifying and maintaining the central values of the organization and the organization's culture
- Assessing and managing the external environment of the organization

Organizational mastery
- Organizational learning
- Double-loop learning
- Continuous process improvement or total quality management (Demming)
- Strategic alignment of the organization with its external environment
- Professional and organization development

Personal and professional well-being
- Physical and mental health of members
- Training and education of members
- Psychosocial support systems of and for members
- Career and succession management and planning systems

Vision/mission/values
- The unit possesses a creative and adaptive vision for the organization.
- The unit possesses mission clarity and specificity and a mission statement that has been developed with input from the members of the team and key stakeholders.
- The unit has a clear idea of its key values and how the structure, processes, and activities of the unit incorporate these. The organization has a basic orientation toward providing an inclusive organizational culture, embraces the notion of stewardship of its resources and mission.
- The organization identifies goals on a regular basis and pursues them in jointly supportive ways.

Organizational structure
- The organization's structure is flexible and based on the vision, mission, values, goals, and priorities that have been established.
- The organization possesses policies, procedures, and job and organizational designs that support the vision, mission, and values.
- The unit possesses and maintains a meeting and communications structure.
- The organizational structure provides role clarity for all its members. The organizational structure incorporates various helpful mechanisms including meetings, documents, job aids, technology, ad hoc structures, and teams.
- Rewards are part of both formal and informal systems and are tied to the inclusive organizational culture, with an emphasis on team performance, and highlight the achievement of goals and the appreciation of the organization's values.
- The jobs within the organization are well-designed to be as enriching and motivating as possible.

TABLE 6.4 continued

Organizational Balancing and Barrier Forces (BBFs)

Organizational processes

The unit has planned and implemented a communications process ensuring that every member will be kept informed of relevant developments and participate in an appropriate way in decision making and other organizational operations.

The organization has a planning and decision-making process that incorporates adaptive strategies and tactics that align the organizational unit with its environment and the pursuit of its vision, mission, and values. Decision making is sensitive to information, participation, and cycle time requirements.

The organizational unit sees the external world as an opportunity in which it maintains a client/patient/customer focus, competes effectively in its market niches, creates internal and external alliances as necessary, demonstrates market and client savvy, and acts to shift and change in response to the challenges that confront it.

The organization has adopted performance standards and metrics.

The organization has developed monitoring and evaluation systems to assess individual, group, and organizational performance that are dynamic and ongoing. The performance management process of the organization incorporates the principles of continuous process improvement. Individual and group performance is managed in keeping with the policies and procedures of the organization.

The members of the organization strive to understand the "big picture" facing the enterprise.

The organization performs routine environmental assessments in keeping with the above processes.

The organization pursues active, adaptive, and flexible conflict management processes to facilitate its operations.

The organization pursues active change management strategies and processes at both leader and follower levels.

The organization actively pursues a motivational strategy that sensitively incorporates Hertzberg's "hygiene" and "motivational" factors in a balanced approach.

The organization actively trains and develops its people.

Leadership and followership

Leadership style is flexible, incorporating participatory and authority-centered strategies as are appropriate to the competitive situation facing the organizational unit and the maturity of the members and operations of the unit.

Leaders understand the requirements for their behavior and the roles they are expected to play.

Leaders pursue self-assessment strategies and try to improve their ongoing awareness of their own individual and unit performance.

Leaders engage in ongoing development of themselves and of key administrative subordinates.

Leaders ensure that career planning and succession management occurs within the organizational unit.

Followers demonstrate mature, responsible, assertive, creative, and collaborative approaches to their behavior in the organization.

Staff members pursue their own professional development in keeping with support from leaders.

Leaders and followers attempt to empower each other in key roles and functions they perform in the organization.

(continued)

TABLE 6.4 continued

Organizational Balancing and Barrier Forces (BBFs)

Followers pursue strategies for improving their self-awareness as a mechanism to improve their organization's performance.
Followers pursue self-assessment strategies to enhance their own development, career potential, and performance.
Both leaders and followers pursue mutual respect in their relationships.
The leadership is capable of pursuing both theory Y and theory X types of behavior as appropriate to the situation and to the maturity of their followers.

Organizational culture

The organization's culture is inclusive in its design and intent, demonstrating the ability to learn about, value, and work productively with the differences individual members of the organizations bring and the resources available to it.
The organization's culture challenges the members to be better than they are and uses conflict, when it arises, in a creative effort to pursue this strategy.
The organization's culture encourages competition outside and support within the organization for mutual achievement of goals and individual achievement of career and professional objectives.
Competition when it occurs within the unit is encouraged to be constructive and as supportive as possible.
The organization's culture encourages and supports inquiring and questioning minds at all levels.
The organization's culture aspires to be free of biased behavior, maintaining an open-minded stance toward people, differences, systems, and other cultures, and does not make untested assumptions about any of the above.
The truth as it is pursued in the organization is based on knowledge, skill, ability, and data deriving from experience rather than on positional or other sources of power.
The organization's culture is less dependent on implicit rules and strives to be more explicit with regard to its norms, values, and behaviors.
The organization actively uses its structures and processes to reinforce the key components of its culture.
The organization does not take its culture for granted, but periodically examines itself to determine if the culture is supporting the organization and its people in accomplishing the missions.

into Stage 3, where they begin to demonstrate symptoms and consequences of regression. Organizations in this stage may correspond to the Phase 2 and Phase 3 organizations described in Table 6.1. Organizations experiencing regressive symptoms most often move immediately into the Stage 4 management process, in which the members of the enterprise make adaptive efforts to respond to the stress or compression constructively. If these efforts succeed, the organization either returns to the state of superresiliency or simply better manages the forces of stress and compression and continues to function. In the event that the adaptive efforts fail, more consequences ensue for the organization and often for its members and stakeholders.

FIGURE 6.4

Stress or Compression
Open systems model of organization.

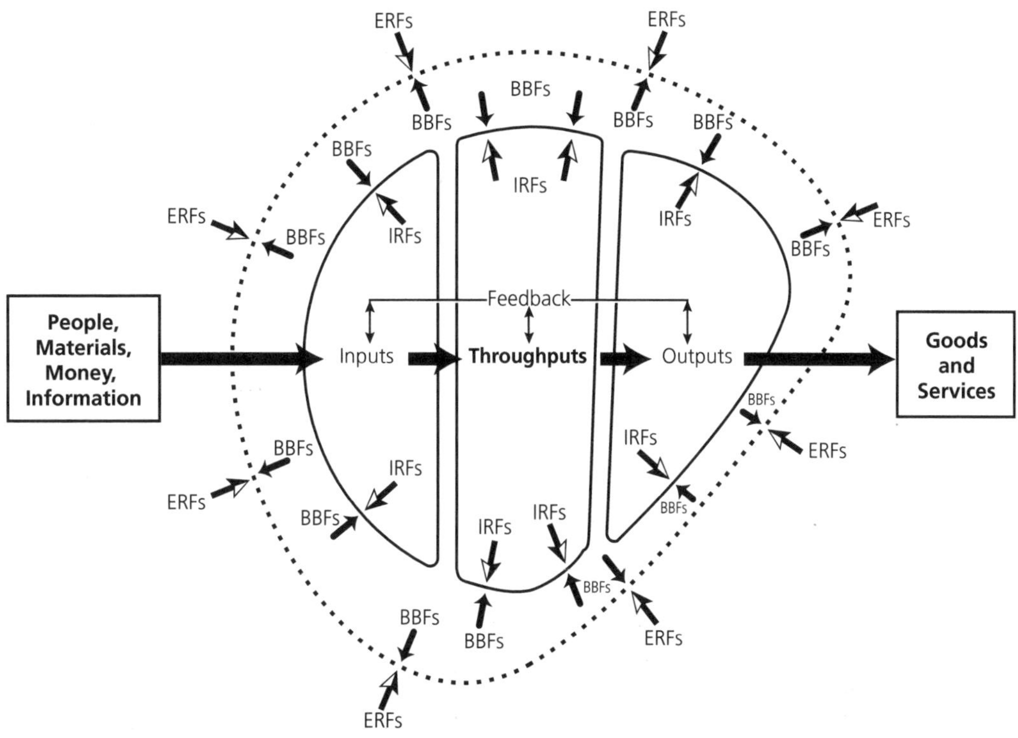

Table 6.5 identifies some of these consequences. For individuals they can include physical and behavioral health problems, stress, career derailment, family problems, and performance problems. Groups and organizational units often experience conflict; decreased performance and productivity; communication and decision-making problems; competitive failure; and in the worst case, unit death and dismemberment. Similarly, large organizational units and entire enterprises can experience market losses; financial setbacks; turnover; and large-scale problems with vision, mission, values, and strategic alignment. Downsizing, spinoffs, mergers, bankruptcy, death, and dismemberment can happen in advanced cases of regression. Finally, there can be significant consequences for communities that host a regressed organization. These effects can include social dislocation, increased unemployment, increased crime, public health problems such as drug and alcohol abuse, increased poverty, increased pressure on government services, environmental degradation, and decreased life expectancy for com-

TABLE 6.5

Potential Consequences of Organizational Regression

- Individual Leaders or Followers
  - Behavioral health problems
    - Mental and emotional problems
    - Substance abuse/dependency
    - Suicide/homicide
  - Physical health problems
  - Stress
  - Burnout
  - Absenteeism
  - Turnover
  - Career derailment
  - Family problems
  - Relationship problems
  - Performance problems
  - Anomie/disillusionment
- Groups and Organizational Units
  - Group Conflict
    - Fight–Flight
    - Subgroup and pairing dynamics
    - Dependency
    - Hostile conditions
    - Open warfare
  - Decreased performance
  - Decreased productivity
  - Decreased group cohesion and conformity to norms
  - Increased deviancy in behavior
  - Increased role conflict and confusion
  - Increased communication, decision-making, and implementation problems
  - Increased internal competition
  - Competitive failure
  - Group or unit death and dismemberment
- Organizations and Large Organizational Units
  - Market losses
  - Competitive failures
  - Financial losses or setbacks
  - Leadership changes
  - Increased turnover
  - Lack of vision or unclear vision
  - Lack of mission clarity
  - Goal conflict
  - Role strain, confusion, conflict
  - Products and services not aligned with customer needs and demands
  - Loss of strategic alignment
  - Loss of political supports
  - Downsizings, reorganizations, mergers, being acquired, bankruptcy
  - Death and dismemberment

TABLE 6.5 continued

Potential Consequences of Organizational Regression

Host Communities and Social Systems
Increased social dislocation and relocation
Increased unemployment
Increased crime
Increased collateral business failures
Increased suicide and homicide
Increased social deterioration
Increased community blight and deterioration
Increased poverty
Increased pressure on government services
Decreased tax collections
Potential environmental degradation
Increased effects of behavioral health problems
increase in divorce
increase in child abuse
increase in spouse abuse
Increased health risks
Decreased life expectancy

munity members. Thus, the consequences of organizational regression can range from the simply irritating to matters of life and death for people, institutions, and host communities.

The suffering caused by these consequences pushes the members of organizations into Stage 6 of their management efforts, in which they make additional adaptive efforts to address both the causes and the results of the regression. Again, if these adaptive efforts are successful, the organization and its people can reestablish better and higher levels of functioning, such as Phase 1 or Phase 2, the superresiliency or normal operations. If they fail, the organizations regress further into Phases 3, 4, or 5. As failures mount, the adaptive efforts of these organizations and their members take on less organized and more sporadic forms, such as firefighting and crisis management. The organizations themselves can become battlegrounds and unhealthy places to work. The performance of the enterprise becomes publicly and visibly poor. The resultant public observation and criticism can make the problems even worse. Often, leadership will be changed frequently to make constructive improvements. However, as an enterprise moves into Phase 5, chaotic organization, it loses adaptive capacity and can suffer permanent losses of its ability to function.

Figure 6.5 depicts these losses of adaptive capacity as injuries and ruptures caused by the regressive process that occur in the fabric of the

FIGURE 6.5

Injury or Rupture

Open systems model of organization.

FIGURE 6.6

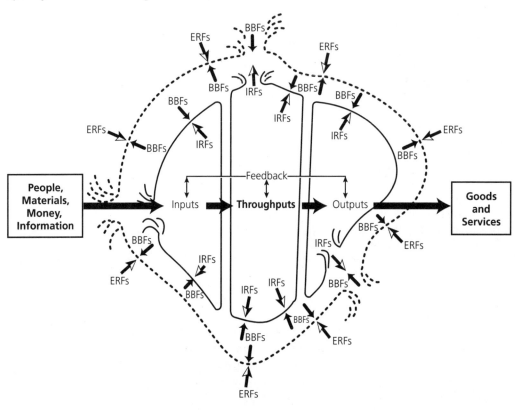

Organizational Death

Open systems model of organization.

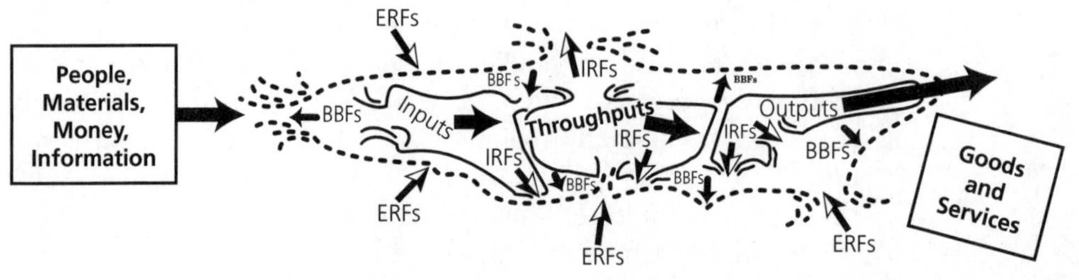

internal structures, processes, contents, and boundaries of the organization. Injuries and ruptures can occur even in superresilient organizations, but typically these are quickly addressed. However, without successful amelioration, the Phase 5 organization begins to reach Stage 9, the point of no return, and significant breakdowns in major systems occur. Staggering losses can accumulate, and the organization can face significant problems in finding resources to address problems and to make adaptive efforts. The organization reaches Stage 10 when these breakdowns permanently cripple its adaptive ability. At this point, these enterprises can be identified as Phase 6, or dying organizations.

At Stage 10, it becomes nearly impossible to salvage the institution. If it is a unit of a larger enterprise, it may be restructured or merged with other units, its resources and responsibilities dispersed. If it is an independent business or a strategic business unit in a conglomerate structure, it may be restructured, divested, or liquidated. In some cases, leaders and stakeholders will file for some form of bankruptcy protection while the functioning assets are realigned in an adaptive and often superhuman effort to restore the company to a higher level of performance. Some do survive at this point, but they are rare. Death rates among organizations of all types are high (Singh, House, & Tucker, 1986), and the process of organization regression described in this model effectively depicts how this can occur over time in any enterprise. Figure 6.6 portrays an open system in the final stage of dying.

The previous summary describes the linear flow most typical of a regressive process. However, viewing Figure 6.1 also provides a way of understanding what can happen in the case of a catastrophic or chaotic regressive process. In these situations, organizations can skip over many of the intermediate stages or steps of regression. The flow diagram on the right side of the figure indicates that in some circumstances, regressive forces can be so strong that all efforts at balance and adaptation immediately collapse and the organization can move directly to chaos or even to death and dismemberment. Adaptive efforts can also be partially successful, resulting in an organization that jumps from a superresilient or normal state into an oscillating or regressive level of function. These chaotic collapses or revivals are most frequent when extreme market or technology changes, competitive challenges, legal shifts or attacks, environmental disasters, or losses of key people occur.

This organizational process parallels that described for individuals in chapter 4. Chaotic attractors and repulsors operate in the behavioral space of an enterprise. The specific patterns described in each phase of regression can be thought of as virtuous attractors or circles in the case of superresilience or normal organizations. However, as enterprises move toward Phase 6, dying organizations, the viciousness of the patterns or attractors of behavior can be extreme and nearly impossible to change.

Regression of Individuals

In chapters 4 and 5, I described the processes, structures, and contents of the behavioral systems of individual leaders. Coaches must understand that attractors and repulsors and the operation of the shadow, psychodynamic side of human behavior through the process of compromise formation remain present even as the concrete issues and problems of managing a complex organization absorb the time and attention of clients. Coaches must remain attentive to these forces precisely because of their effects on the performance of clients and, therefore, on their organizations.

The process of organizational regression described in this chapter metaphorically parallels that of individual regression described by Kernberg (1978, 1979). According to psychodynamic and developmental theory and research, humans normally grow and develop through a series of age-dependent stages. Each stage or period has a set of tasks to be completed, a set of skills to be mastered, and a knowledge base to be attained. Kegan (1982, 1994) described in detail six stages that individuals may go through in their own development: incorporative, impulsive, imperial, interpersonal, institutional, and interindividual selves. He related them to the previous work done by theorists and practitioners such as Piaget, S. Freud, Erikson, Kolberg, McClelland, and others who have attempted to describe and provide similar developmental frameworks. Each stage has a creative, virtuous attractor at its core in the sense that people are naturally drawn to the issues and tasks in them through the processes of development and aging. Let's take a quick tour through each of Kegan's stages as a way of illustrating and understanding some of the aspects of human development. By doing so, we can gain acute insight into what happens when an individual undergoes a behavioral regression. I could do a similar review of the work of any of the other frameworks and accomplish the same thing.

Following Kegan, the requirements for human mastery of the incorporative stage that characterizes infancy pull babies naturally into the use of their reflexes and to their abilities to sense, move, and respond empathically and emotionally to events around them. Children first learn to trust and be dependent on adults for their needs and to interact in a way that guarantees that they will be supported. As children learn and grow, they develop more verbal, motor, cognitive, emotional, and interpersonal skills, and gradually move out of the attractor or state of primary dependency that characterizes the incorporative stage and into the challenges of the impulsive stage.

In the impulsive attractor, children, now typically 5–7 years old, learn to manage their own fantasies, wishes, and needs in the context of the typical family triangle of mother, father, and other siblings. They begin to compete with peers in school and are gradually forced to become increasingly responsible for controlling both behavior and emotion in social situations. These tasks and skills take many years to master, and they slowly give way to the challenges of the imperial stage, which comprises most of adolescence.

In adolescence, individuals truly become responsible for the consequences of their actions; learn to work in more collaborative ways with peers; are challenged to take the needs and desires of others into account, and hopefully build the capacity to have close interpersonal relationships with others. During this stage, we often begin to see the presence of repulsors in the sense that the normal tasks and skills that draw most young people into adolescence quite readily prove difficult, if not terrifying for some. These individuals can remain mired in the previous impulsive stage of development until and unless they are assisted with overcoming their resistance or trouble in entering fully into the struggles and requirements of the imperial attractor.

Assuming that the individual masters adolescence and its challenges, life inevitably draws him or her forward into the tasks of young adulthood, the interpersonal stage. Here, the person learns about mutuality, the ability to give and take in human relationships; about the ability to perform visibly and reliably as an adult in the world; and about better defining his or her sense of personal identity. This stage is associated with going away to college, signing on for a tour of duty in the military, or getting a job, and therefore, truly coming of age as an adult in the world. The time lines for accomplishing the tasks of this stage are looser than in the previous periods, and some individuals can become permanently mired in the intricacies of young adulthood. Again, for some people, mastering these normal skills and tasks can act as a terrifying or mystifying repulsor that is avoided or never fully engaged instead of as a challenging and tremendously rewarding attractor. These individuals may appear to be permanently locked in a state of late adolescence with its self-centeredness, primitive interpersonal skills, and difficulties in assuming adult responsibilities.

Success and competence in the interpersonal stage lead the person to the challenges of the institutional stage. Here, individuals typically move into the world of adult work and relationships. They define career identities; begin to compete broadly in the world; and try to form more permanent adult, loving relationships. They come to grips with ambition, the desire and need to find a life partner and form a family, and the tasks of adult self-development. This period can last for a long time and for some people represents the end of their journey. However, many others will rise to the challenge of moving into Kegan's final interindividual stage.

During this period of development, a person struggles with the challenges of true interdependency, self-surrender and intimacy in relationships, and with defining the work and personal self in the context of a web of human relationships. It is in this final stage that most people become capable of fully developing and using the capacities of human wisdom described in chapter 4. Sufficient experience and skill have been acquired to make reflective decision making possible. Although there are no formal age norms for this stage, typically people struggle to master its intricacies through midlife and beyond. Many people never make it to this stage, and of those that do, not all are able to master its requirements.

As previously stated, Kegan attempted to integrate these stages with the ideas and developmental frameworks of Piaget, S. Freud, Erikson, Kolberg, McClelland, and others. Each of these scholars also made systematic efforts to describe the human developmental journey. No effort will be made here to describe their ideas or approaches; however, all of their work shares certain features, such as the identification of a line of development through time from infancy to adulthood; a set of stages that each have their own tasks, challenges, and requirements; and an implicit assumption that individuals must move forward through each stage if they are to be successful and fulfilled in their lives. Each would also agree with S. Freud, who was the first person to suggest that failure to move forward eventually produces significant problems for those who are not able to do so. Freud and other psychodynamic scholars also demonstrated that individuals can in fact slide from a higher level of human functioning to a previous one under the pressure of external stress or internal conflict. It is this idea that ties individual and organizational regression together.

The model of regression and the regressive process described in this chapter both apply to individual behavior in the sense that people can be defined as complex active systems similar in general structure, process, and some content to organizations. As individuals enter into the struggles of each normal developmental stage, they have internal and external balancing and barrier forces to regression as well as many of the same kinds of regressive forces encountered by organizations. They attempt to cope and adapt within each of these stages, creating the knowledge, skills, and abilities that permit them to move forward with their lives if the barrier and balancing forces are stronger than the regressive forces. However, at any point in life, in fact, at any point in a given day, anyone can experience a shift in this equilibrium of forces, and behavior can swing either gradually or catastrophically into a pattern more primitive and reminiscent of an earlier time in our lives. This phenomenon occurs all of the time in our work organizations. Most often it remains simultaneously mystifying and frustrating, and at times, it becomes infuriating or even dangerous.

A typical example occurs in a work group that might be accustomed to working effectively together under a leader who most often is mature, thoughtful, problem oriented, and concerned with maintaining good relationships with colleagues and subordinates. If that leader experiences increased pressure at home from, say, a troubled marriage, a child who becomes ill, or difficulties with a new and much more demanding supervisor, the mature behavior usually experienced by the members of the team may be replaced by a pattern more reminiscent of young adulthood or even adolescence. The leader may become less attentive to the needs of others, become more self-centered and more demanding, demonstrate less impulse control, and even act out by becoming excessively demanding with others or yelling, criticizing, or regularly arguing with subordinates. The individual may make adaptive efforts that succeed momentarily in restoring equilibrium, but if the underlying troubles remain unresolved, colleagues and subordinates may need to adopt a strategy that recognizes that the regressive pattern may recur or even become a more permanent feature of their interpersonal and organizational landscape, as Phases 3–5 of the regression model suggest.

Coaches are often invited or sent into situations in which individuals and teams have experienced such regressive slips or seem permanently mired in a self-destructive, vicious, and regressive attractor. Individual executives in these situations frequently face career derailment unless they are able to overcome the regressive patterns. Teams can experience the same fate as organizations that cannot stop a regressive pattern. These situations are among the most difficult that a coach can face, and a thorough appreciation of the dynamics of regression can help coaches stay focused on the patterns and processes that must be changed if the individual or organizational client is to succeed and regain career or organizational momentum.

Case Examples

Case material illustrating this model can be discovered in the business pages of any local or national newspaper. In the past several years, Montgomery Ward, a national retail chain in business for over half a century with hundreds of stores, announced that it sought bankruptcy protection in a last-ditch effort to prevent its liquidation and confirmed what many business analysts had been publicly saying—that it had been a dying enterprise. The organization had struggled for many years, making significant changes in leadership, market approach, and financial restructuring, all to no avail. Although I have no information on the internal operations or organizational climate, it is not hard to imagine what the past few years have been like for employees of this corporation. Rumors and public criticism have dogged the company in newspapers and business magazines. If one were to reconstruct the corporation's past 10 years of history, the outline of events and consequences would most likely follow the model of organizational regression outlined above.

Apple Computer is a visible public company that followed the regressive path during the early 1990s. Financial results reported in 1996 and 1997 pushed the accumulated losses of the early nineties well past $1 billion. The board of directors announced yet another change of leadership as the CEO was forced out. The company systematically closed plants, fired thousands of employees, spent lavishly to acquire new assets, and invited company cofounder Steve Jobs to be interim CEO, all desperate adaptive efforts to reverse its regressive slide. As of the end of 1999, these efforts began to pay off as the company returned to profitability with new products and a reinvigorated corporate image. Its stock price rose twelvefold as analysts began to publicly state their belief that the company had a future. Again, I have no information about what daily work life has been like for the members of the company who have survived thus far but, based on experience in other organizations, these kinds of visible consequences often represent the culmination of a great deal of internal symptoms and injuries. Publicly, Apple appears to conform to the description of a Phase 5 chaotic organization that has moved back from the brink and into Phase 4 or Phase 3.

Another example can be seen in a small, fairly successful publishing organization I have served as consultant to for several years. This enterprise produces a monthly periodical under an agreement with a national organization. It has a senior editor responsible for policy and content, a publisher who manages the operations, a small administrative staff, and a few technical editors. The enterprise has been routinely profitable and enjoys a superb reputation. In its stakeholder community, the publication and its organization are international leaders. However, inside the organization, a different picture can be seen. The senior editor has taken a "hands-off" approach to the daily operations. Aperiodic, unpredictable inter- and intragroup conflict between the technical editors and between them and the administrative staff has become a way of life. Despite numerous successful efforts to improve the technical capacity and performance of the organization and to provide for improvements in the economic conditions of the staff, the small management team has been roundly criticized for its failure to meet all of the needs of the staff, to solve ongoing production problems, and to constructively address the conflict behavior of its organization's members. At the end of the assessment phase of this consultation, this enterprise was described as a Phase 3 organization with regressive oscillations that could at times seem normal and at other times present with most of the behaviors of a Phase 4 organization with visible regressive patterns.

General Electric Corporation can serve as a brief example of a Phase 1, superresilient organization. Although it remains dangerous to hype an organization currently experiencing a great deal of success as a model that should be emulated, several features of General Electric's story invite attention. This corporation has survived in the hypercompetitive, industrialized, and capitalistic system of the U.S. economy for a century, one of only a few businesses to do so. The most common types of organizations with longer, successful life spans are churches, governments, universities, certain family-owned enterprises, and some other not-for-profit institutions such as hospitals. The company has often led the way in innovating organizational approaches to market and human performance problems, facing its own regressive experiences and creating adaptive solutions to them. Among companies of its size and level of financial success, it has routinely paid close attention to the management of its human assets, and it continues to do so, despite reports from a variety of sources that the organization can be a difficult place within which to work. In short, its leadership consistently has created a situation in which the balancing and barrier forces available to the organization significantly outweigh the regressive forces that challenge it. All of this has been done in a globally active enterprise with hundreds of thousands of employees, tens of thousands of supervisory and management staff, and an officer corps of approximately 1,500 people. General Electric and other organizations demonstrate that the Phase 1 organization is not just a theoretical possibility, but that they can, with careful work on the part of leaders, stakeholders, and members of the organization, achieve and maintain this state over many generations (Collins & Porras, 1994).

Finally, we can use the example of Ken, first explored in chapter 4, to describe a regressive individual pattern and efforts to ameliorate it. Ken both presented and described himself as hard driving, achievement and action oriented, smart, tough, and willing to fight whenever and wherever needed to accomplish his objectives. Although he could inhibit his aggressiveness with customers and selected others, the passive–aggressive and dependent behavior of his partners often sent him into a regressive rage in which he publicly argued with and even verbally abused them. In turn, they withdrew from him, would not offer assistance when he asked for and needed it, privately criticized him to each other, and seemingly did nothing to encourage the business to grow. Coaching illuminated the broad outlines of this pattern of regression, helped Ken identify creative alternatives, and at least temporarily assisted him to stay with his company and perhaps enabled it and him to work through a difficult transition.

Summary

This chapter has presented a model of organization regression that suggests that the behavior of any enterprise or individual can be viewed diagnostically on a continuum from superresiliency to death and dismemberment. A flow model illustrated that regression can present itself in aperiodic, discontinuous ways that are often difficult to assess and manage. Within the model, organizations and individuals are seen as open systems that regulate internal and external regressive forces with balancing and barrier forces, many of which leaders or management teams can bring under volitional, organizational control. The consequences of regression in organizations can be extraordinarily serious for individuals associated with an organization, for the enterprise itself, and for their host communities.

This model of organizational regression, if examined carefully, is compatible with current theories of organizational adaptation and survival, including ecological theory, structural inertia theory, contingency theory, and resource dependence theory. The model strongly suggests that if leaders pay careful attention to managing internal and external regressive forces and deliberately act to improve the strength of their balancing and barrier forces, the performance and effectiveness of their organizations and of themselves can and will remain high over prolonged periods of time. It provides consultants and coaches with specific ideas about what may be going on in an organization or individual in trouble and what they can recommend to clients to address the problems so identified.

7 Working With Human Emotion and Cognition

The Case of Ann and the Unwanted Job Offer

"I need to get out of the office. Can we have our meeting over lunch?" Ann asked. "Sure, where do you want to go?" I replied. "I don't know, I just need to get away from this place," she replied irritably. We drove a few minutes from her office and settled into a cozy neighborhood restaurant. Ann was one of two executives reporting to the senior vice president for marketing and sales for a medium-sized manufacturing company. She had worked her way up the ranks, having joined the organization 10 years before after completing her master's in business administration. She was a divorced mother of two adolescents, and I had worked on and off with her and several of her subordinates for a few years. Ann excelled at sales and marketing strategy. An intense but reasonably flexible extrovert, she forged strong working relationships with her colleagues and clients and used them to push the business forward in a systematic fashion that was widely recognized and appreciated in the company. In her current position as vice president, she had presided over six consecutive years of growing sales volumes and a subtle but consistent marketing strategy that emphasized quiet and obsessive attention to customers. Most of the company's old clients stayed with them, and these clients referred others based on their excellent experiences with the sales force that Ann directed. After we ordered lunch, Ann took a sip of her iced tea and started to talk.

"I had a meeting with Jeremy earlier this week, and he asked me to take John's job," she said, barely holding back tears.

John was her vice presidential counterpart in the organization. He ran all of the internal, back-office operations of sales and marketing such as information systems, order fulfillment, telemarketing, and relationships with manufacturing. He was fairly well organized and attentive to detail, but he lacked real imagination and drive. His units tended to underperform, although he had cleaned up major messes in most of them since assuming his position. Both Ann and John reported to the senior vice president for marketing and sales of the company, Jeremy.

"I think this is one of those offers you can't refuse," she said.

"What makes you think that?"

"Because Jeremy had that 'it's a done deal' tone in his voice, and he talked in terms of when and how, not if and whether. Nope, I either take this job or I have to leave the company. He's such a cold, self-centered man. He didn't even try to sell the job to me. He just launched into a description of how John's units were underperforming, how he needed to fix them if we were going to hit our new targets, and that he knew I could get them operating at the next level."

"What about your position?"

"My bet is that he has calculated it will be easier to fill my job than John's, and he's probably right," she said, now wiping a few tears from the corners of her eyes with her napkin.

I simply nodded in reply.

"He's brilliant, but he has absolutely no feel for people unless they're customers. It's like we haven't worked closely together for 6 years. I haven't covered his tail, cleaned up his mistakes, and made his numbers. He just dismisses me."

"Did he ask you what you thought?"

"Of course not, he doesn't want to know what I think. It's what he thinks that's important."

"Well, what do you think?" I asked.

"Frankly, I've been too mad and hurt to think clearly. I've talked to a couple of my close friends who both say I really don't have a choice if I want to stay with the company."

"Have you thought about leaving?"

"Sure, but I'm not ready to leave. My two kids are in high school, and I was never one for moving around a lot anyway. My friends are very important to me."

"So, if you take the job, how will it make you feel?"

"It will be humiliating. Oh, he'll put the best face on it, but I go to the back office, out of all of the corporate strategy meetings. I lose all of my working relationships with our key customers and most of my contact with our competitors. In short, I go to Siberia. Everyone will be nice to me, but they all know that this is a demotion."

"Did you say that to Jeremy?"

"Yes."

"And?"

"And, he became his usual awkward, defensive self. He told me that it was not a demotion, that it would look good on my résumé, and that he'd give me a raise."

"But it's still humiliating to you?"

"Wouldn't it be to you? I can't think of anything else. My friend told me about another job, and I'm going to call the guy tomorrow. But I wanted to talk to you first to see if I'm crazy in my response to this crap."

I suggested that Jeremy's request and the way he made it had produced very strong emotional responses in her and that she was having trouble sorting out what was in her best interest from the emotional background noise. I emphasized the disorienting effects that anxiety, shame, and anger can have on human thinking ability and how difficult these feelings can be to cleanse once initiated.

"So, you think I should just take the job and keep my mouth shut?"

"I didn't say that. What I said was that when feelings are running this high it becomes very difficult to make an accurate assessment of what is in your best long-term interest and to act accordingly. The misery that the feelings themselves cause moves us quickly toward action."

"What should I do then?"

"Can I ask you some questions?"

"Sure."

I proceeded to ask Ann a series of questions about her vision of her future, the kind of work she truly enjoyed, how her children were doing and what their plans were, whether she thought Jeremy was wrong in his assessment of what his organization needed, how she would have wanted this to happen, and what she would like to be different. As we explored her answers, it became clear that she really did not want to leave the company and that she thought that Jeremy was right that John would need to be replaced if the organization were going to move forward. Her children were finishing high school and were not ready to go off to college just yet. Although she could readily see herself in another geographic region of the country eventually, she knew that it would be very hard to leave her friends and start over. It was also clear that she had not thought about what she should ask for to make the new position a success for her. In fact, she was so angry and humiliated, she could see nothing positive for herself in the change at all. She had formulated neither a strategy nor a negotiating position, and this was highly unlike her usual professional response to challenges. These were both incredibly strong parts of her professional knowledge and skill base, and it was as though she had completely lost them during the past week.

As we talked over lunch, she started to think out loud about what she should ask for if she were to take the job. She also thought of a way to get the message to Jeremy that she was not happy without jeopardizing their relationship. We talked about his emotional makeup, based largely on her experience with him and my own limited exchanges over several years of coaching in the parent organization. Jeremy was basically an "all-business" kind of person. He had the capacity to think about people and relationships but mostly in an instrumental fashion that allowed him to relate correctly, if somewhat coldly, to everyone around him. He was rarely wrong strategically; he obsessively attended to detail and to making the numbers for the company, so that he enjoyed broad political and professional support in the organization's board of directors. Ann knew that she would need to discuss her feelings with him if she were going to stay. However, she also knew that she would need to do it in a way that did not make him so angry and defensive that it would rupture their working relationship. Through the rest of lunch, we talked in detail about various directions her strategy might take and her potential responses to the offer.

"I'm sick and tired of doing his feeling and thinking for him," she said as we got up to leave the restaurant.

"I think managing up is one of the hardest parts of being in a leadership position, particularly when your boss lacks empathy and an ability to connect with his own feelings. But, there's no real choice from what you've told me," I replied.

"I know, but I don't need to like it. Do I?"

"No, no you don't. You just need to manage it very carefully," I answered as we left the restaurant.

Feeling and Thinking at Work

In most organizations, leaders assume that everyone who works there will think clearly, rationally, and effectively about their jobs and how to do them well. In rare instances, some organizations may provide training in how to think on the job, but formal programs are few. With regard to emotion, leaders typically make no such assumptions. In fact, many—if not most—individuals at senior levels in organizations believe and behave as though emotions have no place at work. The language, logic, and theory of business are couched in rationality, as if by talking only in those terms, human emotion can be obliterated from the workplace. How ironic then, that everyone knows that jobs and work produce extremely strong emotions, both positive and negative. Equally significant, those emotions interact with and influence our ability to think rationally about work. Anyone who coaches managers and executives or who wants to do so should have a good understanding of the basics of human emotion and cognition, how they can influence behavior, and how they can be modified in ways that assist clients to do their jobs more effectively.

The case of Ann illustrates the principal issues nicely and succinctly. Ann was a bright, articulate, and successful professional. She encountered a career and life-challenging problem on the job, a requirement for a catastrophic shift in duties that created enormous levels of emotion in her. These feelings dramatically affected her ability to think clearly about the nature of the problem, alternatives that she might pursue to solve the issues, and even about what was in her best interest. Ordinarily level-headed and even tempered, she was tearful, humiliated, enraged, and fearful about what might happen to her. She was able to express all of these primitive and powerful feelings in less than 10 minutes over lunch and, with some assistance from me, she was able to see how they were influencing her ability to manage the very tricky situation that confronted her. I tried to validate her feelings and talked briefly about their potential influence and, as she responded to a few well-directed questions, she was able to shift her attention to a wider frame of reference that she used well to explore the situation more fully. These types of emotional problems and issues are often the most critical and difficult issues that coaches and consultants face in their work with clients.

Chapter 2 initially introduced these issues as part of the 17-dimensional model of systems and psychodynamics that forms the conceptual foundation for this book. Table 2.8 presented a framework for identifying and understanding goal-congruent and goal-incongruent emotions. Shame, guilt, anger, sadness, disgust, envy, jealousy, and anxiety are the primary incongruent emotions and are most often experienced as negative by all human beings. Similarly, joy, pride, relief, hope, compassion, curiosity, surprise, esthetic experience, and sexual feelings are the positive, goal-congruent emotions. Both sets of emotions fill daily personal and work routines with complexity, richness, and wonder.

Increasingly, scientists and practitioners are exploring the complex role that these emotions have in our daily lives. Although no review of this extensive literature will be attempted here, readers can further their understanding by exploring J. G. Thompson's (1988) description of the psychobiology of emotion. In addition, the pioneering and complex work of Tomkins (1962, 1963), and Lazarus's (1991) update on the developments in the field offer a great deal of insight and understanding. Hillman (1992) and Socarides (1977) explored the therapeutic implications of emotion. Lewis and Haviland (1993) compiled a series of papers illustrating the complexity of thinking on the topic. More recently, Goleman (1995, 1998) caught the attention of the public with his notion of emotional intelligence. Weisinger (1998) and Cooper and Sawaf (1997) extended the notion of emotional intelligence to the workplace, and specifically, to how people in leadership positions can develop and maintain these capacities in doing their jobs. All of this work points to the primary role that emotion plays in human motivation and behavior. If practitioners want to help executives function more effectively in their difficult and demanding worlds, an in-depth understanding of emotion and how it affects their lives is absolutely critical to working effectively with them.

According to Tomkins (1962, 1963), emotion is the primary motivating mechanism of human behavior. It serves to heighten basic drive or need states and is based in neurohormonal activities involving some 50 chemicals that serve as neurotransmitters in the human nervous system and dozens of hormones produced by the various organs of the body. I have often thought of the human body as a large vat of soup, constantly cooking batches of emotional experience for us. The soup is flavored with and determined by the levels of these substances as they are secreted; interact with each other and the organs of the body; and affect the physical, mental, and behavioral lives of people. External events, memories, and the wide variety of human cognitive capacities can both produce and be affected by these physiological components of emotion. People do not tend either to understand or to monitor themselves at these baseline physical levels. In fact, much of the socialization and early learning of humans teaches them to deny, project, repress, and hide their emotional responses to the world. When they do "tune in" to what is happening in their bodies, they are more likely to become aware of the secondary effects that the biochemistry has on physical systems such as respiration, skin temperature, heart rate, sweating, body flushing, pupil dilation, and so forth. Most often, these physiological effects are simply interpreted psychologically as feelings, but many people have great difficulty even identifying the nature of the feelings they are having. As we know, and as illustrated in the case of

Ann, intense emotions lead to and affect behavior even in superbly prepared and wonderfully motivated executives.

Similarly, the work of de Bono (1973), Kegan (1982, 1994), Neisser (1967), Piaget (1971), and many others highlights the complexity of human cognition. Empirical research has demonstrated clearly that the ability to think in people begins at birth. The early stages of development are marked by primitive skills that help organize and integrate experience. As children mature, they gradually begin to perform logical operations that enable them to classify and order the various events, stimuli, and activities that they confront in their daily lives. At about age 11, as they enter into puberty, they develop the basics of a fully logical system of cognitive operations, which enables them to manipulate experience, thoughts, and feelings through a full range of mental shifts from negation and identity through union and disjunction. In other words, these logical operations enable the adolescent to tell how events, activities, and experiences in the world are alike or not alike. They also support the creation of alternatives and the ability to see reversals, nuances, differences, and other forms that a thought, an abstract principle, or an interaction with another person in the world might take.

Kegan (1994) delineated five levels of consciousness or meaning-making with their underlying cognitive structures. The first rests on a single point of view and the immediate internal and external experiences of the person. The second involves the ability to form durable categories of events and relationships. Individuals can understand roles and relate with a "tit-for-tat" framework. They collect data and can reason with cause and effect. The third level uses cross-categorical and transcategorical modes of cognition. People with this type of consciousness relate to others in a mutual fashion and are conscious of the roles that they play or are required to operationalize. They can make hypotheses, formulate and function according to values, and make inferences and draw generalizations. The fourth level entails an understanding of systems and complex interrelations of categories. Abstractions, formulations of positions and ideas, and the ability to maneuver within multiple systems of thinking characterize this level. Individuals with fourth-level consciousness can self-regulate their emotions and behaviors, create and recreate their identities, and act autonomously or with mutuality. The fifth and final level of consciousness uses transsystem and transcomplex cognition and structures. Individuals reaching this level operate in and through the dialectic, forming, understanding, and playing through paradox, contradiction, complexity, and polarities. Relationships between the self and others are interpenetrating and interindividuated. People at this level can create and recreate themselves, their relationships, their roles, and their performances. Kegan suggested that these levels of consciousness are developed through time. Thus, infants, toddlers, and young children tend to use the first and second types of consciousness. Adolescents progressively develop the third. Many young and middle-aged adults acquire the fourth level, but not everyone. In fact, the research that is available suggests that the majority of people do not consistently reach this level of consciousness. Kegan also believed that many of the requirements of our demanding workplaces are embedded in a capacity for fourth-level meaning-making activities and that this explains why so many people are so distressed in their work. This probability has significant implications for coaching executives. And finally, some individuals grow sufficiently to be able to access and operate in the fifth level of consciousness. These concepts can be useful when assessing the type of cognition and interpersonal relationships of a coaching client.

Kramer (1990) described a model of wisdom based on the integration of cognition and emotion. She suggested that there are four types of thinking: presystemic, intrasystemic, intersystemic, and integrated or autonomous. Of relevance to our coaching work, the intrasystemic, intersystemic, and integrated types are further described as absolutist, relativistic, and dialectic. In absolutist thinking, people place the emphasis on creating rigid dichotomies in which events, people, and thoughts are categorized, classified, and responded to as if those acts of classification and categorization are all that are required for managing them effectively. People, behaviors, and experiences can thus be seen as right or wrong, good or bad, friends or enemies, successes or failures, and responded to solely in those terms. Relativistic cognition, a more advanced type of thought, allows a person to consider that knowledge, human experience, and thinking are embedded in an environmental, interpersonal, cultural, and emotional context. This allows an individual to consider that judgment and decisions can be subjective and that other perspectives can be valid and contribute to a more elaborate understanding of what might be happening. This enables an increased range of ideas to be generated about what might work in response to events. Finally, autonomous thinking is characterized by the operation of dialectic cognition. In this form of cognition, paradox, polarities, complexity, symmetry, asymmetry, uncertainty, creativity, divergent and convergent approaches are routinely considered and appreciated as the person who operates dialectically attempts to find, define, and solve both structured and unstructured problems in the world. Appreciation of these types of cognition can significantly increase a coach's ability to help clients assess what is happening in their inner and outer worlds.

Research suggests that wisdom is not expressed much before people enter into their third decade of life (Sternberg, 1990). Jaques and Clement (1991) delineated clearly how cognitive capacity and complexity affect a person's ability to lead in organizations. They further suggested that leaders without the highest levels of cognitive complexity have restricted ability to analyze and integrate the enormous amounts and variety of data that modern organizations create and consume.

Kets de Vries (1984, 1987), Langs (1973, 1974), Kilburg (1997), Schwartz (1990), Czander (1993), Diamond (1993), Levinson (1981), and many others have demonstrated that human emotion interacts with the human ability to think and perform work and that the role of emotion must be carefully managed because it can literally destroy individual people and entire organizations. Kramer (1990) suggested that individuals do not become wise unless thought and feeling, cognition and emotion, are integrated as they try to solve the problems they encounter. Her model of wisdom assumes that over a substantial period of time a person develops the ability to be aware of and understand how emotions work, both consciously and unconsciously, and that he or she can think dialectically with nuance and an appreciation of polarities, complexity, and paradox. Based on these abilities, individuals can then engage in wisdom-related processes such as recognizing both individuality and relatedness, identifying context, interacting with others effectively, understanding and creating change and growth, and paying attention to both affect and cognition. These processes in turn power the functions of wisdom, which Kramer saw as solving the problems that confront humans, providing advice to others, managing social institutions including groups and families, performing reviews of one's life, and engaging in spiritual introspection. She asserted that people who are able to use these processes and perform these functions well are better able to adapt successfully in the world, solve unstructured problems, surmount difficult challenges, and work through the various crises of adult life.

One can readily understand and see how these forms of emotion and cognition emerge and influence the behavior of individuals, groups, and whole organizations. Leadership and managerial competence increasingly are being extended into these realms (Cooper & Sawaf, 1997; Weisinger, 1998). Coaches and consultants who work with leaders and organizations will increasingly need the ability to help them appreciate the problems that disordered emotion and cognition can create and to change regressive, dysfunctional patterns. Let us examine some of the more common types of patterns I have encountered in organizations.

Vicious Circles and Dysfunctional Attractors

Following the discussion in chapter 4, I have come to believe that problem patterns of cognition and emotion can operate for individuals, groups, and organizations as dysfunctional chaotic attractors. It is easier for clients to understand them as vicious circles. Their chaotic nature can be seen in the relative ease with which a person or group functioning on a mature, effective, and advanced level one day then, under the pressure of changes in the equilibrium of regressive and balancing forces, rapidly shifts into a problem pattern (see chapter 6, this volume). In this section, I describe some of the more common vicious circles I routinely encounter.

SHAME, RAGE, AND ACTING OUT

Based on my clinical and consulting experience, I believe that the most difficult emotional state for the average person to master is shame. The feeling is enormously intense, producing a pronounced sense of worthlessness and unlovability, in that the person experiencing it feels as though nothing he or she says, feels, or thinks; has done; or can do is good enough (Nathanson, 1987; Schneider, 1992; Wurmser, 1981). People cannot experience this feeling for long periods of time without profound consequences psychologically, physically, and socially. As a result, they move quickly to restore some sense of good feelings about the self. In most people, efforts to reduce shame occur unconsciously and almost instantaneously. Most often, the person being shamed or feeling ashamed becomes instantly angry. Depending on the individual's acculturation and socialization, the anger can be expressed verbally in arguments; nonverbally in silent, sullen withdrawal; other passive–aggressive behavior; or physically in acting out. Situations involving competitive risk and failure, performance-based feedback, affiliation, and relationship development constitute fertile ground for the production of shame and its self-protective cousins, anger and rage.

One need not look far in the life of an average leader to find examples. Providing feedback to individuals or groups about performance that has fallen short of expectations is perhaps the most common experience. Subordinates often become angry, argumentative, and uncooperative when they are told that they need to improve. Similarly, when sharp differences of opinion about business tactics or strategy, the allocation of resources, or of work assignments arise publicly, people often treat each other with profound disrespect that produces shame. For others, fears of being seen as weak or of being discovered to be inadequate can generate intense shame without anyone else saying anything. Active and passive aggressive cycles of conflict frequently arise in these situations. It can be extremely difficult for people having these experiences to neutralize their self-protective anger long enough to recognize that a shame-based emotional event may have caused the anger. When the anger goes unchecked and results in acting out verbally, nonverbally, or physically, further injuries and insults can deepen and extend wounds, increase shame, and consequently produce more anger. These positive feedback loops are the most dangerous for individuals, groups, and organizations because of the ease with which they can lead to physical violence or its organizational equivalents: sabotage, theft, lying, revenge, and noncooperation (Giacalone & Greenberg, 1997; VandenBos & Bulatao, 1996).

SHAME AND SADNESS

An equally difficult pattern involves the sequential or simultaneous experience of shame and sadness. People having these feelings most often describe events in which they felt both rejected and abandoned. The accompanying experiences of powerlessness, emptiness, helplessness, despair, and despondency leave the average individual feeling so desperate and agitated that profound depression and immobilization can result. This can occur in groups as well. When this pattern of desperation occurs in groups or large numbers of employees, motivation for work all but disappears; time and attendance problems increase; productivity, loyalty, and organizational commitment decrease; and organizations frequently fail. These patterns occur often during downsizings, mergers, market failures, prolonged periods of stress-inducing work that goes unrecognized, or when being passed over for promotion or plum assignments. Events outside of work can also cause this pattern to emerge. Many individuals come to work in organizations already experiencing this state of desperation based on past or present personal experience. Helping individuals or groups to mobilize out of the desperation can prove challenging. At times, the desperation can also lead to the anger and acting out described above, and this also can be an extremely volatile and dangerous combination.

SADNESS AND GRIEF

As Handy (1994) eloquently pointed out, the world of organizations has changed permanently. In many enterprises, the nature of the psychological contract now specifies that there will be no permanent tie or bond with the individual employee. Companies feel free to hire and fire people as economic conditions or strategy dictate. People are left to their own devices to cope with whatever happens to them. One of the major difficulties with this approach is that it completely ignores the fact that people form emotional bonds with others and with organizations naturally and without any exterior motivation. Most people want to be loyal and attached. When attachments are broken, the average person experiences it as a major loss in life. During this time, it is natural for them to feel sad and to go through a period of time in which the losses are grieved. Sadness and grief reactions are among the most powerful emotional states that humans can experience. They often lead to clinical depression which, in its worst forms, can be one of the deadliest diseases a human being can face. Suicide gestures, attempts, and successes are routine events in the more profound forms of depression. When depressed, human beings can become immobilized by powerful experiences of hopelessness and helplessness, which can lead to tremendous problems in attention, motivation, and productivity at work (Beck, Rush, Shaw, & Emery, 1979).

Executives in modern organizations often either deliberately create such grief-producing events in the lives of their enterprises or cope with the effects of them. In some organizations, coping with loss and the associated depression is rapidly becoming a chronic problem, as leaders treat their employees as a contingent workforce to be hired and dismissed as they see fit. An extended period of grieving and an associated depression can be difficult to surmount. Yet, the world of the modern organization expects all of its members to incorporate such losses and events rapidly and to maintain productive and even creative work. In my experience, this is an extraordinary and unrealistic expectation, but it is real. Harry Levinson (personal communication, 2000) is fond of saying that "all change involves loss, and all loss must be grieved." In our coaching work with executives, we must be alert to significant shifts that have occurred in their work or personal lives and to the sadness, grief, and depression that can naturally follow.

FRUSTRATION AND ANGER

Another common and potentially dangerous emotional pattern that happens in executive work settings is the experience of anger in the face of an immediate frustration or a chronic pattern of events or interactions that induce frustration. Humans are goal driven, and when goals are not reached, frustration can often occur. Think of the feelings that are aroused when we stand in line too long, do not receive something that was promised, or expect something that never materializes. Usually, there is a brief period of frustration followed quickly by a flash of anger. As I described above, the anger can take many forms from remaining suppressed and unexpressed to physical violence.

The world of work creates an endless stream of opportunities to experience frustration and thus to create anger. Increasingly, there is a leadership expectation of perfect performance. Six Sigma total quality programs create explicit goals of one mistake or error per million operations. Many companies are embracing these standards and driving their employees through extensive training and quality improvement programs. Often, financial incentives are tied to production efforts. Simultaneously, other initiatives such as just-in-time manufacturing and minimal or no inventory techniques are being used to drive down costs and maximize profits. As these methods are implemented with "lean and mean" workforces, small unpredictable events can have significant, often catastrophic effects on production. An unpredicted strike at a key parts plant, a key worker who stays home with a sick child, a colleague whose attention wanders during a production run, or a simple human error can frustrate the expectations of everyone involved. This frustration often flashes into anger (Tavris, 1982; Weisinger, 1985). When these events occur in a diverse workforce in which different values, attitudes, beliefs, and norms govern the expression of these feelings, misunderstanding and mismanagement often occur. This is especially true when the members of the work team are not well prepared to identify and manage strong emotions when they arise. Coaches often are pulled into such circumstances by their clients as they face real problems at work.

FEAR AND ANGER

A similar pattern that frequently appears in work settings evolves when people become afraid and then cover their fear with expressions of anger. Fear and anger are both emotions designed to motivate quick action in humans. Fear tells people that they are in danger. Physiologically, it prepares the body to flee from the source of the threat or to engage in self-protective combat. Similarly, anger and the accompanying aggression also prepare the person to meet a life-threatening challenge. People are usually perceptive about what might be threatening to them, and anticipatory anxiety can strike anyone at any time (Sheehan, 1983). Often, humans experience the anxiety and fear at an unconscious level well before they become aware that they are afraid. For many people, the combination of fear and anger leads them to psychically or physically flee from a threatening environment. For others, it leads to covert or overt conflict. In worst cases, it leads to open combat. Patterns of fight and flight are also frequent results from this combination of emotions for both individuals and groups. When people engage this pattern, episodes of open conflict and even combat in various forms are followed almost immediately by withdrawal from any form of angry expression. The situation can appear to be calm on the surface, but the reality is that the pattern of flight connects intimately to the overt aggression. The withdrawal signals only that the cycle is continuing.

FEAR ALONE

Human beings have a nervous system that ties them intimately to what goes on around them. The average person constantly gauges events and circumstances according to the degree to which it poses a threat. The ability to perceive and respond to external and internal cues that signal the potential for danger and injury is hardwired at birth. Fortunately and unfortunately, people only need to think about or unconsciously sense that a threat of some type exists and a whole cascade of physical and psychological events occurs that creates the experience of fear. Fear, like every other emotion, is usually experienced along a continuum with slight discomfort or worry on one end and full-blown panic on the other. For most people, introduction to someone new or entry into a new situation can create milder forms of fear or anxiety. The feelings may include a vague sense of discomfort or irritation that cannot be explained and often does not rise to the level of conscious awareness. This is a common experience, shared by most people. The other end of the continuum consists of exposure to events that may be life-threatening. Being robbed at gunpoint, told that one has a potentially fatal disease, or that a job that is both needed and loved may be taken away can induce the most profound experiences of panic. Again, the physiology of this emotion consists of a complex web of neurological and hormonal interactions that can evoke profound subjective states of feeling for any person.

The world of work produces many situations that can evoke fear or anxiety responses. Some more common events include participating in a performance review; being told that one's job has been eliminated; getting a new supervisor, colleague, or subordinate; receiving a challenging assignment, joining a new organization or group; and working with a difficult person. Most people cope reasonably well with modest levels of fear because they have a great deal of experience with these feelings in a wide variety of circumstances. Many individuals relish the experience and constantly seek high-risk job assignments, adventure sports, or even extreme physical or emotional challenges. As unbelievable as it seems, climbing Mt. Everest has become a tourist attraction, with dozens of adventurers literally taking their lives in their hands each year. However, fear and anxiety can overwhelm anyone at any time.

The most frequent responses that I see as a result of simple states of fear in people on the job are being timid or uncertain about what to do; a willingness to gossip, to triangulate their communications with others not directly involved, spread rumors, and use the grapevine to express the emotions and speculate about a situation rather than explore things creatively and directly; and a lack of ability or unwillingness to experiment or try new behaviors. These behaviors can be fatal in modern, fast-paced organizations that are constantly changing and require that all employees be willing to embrace what is new and even difficult. Managers and executives who become timid and fearful in such situations never make it onto the fast track for promotion. Even those that do rise quickly in organizations may have either quiet moments or extended episodes of crippling panic. Fear responses can be a particularly vicious circle for leaders because of the levels of uncertainty that exist in the decisions and circumstances that they frequently face. Coaching them in these situations can be challenging.

FEAR AND SHAME

The final vicious emotional pattern involves the sequential or simultaneous experience of fear and shame. As described above, both feelings can exist in mild forms that signal the average person that there are risks in a situation or that danger may exist. Shame connects people closely to how they are being judged by themselves and others and to the degree to which they are being supported and even loved. Humans typically are exquisitely attuned to their level of shame. People are also capable of becoming afraid of other feeling states. I have found this to be particularly true of shame. The mere anticipation of an embarrassing situation or event in which failure or public exposure may be a risk can produce significant amounts of discomfort. In worst work-based cases such as public-speaking phobias or writer's block, people can actually become completely paralyzed. I have personally witnessed an extraordinarily talented executive become completely speechless on a stage. A colleague who watched him spend several humiliating minutes of silence at the podium in front of several hundred people recognized that his friend was completely panic-stricken and unable to continue. He then escorted him back to his seat.

Thus far, I have described many of the workplace challenges that connect subtly and intimately with self-esteem and shame. Pride and shame exist on opposite ends of a continuum for every person in an organization. Pride can lead to a vicious circle in which a prolonged pattern of success creates a state of hubris in which individuals and work teams come to believe that they are omnipotent and cannot fail. They truly expect their judgments to be correct in every circumstance and can refuse to hear, read, or see disconfirming information. Paradoxically, these individuals and groups can be uniquely attuned and ultrasensitive to shame and are often completely intolerant of the feeling. They react violently when forced to experience it. As a result, they constantly scan their worlds for the presence of events, people, information, and developments that could produce shame. Whenever they perceive that shame might be possible, their anxiety levels spike high, and they move quickly to deal with the threat. In some organizations, leaders who live in this vicious cycle become virtually intolerant of information that might disconfirm their interpretation of events. Subordinates quickly learn not to disagree with or challenge them because of their propensity to act out the fear aggressively. As a result, the executive and the entire team can lose touch with reality as everyone plays a game of the "emperor's new coat." No one dares to tell the truth. This is a common and troubling version of the shame–fear vicious circle.

Coaching in these situations can require the utmost tact and sensitivity. When vicious emotional circles operate in an individual or group, they make reality testing and higher order thinking difficult. Under the pressure of strong feelings, people have a greater tendency to act out in ways that can injure themselves and others. These injuries can lead immediately to more strong feelings, creating a positive feedback loop from which it can become virtually impossible to escape without assistance.

The vicious circles described above represent some of the most common patterns that I have experienced in my own practice. However, everyone who wants to coach executives must realize that the emotions of people are extraordinarily flexible, easily aroused, and conditionable. Human beings learn through their emotions and they learn fast. Each one of these goal-incongruent emotions can elicit the others, and complex and highly nuanced patterns exist in virtually every person. One goal when coaching is to help clients become aware of their own emotional patterns and learn how to use them constructively.

ABSOLUTIST THINKING

In my experience, one vicious pattern of cognition that deserves discussion is absolutist thinking. As previously mentioned, Kramer (1990) described absolutist thinking and differentiated it from either relativistic or dialectic thought. When humans use this form of thought, they force themselves to define their worlds in categorical or dualistic terms. Events, feelings, ideas, people, and experiences are divided into opposing categories. Reality takes on a surreal tone as anything that is said or done becomes immediately all good or all bad, right or wrong, stupid or smart, rational or irrational, true or false. Logical processing of information or experience becomes impossible because the only permissible cognitive act involves simple classification. Categorical thinking can be extraordinarily powerful and can create a maddingly magical organizational and interpersonal world. Discussions with individuals or groups using absolutist thinking are only possible when agreement is reached early about the categorization scheme being used to define the experience. Further elaboration and definition of the category is then permissible. However, efforts to challenge the category, stretch the boundaries of the conversation, or simply disagree often are met with real resistance, often expressed as strong emotions, including shame, anxiety, and anger. Creative exploration of alternatives, acquiring additional perspectives, or even empathic embrace of the experience of others becomes impossible when this vicious circle operates.

Absolutist thought contrasts with the relativistic and dialectic thinking described above. In these modes, the points of view of others are deliberately embraced, explored, and often enjoyed for their subjective perspective. Using dialectic modes of thinking requires the creation of polarities, the appreciation of nuance and complexity, and the ability to incorporate paradox as events and ideas are explored. Absolutist circles make such thinking impossible.

Jaques and Clement (1991) provided a complex formula and intricate set of descriptions and definitions of cognitive complexity as it operates in individuals and executives. They identify four types of cognitive processing: assertive, cumulative, serial, and parallel (pp. 52–53). In addition, they suggested that information is ordered in four levels of complexity: concrete things, first-level abstraction of verbal variables, second-level abstraction of concepts, and third-level abstraction of universals. These types of processing and levels of information increase in complexity from lowest to highest, that is, assertive processing of concrete things through parallel processing of abstract universals. They further suggested that these two sets of concepts can be combined to help assess the capacity of any manager or executive to process information and make decisions along various time lines from what needs to be done tomorrow to what might occur 50 or even 100 years in the future. They suggested strongly that individuals who can process only in the assertive mode with concrete things, or first-level abstraction of verbal variables, are unlikely to make strong, visionary leaders. This represents an accurate description of someone mired in a vicious, absolutist circle of cognition. Jaques and Clement's (1991) framework also suggests that there may be other vicious cognitive circles that can trap leaders in cumulative or serial patterns of information processing using only concrete things, verbal variables, or concepts. They suggested that information-processing ability can be modified by coaching, training, teaching, mentoring, and counseling. These and other techniques can be used by coaches to help a client move out of an absolutist-thinking mode and toward dialectic frames using parallel forms of information processing with flexible access to all levels of complexity of information. I believe firmly that coaches must be able to tune into these modes of thinking as they interact with their clients for both diagnostic and intervention purposes.

When I have been invited to coach someone in trouble in an organization, most often I have found one or more of these vicious circles or attractors operating strongly in the client. In Ann's case example, she clearly felt mired in shame and rage. Initially, she simply found it impossible to understand how Jeremy could so easily dismiss her feelings and misunderstand what was important to her. Her anger at him surged to the surface repeatedly during our conversation. If she had stayed anchored in those emotions, she could not have extended her understanding of his motivations, her own positive, if somewhat limited, options in the situation, and the nuances of how she could define and implement a strategy to help herself. As previously described, my strategy during the lunch was to provide a safe containment and first make sure that she became as aware as possible of the full extent of the various dimensions of the situation. I empathized completely with her position and did nothing to challenge the validity of her feelings and thoughts. This brought a torrent of uninterrupted responses from her that lasted for more than 30 minutes. I then sought her permission to ask some related questions. During the next hour, Ann progressively explored with me many other features of her reactions to the situation, what she could safely discern and speculate about Jeremy's thoughts and true feelings about her and the state of the organization, and even more importantly, the consideration of an array of additional strategies and tactics for managing her behavior.

Over the course of the next 4–6 weeks, I talked with Ann several times about what she felt, thought, and was doing to manage herself. Ultimately, she took the position Jeremy offered her after negotiating an appropriate title, a significant raise in pay, and some changes in job duties that would enable her to do some of the things that she loved to do and after she pushed him to further understand the nature of the sacrifice that she felt she was being asked to make for the organization. He was unable to truly understand or empathize with her but listened carefully to what she told him. This ability to at least hear her out on her concerns created sufficient good will that the changes were made without her leaving the job. It was notable that Ann created the circumstances in which this conversation took place. Without her skillful maneuvering in the situation, it was unlikely that Jeremy could have recognized what needed to be done to implement his own strategy.

Virtuous Circles and Functional Attractors

Again following the conceptual foundations we explored in chapter 4, I want to spend a little time discussing virtuous circles. When coaching executives, we tend to take them for granted when we find them operating in our clients. Yet, it is as important to understand how these goal-congruent, positive emotional and thinking patterns work as it is to understand their powerful and goal-incongruent cousins. Without an intimate knowledge of these circles, coaches are unlikely to know what they are trying to help their clients develop by way of new knowledge or skills. The clearer I am about what I am trying to do with clients, the easier it is to work with them and the more comfort I experience in my role. The following explores five virtuous patterns or attractors. Some of their characteristics have been described in the previous section by way of contrasting them with their more dysfunctional counterparts.

CURIOSITY

Humans are by nature curious. From the earliest days of an infant's life, the primary job is to explore the world and progressively master both him- or herself and the environment. Children naturally forge alliances with people to help them in these tasks. They learn almost immediately how to elicit responses from caretakers. Contrary to popular conceptions, they are active learners, with many built-in skills and abilities (Stern, 1985). As described in chapter 6, Kegan, Erikson, Piaget, and other lifespan developmentalists have provided detailed maps of the various challenges and types of learning that people must attack and master throughout their lives. In each developmental stage, individuals who are able to systematically engage and use the positive, goal-congruent emotion of curiosity experience a considerable advantage over those who cannot.

It is both easy and pleasurable to watch toddlers explore the world; they are natural adventurers. They want to see, taste, touch, hear, and embrace almost everything with which they come into contact. Indeed, they are so good at being curious and exploring that an industry has developed that helps parents protect them from their positive instincts. Plastic inserts for electric outlets, latches on cabinet doors, stickers on household chemicals, intercom systems, and other forms of technological inventions help parents keep their children from harm as they discover and explore.

This most positive emotional pattern enhances our lives as we age. However, social and emotional experiences can teach people to inhibit curiosity. Trauma, chronic shaming, failure, or lack of psychological or social support for exploration and experimentation can either temporarily or permanently inhibit curiosity. The vicious circles described above certainly restrain anyone from being interested in what is happening when the experience is noxious, injurious, or traumatic.

I believe that the most successful executives have learned to exercise the virtuous circle of curiosity in every situation that they face. These extraordinarily resilient individuals view crises and catastrophes as learning opportunities that they attack with enthusiasm. Life to them is an endlessly unfolding puzzle or mystery. They make part of their mission in life to explore the mystery and try to solve the puzzle. Their ceaseless curiosity helps them create meaning even in the most trying of circumstances. Mergers and acquisitions become the equivalent of climbing Mt. Everest. Job changes and new assignments are relished for their novelty and the opportunities for growth that they create. Emotional, interpersonal, and business conflicts provide the foundation on which human and organization development are constructed. As a coach, I know that my efforts will be both successful and rewarding when clients ask me a lot of questions, challenge my views, seek out opportunities to read and learn on their own, and make recommendations to me about what I might find useful to read or explore. In these situations, the virtuous circle of curiosity adds tremendous power to the containment and the basic coaching stance toward the client. When harnessed properly, it becomes a virtual torrent that both the client and the coach can ride to new insights, use to experiment with new skills, or count on to help them maneuver through some tricky territory. Coaches must help clients engage and master their curiosity if they want to be successful.

JOY

Joy is a similarly powerful and goal-congruent emotion that can be a self-reinforcing virtuous circle. The human experience of joy consists of feelings of delight, happiness, and pleasure. The emotion can arise spontaneously when a person meets a long-lost friend; has a wonderful, if unexpected, conversation with a colleague; obtains a long-sought objective; or exercises knowledge, skills, or abilities in new ways. Even more importantly, joy can be deliberately encouraged and created as an emotional foundation on which to base one's interactions with the world.

Quite often in my coaching assignments, I know how easy it will be to work with someone by the frequency with which they spontaneously smile and laugh. If someone is able to view their most troublesome problems and difficult challenges with a twinkle in their eye, I know that it will be a pleasure to work with that person. I have come to believe that it is easier for humans to move forward, explore new territory, accept negative news or feedback, or heal from wounds the world inflicts if they are able to create joy for themselves. Hints about this capacity or ability to use this virtuous circle come from answers to questions such as, Is there anything that truly excites you in your work or life? What makes you happiest? Do you have hobbies or an avocation that you enjoy? What have been some of the most joyful moments of your life? What do you, your team, or your organization do best? This line of questioning follows the precepts of appreciative inquiry outlined by Cooperrider (1996), Hammond (1996), and Hammond and Royal (1998). Approaching clients in this way can readily move them into a place of joy from which further exploration becomes much more possible than from any of the vicious circles described above.

LEGITIMATE SELF-DEFENSE

This goal-congruent, virtuous circle comprises a set of emotions and behaviors that most people have developed during their lives and exercise with more or less expertise and sensitivity. I raise it here not so much because it is a true, unique emotional state or pattern of thought, but because it logically fits and is important to executive development and survival.

Modern organizations are hypercompetitive places. Most of the people in management and executive positions are ambitious and achievement-oriented. They have spent their lives striving to succeed, win competitions, and better themselves. In my experience, the vast majority of them are prepared to and do play by the rules. That is to say that they are reasonably cooperative, will try to help a colleague do his or her work, and will work to repair damage when it has occurred. However, a few individuals in almost every organization may have learned to compete unfairly or do not believe that rules or norms apply to them. In worst cases, they may be hyperaggressive and malevolently destructive. More commonly, they simply push their own agenda with no true regard for the consequences to colleagues, subordinates, superiors, or even the organization as a whole.

When confronted by one of these people, or the organizational equivalent, a competitor who deliberately tries to put an organization out of business, self-defense is in order. This virtuous pattern uses the anxiety aroused by perceived or experienced threats to generate a sufficient amount of anger to guarantee vigorous action. It may be accompanied by acute feelings of shame if failure or rejection have been encountered. It may also be tinged with sadness if losses must be incorporated, as when business reversals require a company to lay off workers or restructure itself. Interestingly, anticipatory guilt, which is a difficult emotion to manage, may be aroused because self-defense may require aggressive actions toward others. These can become specific, injurious acts that most people have been socialized to avoid. Guilt is most often experienced when a transgression of some sort has been committed and, at its worst, it can cause a profoundly debilitating depression with the potential for suicidal ideation, attempts, or successes. A complex array of behaviors may be used in effective self-defense. Effective communications, conflict management, problem solving, creative thought, shifts in relationships, alliance building, constructing new products or services, political maneuvering, limit setting, and open legal combat are just some of the tactics that individuals and organizations might use to protect themselves.

One of the most common situations in which self-defense should be used by managers and executives comes when a subordinate or a reporting unit systematically or deliberately underperforms. Incomplete or poor work, ineffective implementation, or repeated missing of goals are sufficient grounds for some type of vigorous action by a leader. Most organizations have guidelines about how to deal with underperforming individuals in their disciplinary policies. No such systematic advice is usually available when an entire organizational unit fails. Nevertheless, it is always necessary to act to halt a regressive slide in an individual, a group, or organization. Assisting clients to discern situations in which self-defense is required and develop strategies and tactics to do so are among the most complex tasks that a coach may face. It is difficult to stay in the positive circle of self-defense and not regress into some of the most serious forms of vicious circles described above. Creating enemies is easy to do (Keen, 1986). Turning around negative situations requires delicate and difficult work that invokes the highest levels of skill, patience, and prudence for both clients and coaches.

LOVE AT WORK

Few books on management or leadership raise the issue of love as it pertains to the world of work. As many authors and leaders say, "business is a serious business." However, in my experience, leaders and managers frequently tell me that they love their jobs, their careers, their colleagues, and even their organizations. I believe this is natural and that it has a long-standing history in human affairs. We readily believe an artist, musician, engineer, or athlete who says "I love what I do." Such messages engender no questions, challenges, or cynical remarks. We understand that people who have invested so much time and energy to become excellent at what they do would probably feel deep devotion, affection, and attachment to it. It becomes disconcerting to think of someone in an executive position feeling this way, but many do. For the most part, the language of love has been systematically excluded from the world of work. Yet, when working with high-level people or people with potential, coaches are trying to help them unleash passion for what they do and who they are in their work roles.

Maccoby (1976, 1988) discussed the motivational factors underlying the performance of people in the world of work. He emphasized the role of *value drives*, which he defined as "energized patterns of perceiving, thinking, wanting, and acting shared by members of society" (1988, p. 53). He identified eight value drives that energize people's performance in the workplace: survival, relatedness, pleasure, information, mastery, play, dignity, and meaning. Each of these in turn has a subset of descriptive values that helps to illuminate the category. For example, "relatedness" has such value features as attachment, care, protection, recognition, communication, sociability, and community. "Pleasure," he suggested, has comfort, sex, tasty food and drink, exercise and rest, novelty, fun, and beauty as major components. Within this framework, love as expressed at work is a complex, value-driven emotion that allows individuals to invest themselves in their relationships, roles, and tasks in an uninhibited and passionate way. In its best and most intense forms, it leads individuals and work teams to value both their jobs and each other and to experience true pleasure and passion as they perform.

Assisting clients in finding and expressing these value drives, in experiencing and creating a love of who they are and what they do is, I find, the greatest challenge and highest reward in coaching. Watching someone move from living in vicious circles of fear, shame, sadness, rage, and absolutist thinking to a place in which they can love themselves, what they do, and who they do it with is a truly joyous experience. When clients can reliably create virtuous loving circles for themselves, I know that they can and will succeed at whatever they attempt.

SEX AT WORK

Human sexuality is not a simple, single emotional state; rather, it involves complex patterns of thought, feeling, and behavior. However, virtually all adults can readily identify when they are sexually aroused, and there is no way to determine when and with whom such arousal might be experienced. One needs only to read the headlines of the daily newspapers to know that sex is a human experience in the world of work. Many romantic relationships begin on the job. Sexual harassment, the worst form of sexual expression at work, is widespread, illegal, and enormously risky for organizations and participants. I have had any number of experiences with coaching clients in which sex needed to be discussed.

I put it in this section on virtuous circles because for most people most of the time sex remains appropriately under the surface of their relationships at work and provides additional motivation in many situations. Psychodynamic theory and most of human experience suggests that such feelings can be effectively expressed indirectly through creativity, play, hard work, and effective relationships. Sex does not need to be directly experienced, discussed, or engaged in to play an important role in how people work and perform. Becoming attracted to a colleague, enjoying his or her presence, and having fun in a mutual work assignment can enhance performance. However, it remains a difficult and tricky issue.

On the positive side, many people find their spouses or significant others on the job. They successfully court each other, maintaining appropriate boundaries and performing their duties well. Even when such a courting relationship dissolves prior to marriage, the majority of the participants and their colleagues manage these situations with reasonable dignity and minimize any damage to each other or to their enterprise. Some organizations are well known for being places where colleagues date each other, form attachments, and manage to do so reasonably well most of the time.

However, sexual feelings and behavior at work can have a negative and corrosive influence on participants and on the organization as a whole. Despite laws and regulations that create stiff penalties for harassment, it continues both overtly and covertly in the workplace. It represents a perversion of the constructive aspects of sexual experience on the job. Sexual harassment leads to career derailment, huge legal bills, serious financial penalties, and mental and physical illness. When sex invades the workplace negatively, men and women can become inhibited, terrified, and enraged. Acting-out behavior up to and including homicide are possible. Disaffected or unrequited lovers can make life difficult for the targets of their affections and for everyone else around them. In the worst cases, ex-lovers have shown up at the workplace and killed their estranged loved ones and colleagues who might be there with them.

A significant problem is always created when a supervisor engages in a romantic relationship with a subordinate. Others in the same workplace can become anxious, jealous, and angry. This is especially true if there are any perceived special treatments such as promotions, raises, or perks such as travel. At the very least, such a relationship unleashes a torrent of voyeuristic speculation and gossip. If participants are married, colleagues can be drawn inadvertently or by design into a pattern of corruption and deception that creates risks and resentments all around.

Coaches must be ever vigilant about the presence of sexual expression in clients and for what may be happening in their environments. Helping them become attuned to sexual feelings and the dynamics of human relationships that might be influenced by these emotions is one of the most complex and challenging jobs any coach will face. It is extremely important that coaches are clear about their own values and boundaries in the area of sexual behavior. Frequently, the coaching relationship itself may have overtones or undertones of sexuality as a strong attachment forms and a productive relationship ensues. This will rarely become an overt issue or problem. However, it is possible that a client may become so attracted or attached that some discussion may be initiated. These can be extraordinarily difficult. Under no circumstances do I believe that it is appropriate for a coach to become romantically involved with a client. As soon as that issue comes into colleagues' view, coaches are obligated to seek assistance for themselves in determining whether the coaching alliance is in jeopardy and what constructive steps should be taken. Similarly, if a client expresses an interest, immediate consultation should be sought about how to manage the situation. If it cannot be worked through successfully, the coaching relationship may need to be terminated and the client referred to someone else.

I do not want to convey the impression that I condone or encourage sexual feelings, expression, or relationships at work. Rather, I am a realist; I have witnessed virtually every kind of situation involving sex on the job. I often see the kind of teasing and flirting that can enliven relationships and dull repetitive tasks. I have similarly witnessed and helped individuals, work groups, and organizations deal with stalking, the threat or aftermath of homicide, spouse abuse, and the most heinous overt forms of sexual harassment. Wherever people gather, they bring all of themselves along, including their complex sexual natures. Coaches must be alert and adept at sensing, assessing, and working with these emotional situations.

Coaching With and About Emotions and Thinking Patterns

When establishing and working in coaching relationships, it becomes inevitable that emotions will be experienced by both parties. Coaches must prepare to confront and manage these most challenging and interesting aspects of human behavior. The basic approach that I take in coaching on emotional or cognitive content does not vary much from that which I use with other content. In chapters 4 and 5, I emphasized the importance of building a containment—a safe, bounded, goal-directed relationship—in which clients and their coaches can explore and experiment securely. I also suggested that the basic task for clients consists of building their capacity for self-awareness and self-regulation (Carver & Scheier, 1998). In addition, I described how the flow of a carefully managed coaching session can and does help a client focus his or her attention on the most salient aspects of the work of the moment. Using the circle of awareness repeatedly improves clients' ability to reflect on events, situations, relationships, challenges, conflicts, and roadblocks to developing new knowledge and skills. All of these basic approaches and skills are needed when coaching on emotional issues.

The first task that coaches face in helping clients with emotion and cognition consists of helping them establish a language to use in discussing emotions and thinking patterns and a basic knowledge of what they are, how they work, and what their purposes are. It constantly surprises me how uninformed even the most sophisticated executives are about the most basic issues of emotion and cognition. So, when initially entering into the emotional and cognitive terrain of an executive's world, I try to make sure that both the client and I understand terms and how we will use them. I frequently provide a short description of the primary emotional states and cognitive approaches. I emphasize that emotions can substitute for each other; protect us from being aware of thoughts and other feelings, or serve as defenses; and even complicate and mask underlying conflicts. I also suggest that emotions can conflict with each other, as when a leader becomes angry at a subordinate for poor performance but may be inhibited or conflicted by anxiety, guilt, or shame when it comes to confronting that person and working through to a clearer set of expectations or limits. I also describe the continuum of human thinking patterns from the most primitive to the highly complex, parallel-processing, universalist principle dialectics that coaches wish to see in clients.

Once I am reasonably sure that the client and I share some of the same basic knowledge, I then use the process of a session and the circle of awareness to conduct an inquiry—one hopes an appreciative one—into how the client thinks and feels about the issues or situation being confronted. I specifically ask the client to try to identify the presence of different feeling states. Usually, it is obvious to me what type of cognitive processing strategies are being used, particularly when absolutist or concrete patterns are present. In these situations, categorical relationships between events and people are most common. Extreme adverbs such as *always, never, most,* and *least* arise spontaneously. Adjectives paint either a bleak negative landscape or an overidealized positive one. Information sources are extremely limited and almost always are used to confirm the basic viewpoint that the client has established. It becomes equally obvious when an executive uses advanced, parallel dialectics. Complex chains of logic, multidimensional streaming of causal pathways, rich, often paradoxical and conflicting sources of data are described; causes and solutions are almost always seen as incorporating a knowledge and appreciation of polarities, alternatives, potential risks, and advantages.

I always find it easier to coach clients who function cognitively in parallel and dialectic modes. Providing them with emotional information and setting out to explore the world of feelings may engender defenses and conflicts, but I am usually assured that the client and I can reasonably sort out what may be going on when a stumbling block arises. Unless the emotions, defenses, or conflicts being confronted are strong, these clients can often be easily moved from a vicious circle into the exploration of a more virtuous one. This is not the case with absolutist thinkers. They often require a great deal of time to incorporate emotional information. Even if they are able to identify feeling states, they tend to focus on positives or negatives. When they are immersed in either a vicious or virtuous circle, they prove difficult to move and frequently fall back into their most comfortable, or in the language of computer programmers, default positions. Careful attention to timing, maintaining the containment, and coaching tenacity may be required to move individuals stuck in absolutist thinking patterns who are also mired in vicious emotional circles.

I have found many other techniques can be helpful when coaching on these issues. At the end of this chapter are brief descriptions and exercises using goal setting, metaphors, and reframing methods with clients.

Ann's Job Offer

As a way of further exploring coaching on emotional and cognitive material, I close this chapter with a brief examination of the influence of subsequent coaching sessions in the case of Ann. Ann scheduled a follow-up appointment with me approximately 2 weeks after the first. When she arrived, she looked much less agitated than the previous time I had seen her. She started out by reporting that after our first discussion, she had talked to several individuals who knew Jeremy well. She communicated some of her concerns to them in the most diplomatic language that she could muster. This strategy worked well for her. Her back channel communications elicited an invitation to lunch by Jeremy.

"He really tried. He really did. But he just doesn't get it," she said, describing how the interaction had gone.

She smiled and shook her head as she said this to me. She explained that she had come to more fully understand that what she had seen and experienced as a more full and complete partnership between her and Jeremy had been much more limited and instrumental for him.

"I'm sure now that he has no idea of what effect his offer and behavior had on me."

"Did you raise it with him?" I asked.

"Oh, I tried several times and in a couple of different ways. He just didn't want to go there."

"Or, perhaps he couldn't," I replied.

"Why do you say that?"

I proceeded to discuss the role of defensive behavior and what some of the emotions might be for Jeremy in such a discussion. This led us to explore some gender differences in the experience and expression of emotion. We discussed the difficulty that some men have both experiencing and expressing emotions beyond anger and competitive strivings. I was sure that Jeremy found it difficult empathizing with others because he did not want to feel what they were feeling. Ann and I talked about the pros and cons in this pattern for leaders. On the one hand, it enabled Jeremy to cooly evaluate the needs of his organization, assess alternatives, and conclude rationally that Ann was the logical answer to a large-scale problem that he and the organization faced. On the other hand, his inability to empathize, see his action in the context of his relationship with her, and correctly evaluate the potential impact on Ann led him to handle the interaction very poorly.

"He could have had me. All he needed to do was to value my contribution a little more, spend a little time persuading me about the importance to the organization, recognize the potential adverse effects that this move could have on my career, and offer to ensure that the downside would be kept to a minimum. Instead, he simply apologized indirectly and tried to persuade me that he had been right all along. I had to steer the conversation away from the job change just to keep from getting mad all over again."

We talked about her emotional reaction, and she said that she was still angry, but that she had no true alternative to accepting the offer. We spent most of the rest of the session discussing her bargaining position and how she could maximize the gains from the changes. She became clearer and more focused during this talk about what she could reasonably seek as part of the new deal.

During this session, Ann readily appreciated the complexity, paradoxes, and polarities that the situation had produced for her. Our discussion moved easily from one extreme to its logical opposite. She described her desire to leave, the steps she had initiated, and others that she would take to get out from under a job that she knew she could do and that she anticipated she would hate.

Approximately 3 weeks later, Ann and I met again. She described the details of the deal she had negotiated with Jeremy. She had agreed to accept the position, and steps were under way for her to assume her new position in a few weeks' time. We reviewed this process, its effects on her current work and relationships, and the need to make time to work through the feelings involved in leaving a job that she loved to take on one about which she had ambivalence. Ann also shared with me the activities that she had initiated to begin a job search that would eventually lead her out of the position. She seemed determined to make the best of her current situation and equally driven to find a position more to her liking. We discussed the difficulties of these conflicts and some of the likely pitfalls that might await her as she made her transitions and continued to explore alternatives. I can truly say that all of her considerable cognitive faculties and professional skills were fully engaged in what can only be described as an effort to defend herself against Jeremy's insensitive but ultimately rational treatment of her as a subordinate.

Coaching in this situation enabled Ann to correctly identify the complex array of issues and her responses to them. I am also sure that she was able to safely explore and express many of her emotions such as anger, shame, anxiety, and sadness without becoming mired in a vicious circle with any of them. She was able to move into both curiosity and self-defense as she simultaneously negotiated her new position and maneuvered to search for something more to her liking. At various times during our sessions, I used metaphoric thinking, reframing, and goal clarification to help her figure out what she was experiencing and what she needed to do. Without such coaching, I doubt that her response to the job crisis would have been nearly as constructive.

This case provides an excellent example of how even a potentially positive event like being offered a new job with a significant salary increase can elicit strong negative emotions at work. Left to their own devices, people usually cope with such events using their typical knowledge and skills. If they remain unaware of the effects of their emotional reactions, particularly the ability to descend into a vicious circle, coping can become stereotyped and, in the worst cases, destructive. In cases in which people are accustomed to acting out emotional responses either actively or passively, individual, group, and organizational regression becomes likely. Coaching that incorporates a sensitive understanding of these patterns and potentials can halt regressive slides and help move clients forward in much more positive and constructive directions.

When Strength Becomes Weakness

I would like to add one final note in this chapter. These patterns of emotion and cognition are often experienced by clients as strengths that they have spent a great deal of time developing. One approaches them with caution and respect when seeking to negotiate change. I have found it useful to suggest to clients that the pattern of behavior being addressed *does* represent a strength in many situations. However, I also stress that strength overused or misapplied can become a weakness. Metaphors can be useful in making the point by suggesting such ideas as "it's like trying to take an engine apart with just a screwdriver," "do a complex painting with only one brush," or "write a novel using only 100 words." Clients who can begin to understand that they need to develop their weaknesses and at times refrain from using their strengths are most often those who increase their resiliency. Those who cannot do so often blunder into difficulties with the best of intentions, using only that knowledge and skill with which they are most adept.

EXERCISE 7.1

Gaps Analysis

In this exercise, adapted from Peterson and Hicks (1996), clients are asked to explore both their own and others' views of them. As part of a homework assignment, they assess where they currently are in terms of their abilities and where they want to go in terms of their goals. They are also asked to identify several key informants, including their immediate superiors, colleagues, and subordinates, and to explore with these individuals how they are seen and what is expected of them. The following format allows a client to fill in the cells, providing a succinct picture of their current status.

Leader/Manager Gaps Analysis

	Where You Are (abilities)	**Where You Want to Go (goals)**
YOUR VIEW	What Can You Do?	What Do You Want To Do?
	1.	1.
	2.	2.
	3.	3.
	4.	4.
	5.	5.
	6.	6.
	7.	7.
	8.	8.
	9.	9.
	10.	10.
	Perceptions	**Standards**
	How Do Others See You?	What Do Others Expect of You?
OTHERS' VIEW	1.	1.
	2.	2.
	3.	3.
	4.	4.
	5.	5.
	6.	6.
	7.	7.
	8.	8.
	9.	9.
	10.	10.

Once the matrix is drafted, the coach and the client can explore the gaps between where they are and where they want to go and between what other perceptions of them are and what standards or expectations they confront. The following questions and issues can guide the mutual exploration:

Self-Analysis

- What gaps do you perceive?
- How serious are the gaps, and what is the priority for attention?

EXERCISE 7.1 continued

- Which stimulate the most resistance/discomfort/defensiveness?
- Which would have the biggest impact if addressed or changed?
- Which is the client most motivated to address?

Objective Observations

- Explore goals vs. perceptions, goals vs. standards, perceptions vs. standards, abilities vs. perceptions.
- Use methods of appreciative inquiry and rely on containment.
- Be alert for psychodynamics—emotions, cognition, conflicts, and defenses.

During the exploration, the coach can assist the client in identifying and establishing priorities for action and behavior change based on the assessment and the gaps that are identified. The following issues and steps can assist in the process of narrowing the list of potential steps and developing a concrete plan:

- Explore the client's personal incentives (be better in current job, prepare for a new job, improve satisfaction, create meaning and value in work, expand or achieve potential).
- Explore the organization's incentives (what is critical to success in the organization, to help the organization make a change, to enhance competitive position, to fill holes).
- Narrow the list (assess return on investment—rate difficulty of goals; assess costs—money, time, effort, organizational support; look at cost vs. payback).
- Choose one or two to develop a plan.

Use the priorities and the process to develop a plan. Consider the following questions when constructing it:

- Does it focus on one or two goals?
- Can he/she work on it and think about it every day?
- Does it anticipate barriers/roadblocks to implementation?
- Does it create daily activity and action? Does it involve distributed practice, proximal and distal learning?
- Does it actively incorporate learning? Time and structure for reflection? Learning records? Barriers and defense analysis?
- Does it document progress? Identify sources and efforts to obtain feedback? Measure progress toward goals? Identify sources of support and nourishment?
- Is it flexible? Does it adjust to changes in the client or organization? Adapt to changes in competency? Incorporate methods of assessment?

EXERCISE 7.2

Use of Metaphor in Executive Coaching Sessions

Lakoff and Johnson (1980) suggested that metaphors are extremely common in the experience of everyday life. They further suggested that the underlying conceptual structure of human understanding and communication rests on the use of metaphor. In working with clients in executive positions, using an understanding of metaphor to help identify current modes of emotion, thought, and action can be extremely useful. As stated by Lakoff and Johnson, "the essence of metaphor is understanding and experiencing one kind of thing in terms of another" (p. 5).

An example of how a client might be using metaphor to describe his or her current situation is as follows:

> I had a fight with one of my subordinates yesterday. She was making claims that were indefensible. Every point that I raised she disputed, but my criticisms of her performance I believe were right on target. I successfully defended myself and shot down all of the arguments that she was making. I left the conversation feeling as though I had been able to win.

The underlying metaphor for this exchange between a supervisor and a subordinate clearly consisted of communication as a "war." The supervisor used a variety of words that a coach could readily identify with the underlying metaphor. These included *fight*, *indefensible*, *disputed*, *right on target*, *defended*, *shot down*, and *win*. The use of this language and of the metaphor "communication and relationship with subordinate as war" has major implications for the ongoing ability of this client to supervise the individual. To help a client become more resourceful, become aware of both emotional and cognitive patterns, and therefore more competent and flexible in this situation, the coach can begin to help the client understand how metaphors can shape assumptions, values, attitudes, beliefs, thoughts, feelings, defenses, conflicts, and behaviors. The following steps can be used by a coach to help a client become more aware of the metaphors that are being used and to identify and select alternatives that may improve his or her ability to work creatively in the situation:

1. Use the stages in a coaching session.
2. Use the circle of awareness.
3. Use the frames for attention.
4. Focus on consistent or episodic use of metaphoric language by a client to describe an event, problem, person, process, or structure. Some examples of such language follow.
   - Talking to him is like banging your head against a wall.
   - That was a disaster.
   - It's a train wreck.
   - She sits on a throne.
   - We're at a crossroads.
   - We're spinning our wheels.
   - We're stuck in the jungle.
   - The ship is sinking.
   - We're rearranging deck chairs on the Titanic.
   - He's a rat, snake, tiger, bear, rabbit.
   - We're on the rocks.
   - I'm dying here.
   - It's like talking to the wall.
5. Make the metaphor real, visible, and discussable—"get it on the table."

EXERCISE 7.2 continued

6. Invite the client to examine/explore the implications of his or her metaphor.
7. Inquire if the client would like to examine alternative metaphors to describe the event, person, problem, process, or structure.
8. Use the technique of reframing (see Exercise 7.3) if the client seems stuck.
9. Be prepared to manage emotions, defenses, and conflicts that may underlie or be attached to the metaphor.
10. Invite the client to brainstorm alternatives.
11. Have the client try to use one or more of the alternatives to re-explore the issues that he or she is working on with you.
12. Create a dialogue on how the alternative metaphor changes the client's perspective, attitudes, feelings, thoughts, and behaviors. Use the ladder of inference (Exercise 9.1) to clarify the steps and stages through which the metaphor may influence the client's current situation and behavior.
13. Develop an agreement with the client to experiment with the new/revised metaphor as he or she approaches the situation, person, problem, etc., again.
14. Using the circle of awareness at a subsequent session, evaluate the outcome of using or practicing with the alternative.
15. Make changes as necessary.

EXERCISE 7.3

Reframing

Individuals, groups, and organizations can readily create frames within and through which they interpret and build their understanding of reality. These frames may incorporate symbols, metaphors, values, attitudes, beliefs, goals, history, emotions, patterns of thinking, defenses, conflicts, and other ways of interpreting experience. They often exist outside of conscious awareness, and they can significantly influence behavior. Coaches can help clients identify and modify these types of frames. The following methods can assist in this process:

1. Identify the existing frame. Examine underlying goals, symbols, metaphors, values, assumptions, beliefs, attitudes, conflicts, defenses, emotions, thoughts, behaviors.
   - Explore the natural history and current adaptation value of the existing frame.
   - Invite the client to examine the existing frame through different levels of reflection (see the circle of awareness, chapter 4, this volume).
2. Test the current frame against current reality and client goals.
   - Invite the client to explore the consequences of continued use of the existing frame.
   - Invite the client to challenge the existing frame with other sources of information, ideas, and experience that may lead to a shift in perspective.
   - Challenge the client to defend the validity of the existing frame in light of what has been explored.
   - Ask the client, "How is your existing frame of reference getting in your way?" "Is this existing frame truly useful to you in your current situation?"
3. Work together to revise the frame
   - Explore different values, assumptions, symbols, metaphors, beliefs, attitudes, behaviors, emotions, defenses, and thoughts that might be applied to the situation.
   - Ask the client, "What would you like to change or be different?"
   - Have the client restate the revision of the frame of reference as he or she has come to understand it.
   - Ask the client to consider the consequences of applying the new frame of reference.
   - Work with the client to construct a useful practice or homework assignment.

8 Working With Client Defenses

The Case of the Venomous, Controlling Spider

I sat in one of four chairs gathered around a table in Carl's office with him and two key subordinates. He was my identified client in a financial production unit that processed large amounts of data and forms. I had been invited in by Carl after discussions with his supervisor, who had expressed concerns about repeated complaints from some of his subordinates. They had reported many examples of mistreatment and ineffective administration. After numerous assessment activities and a comprehensive set of recommendations as part of the consultation project, I had settled into a routine of coaching both Carl and his key subordinates. Joint meetings were scheduled monthly and were supplemented by individual sessions with each of the three professionals. These activities had been going on for about 1 year. The three members of the management team had acknowledged that they had made some progress and that Carl had improved by changing some of his more troubling forms of behavior, such as retreating into his office to play video games, ignoring mail and telephone calls, and avoiding anticipatory or planning activities.

Despite Carl's behavior, the entire unit enjoyed a stellar reputation. The majority of the staff members were experienced, talented, and dedicated. They took great pride in doing their jobs well and seemed to function well with each other and other organizational units. The staff neither needed nor wanted major amounts of direct supervision, but they unanimously agreed that the organization could do even better if Carl could somehow improve and become a more productive leader.

My individual sessions with Carl had been difficult. I gave him the feedback that the assessment produced, and he systematically minimized the critical findings. He acknowledged that he had been through a tough time in his personal life during the past 2 years, and that sometimes he had difficulty generating enthusiasm for work. He emphasized the unit's reputation, the lack of external criticism, and a long-standing history of excellent performance. He took pride in the competence of the staff and the relatively low turnover rate, and he repeatedly returned to that statistic to suggest that the complaints were being expressed by a small minority of the staff. With the visible concern and external scrutiny from his supervisor an ongoing issue, he had agreed to some of my recommendations, including coaching for himself and key staff.

Late in this particular session, the four of us were talking about how they worked together. Pat, the unit's director of administrative operations, had voiced concerns repeatedly in several sessions that Carl changed his mind frequently, had difficulty anticipating events, and was often unresponsive to requests unless they were repeated along with sometimes forceful prods to complete tasks. John, the technical supervisor, had emphasized Carl's lack of willingness to delegate tasks and activities fully or in a time frame that made task completion a reasonable possibility.

"He sometimes drives me a little crazy with the way he does things," John said, taking a major risk in the session.

"Try to describe what you mean by that," I replied.

"Well, what Pat says is true. Carl waits and waits until the last minute to do things. When I give him something to review or suggest that we need to discuss something, he won't respond right away. Often, I think he's simply forgotten about it or that he doesn't care."

"What's your response when that happens?"

"I get really frustrated."

"Anything else?"

"Yeah, sometimes it makes me angry. I can't do my job correctly when he waits like that. It makes me crazy."

"What happens then?"

"Well, it depends. If I remind him a lot, he'll eventually get around to doing something. If I don't remind him, nothing will happen until a deadline is missed, and someone calls upset or angry because we haven't done what we were supposed to do. Then he gets all huffy and comes looking to find out what went wrong."

"And?"

"And, then he usually blames me."

"Or me," Pat echoed.

I looked at Carl who sat scowling, with folded arms and crossed legs.

"How does this sound to you?" I asked Carl.

"I don't think it's true. Just last week, I came into John and asked him to take a walk with me. We went out and had a great discussion about the report that was due. He didn't seem upset to me at all. He didn't say anything to me."

"John?"

"Oh yeah, what he says is true. He came in, and we took the walk. We had the talk, and it was quite helpful, just as he said. What he didn't say was that we knew 6 weeks ago that the report was due. He didn't mention that I had asked him every week what he thought we should do, and he wouldn't give me any time to talk about it. I didn't want to have us look bad, so I went ahead and prepared something that I thought would do the job."

"You didn't tell me that," Carl jumped in critically.

"You're right, Carl, I didn't. You were very clear about what you thought we should do, and you asked to see my draft by the next day."

"What happened then?" I asked John.

"I had to work until 3:00 a.m., and I missed my daughter's music recital. I put the draft report on his desk at 3:00 p.m. the next day, and then I went home exhausted."

"Anything else?"

"He had to throw out 2 weeks of work that he had prepared," Pat answered for John.

"I didn't know that," Carl answered defensively.

"I don't think it would have mattered anyway, Carl. You would have told him to use what he had done and put it in the way you wanted. You always want to control things, and this is just a small example of what goes on around here all the time," Pat replied.

"Could you have delegated the construction of the report to John earlier?" I asked Carl.

"I'm responsible for everything that goes on around here. I need to be involved to make sure that things go right."

"So, even though you trust John to draft the report after you've talked to him, you still feel like you need to be involved."

"Sure, don't you think a manager needs to be accountable? After all, you've been talking to me for months about that stuff."

I sensed the challenge with Carl's remark and recognized that both John and Pat had escalated their level of involvement and risk-taking. This was the first time in nearly a year of monthly meetings that feelings were very close to the surface in a discussion of a recent example of their issues.

"Of course managers must be accountable. However, it's important to be reasonably clear about the type of management style and decision-making process you want to use."

"What does that mean?"

I went on to explain Likert's (1967) view that management and decision making can be viewed along a continuum from malignant dictatorship to full participation and democracy. I also briefly described Hersey and Blanchard's (1977) situational leadership model, trying to provide some concepts and to move the conversation toward working on finding problems and solutions and away from the shame–blame game.

"It seems to me that what John and Pat are describing is a management and decision-making style that keeps you involved in everything. With your tendencies to take time to mull over things and procrastinate a little, it can be very frustrating for mature colleagues who are ready, willing, and able to implement your orders. It's like you've evolved a hub-and-spoke model. All information and decisions must flow to you at the hub. When you do decide, information and orders then flow back out."

"That's a good description of it. I like that," Carl said.

"As with any model though, it has its strengths and weaknesses. In this case, you get the information and control you feel you need, but the spokes are saying that they don't get information or decisions back from you in sufficient time to implement properly. The results are high levels of frustration, inefficiency, and tension between the three of you."

"What's wrong with needing to see the report that John produced before it goes out?"

"Nothing, except that you sat on it until yesterday when you finally got around to reading it," John said, visibly trying to keep his voice even and the emotional edge that he clearly felt under control.

"And, you wouldn't have done it yesterday if I hadn't reminded you four times," Pat added.

"What happened?" I asked.

"He got mad and blamed me when the person who asked for the report finally called him," John answered calmly.

Carl said nothing in reply. This was one of those moments that come in coaching sessions when major possibilities for change and growth rise to the surface. Everyone in the room knew that the issue had been fairly raised, and that Carl now looked squarely at the need to modify his behavior and approach.

"Well, what's the alternative?" Carl asked.

"What do you need to be different?" I replied turning to John and Pat.

They proceeded to state explicitly that they wanted Carl to trust them more and to delegate the work clearly and consistently. They said that they were ready to take more responsibility, that they knew their jobs well, and that Carl could be freed to focus on longer term issues that he was both good at and interested in pursuing. If the existing model were to continue, they were equally clear that they wanted him to respond in a more timely fashion and stop blaming them when things did not work correctly or on time.

"It sounds to me as though you have a clear preference to work in a more participative way and with stronger delegation," I tried to clarify.

"I think it would work better, with less tension, and Carl could do the things he's really interested in pursuing," Pat answered.

"More work would get done," John responded.

At that point, we all turned to Carl. After a brief silence, he proceeded to give a long speech defending himself and his approach. He returned to his mantras about the lack of turnover, the positive public response to the unit's work, and the expertise of the staff. He said that he had talked to the person who was upset about the delay in producing the report under discussion. He reported that the individual was extremely pleased with what he got from them and that he seemed to understand the time delays involved. He suggested strongly that I wanted him to take steps in the direction of letting things go and that he was uncomfortable with turning control over to the staff when he was both responsible and held publicly accountable by everyone.

I responded by pointing out that there were in fact several options being discussed and that he simply had to choose which model best suited his preferences and the needs of his staff. I summarized the difficulties that they were having and suggested that, given the maturity of his colleagues, the level of frustration and performance problems would likely continue or escalate unless he made some changes. At this point in the session, we went through several rounds of reviewing the situation in general, his views of the performance of the unit, and what he was most comfortable pursuing. With each iteration, Carl increasingly built his case for maintaining the status quo. He presented layer after layer of reasoning and explanation, each of which basically repeated his core themes. I found the performance masterful, depressing, and supremely self-contained.

"It sounds to me you are saying in a number of ways that you see no real reason for changing what you are doing in your approach to management. The unit performs well enough, and the feedback is not so poor that your boss will take major action," I said trying to define the situation clearly.

"I think that's right," Carl replied.

"So, regardless of the consequences for your key people, the feelings and problems we've been discussing together for the last year, and your previous commitment to working together, you simply want to keep things the way they are."

Carl paused for a moment. He looked at John and Pat, and then he turned to me.

"Yes, that's what I'm saying."

I made several attempts at pointing out that this position indicated a strong defensive response to the challenges of change, to which he replied that was exactly the case. He said clearly and in several ways that he saw no need to go farther with the project, that we had accomplished a number of things that were helpful, but that further sessions were not indicated. We spent several more minutes talking about the situation, and I indicated that with no intention to change anything I was not sure there was a reason for continuing the coaching sessions. Carl agreed with me. I could see the disappointment and frustration in the faces of John and Pat. Nonetheless, with a total lack of motivation by Carl and the goals of the coaching declared publicly moot or completed, I could see no real alternative to withdrawal.

In keeping with the written agreement that I had with Carl, I suggested that he inform his supervisor that we were bringing the project to a close. I said that I would also communicate that fact to the supervisor and would leave it to him to explain, because our confidentiality agreement committed me to keep the content of our work private. I also clarified that I would be willing to continue to meet with John and Pat should they find it useful. Carl seemed happy to permit this to continue. I quickly reviewed with them what they thought we had accomplished in the approximately 18 months that we had worked together. Despite the palpable tension that continued in the room, Carl, John, and Pat were all able to discuss the gains that they had made. I agreed with them, then reiterated my concern that without additional changes, further improvement would prove elusive. I said I would be happy to resume working with them as a team when and if Carl changed his mind.

I left Carl's office both frustrated and pleased. After months of work, I knew that we had reached the only possible conclusion. Carl would and could not go further. The confrontation that occurred in the meeting was, I knew, fundamentally healthy because it specified the location and type of trouble that they would continue to have. With a clear agreement to stop, I could feel free to redeploy my time and attention to other clients who might be more interested in growth. Once again, I marveled at the complexity and effectiveness of human defensive behavior and the difficulties of working with and through these self-protective operations. I knew that Carl and his staff could do better than they were, but as frustrating as it was, I also knew that he would take no additional steps to change in the present situation. Whatever it would take, I understood that my knowledge and skills could move him no farther. Constructive withdrawal in the face of such protracted and entrenched defenses is often, I believe, a reasonable course of action open to a coach.

As I walked down the hall toward the door, Pat caught up to me.

"You were right about the hub-and-spoke thing, but I think there's a better way to describe it. He's more like a spider in the middle of his web, and we're the poor insects who get caught and sucked dry by him. I really need to get out of here," Pat said, visibly shaken by the meeting.

I referred Pat to a resource specializing in career transitions and offered to talk further about what might be possible. Then I left the building.

The Self-Protective Behavior of Human Beings

As discussed in chapter 2, almost every person has and uses emotional, cognitive, and behavioral methods to defend him- or herself in the world. Conte and Plutchik (1995), A. Freud (1966), and Valliant (1977) have provided comprehensive descriptions and coverage of the types, issues, and methods of operation of what psychotherapists call *ego defenses*. Defenses have several major purposes. They are one of the primary means through which humans experience and explore the events in their lives. Along with other physical, cognitive, emotional, and behavioral skills, defenses provide organized ways to master the tasks of adapting to the challenges and demands of the external world. They permit people to integrate their internal experiences in ways that they can understand and tolerate emotionally. Defenses help regulate emotional experience and expression; they have a unique role to assist in keeping the anxiety that is naturally generated by being alive within tolerable limits. Finally, they provide a foundation on which every person constructs his or her understanding of the world. In other words, defenses permit and often unconsciously guide the definition and expression of meaning in each person's life.

Defenses arise naturally in the course of human development. Within an information-processing model, they can be thought of as master programs that each person seems to have embedded in his or her biological hardware. These programs manifest themselves throughout our lives and direct the emotional, cognitive, and behavioral subroutines that enable people to live and survive more or less comfortably in the world. For most people, these defenses operate largely unconsciously, dictating their organizing principles silently but extremely effectively. The average person usually cannot and does not become aware of this guidance and the sometimes self-limiting, sometimes self-expanding impact that it can have. Following the ideas suggested in previous chapters in this book, we can see human defenses as both vicious and virtuous circles, or as *attractors* and *repulsors* in the language of complexity theory. We can also understand them as either inhibiting or facilitating the development and day-to-day use of human wisdom.

Defenses seem to follow a normal trajectory as each person grows. Virtually everyone that I have encountered in my career seems to have his or her full complement of defensive operations, but as in most areas of human behavior, each person tends to have stronger and weaker methods, or preferential, modes of defense. Table 8.1 presents an elaborated list of the majority of psychological defense mechanisms identified in Table 2.7 (see chapter 2, this volume). Since being first described by Sigmund Freud (1893) and expanded by his daughter Anna (1966), a great deal of research has been performed that has validated the existence and explored the organization and operation of these most complex and interesting behavioral patterns. Although a thorough treatment of this topic is beyond this book, I make several major points that are relevant to the coaching of managers and executives.

First, as briefly described in chapter 2, defensive operations arise from developmentally oriented interactions between a person and his or her world. Defenses have cognitive, emotional, and behavioral elements that are beautifully complex. Tables 2.7 and 8.1 array the defenses from the earliest, most basic, and primitive type through to the most complex and usually latest to develop. Thus, the first and most basic defense to develop is denial, a disavowal that aspects of external or internal reality exist. This is accompanied by splitting, a mechanism that allows an infant to create and distinguish between dichotomies in the world. Through splitting, experience can be divided into good and bad, right and wrong, the extremes of continua, or unreconcilable polarities. Denial and splitting provide a young child with powerful, if primitive, tools with which to begin to organize the complex, difficult, sometimes painful, and usually anxiety-arousing experiences of being in the world. Through both they learn to control some of the misery that life can create either by shifting their attention away from noxious events and sensations or by organizing them into absolute categories that present easier choices about how to cope with the negative or positive effects. These mechanisms correspond with Kegan's (1994) first level of human consciousness and meaning making.

TABLE 8.1

Definitions and Descriptions of the Major Psychological Defenses

Defense mechanism	Definition/Description
Denial	A pattern of disavowing thoughts, feelings, wishes, needs, or external reality factors that are intolerable at a conscious level.
Splitting	Separation of external reality, experience, thoughts, feelings, wishes, or needs into two absolute categories—one all bad and not part of the person and one all good and part of the person.
Distortion	Systematically shifting elements of external reality, experience, thoughts, feelings, wishes, or needs to ones more consciously compatible with and acceptable to oneself.
Projection	Taking parts of external reality, experience, thoughts, feelings, wishes, or needs that are unacceptable to the self and rejecting them and attributing or projecting them to or onto other people.
Projective identification	Taking parts of external reality, experience, thoughts, feelings, wishes, or needs that may be consciously unacceptable to the self and acting as if they are present in and being expressed by another person.
Hypochondriasis	Persistent and obsessively anxious attention to aspects of physical health or bodily functions that may be experienced as symptoms of various diseases and disorders but that are largely imagined.
Passive–aggressive behavior	A pattern of aggressive behavior largely demonstrated in forms such as pouting, obstructionism, procrastination, intended ineffectiveness or inefficiency, or stubbornness.
Masochism	A pattern of choosing self- or other-inflicted pain or discomfort usually because the anxiety of not doing so is experienced as more painful. May occur in the context of sexual activity, work, or interpersonal relationships. Very prevalent in people with addictive disorders or those in caring relationships with them.
Acting out; criminality; perversion	Expressing reactions to external reality, experience, thoughts, feelings, wishes, or needs in actions or deeds rather than in fantasy, words, or other forms of symbolic expression. Extreme forms can involve criminal activity or acts of perversion.
Sadism	A pattern of choosing to inflict pain or discomfort on others usually because the anxiety of not doing so is experienced as more painful. May occur in the context of sexual activity, work, or interpersonal relationships. Very prevalent in people with addictive disorders or those in caring relationships with them.
Dissociation	A process through which the actual emotions and emotional significance of events in external reality, personal experiences, thoughts, feelings, wishes, or needs are separated from conscious memory and may be lost to the person for a long time. Usually occurs in situations in which trauma has occurred.

(continued)

TABLE 8.1 continued

Definitions and Descriptions of the Major Psychological Defenses

Defense mechanism	Definition/Description
Derealization/ depersonalization	A process in which a person experiences feelings of unreality, loss of contact with the body or other feelings, or of being estranged from people or surroundings. Often occurs in threatening or traumatic situations.
Isolation	A process in which unacceptable, anxiety-arousing thoughts, impulses, feelings, wishes, or needs are separated from the original memory or the actual experience and thereby lose the emotional charge or threat.
Detachment	A pattern of being or becoming physically or emotionally aloof or distant from people, events, conscious experience, history, or unacceptable unconscious conflicts, external reality, personal experiences, thoughts, wishes, or needs and the emotions that they may generate.
Intellectualization	The use of logic and reason to protect oneself from confronting or experiencing unconscious conflicts, external reality, personal experiences, thoughts, wishes, or needs and the emotions that they may generate.
Rationalization	The effort to justify, make understandable, acceptable, or reasonable through plausible explanations, or descriptions of motives or behaviors, unacceptable unconscious conflicts, external reality, personal experiences, thoughts, wishes, or needs and the emotions that they may generate.
Obsessions	Persistent unwanted thoughts or patterns of thinking that cannot be ignored or eliminated by reason that are related to unacceptable unconscious conflicts, external reality, personal experiences, thoughts, wishes, or needs and the emotions that they may generate.
Compulsions	Persistent, repetitive, and unwanted impulses or urges to act in a fashion at odds to the person's normal or acceptable way of behaving that are related to unacceptable unconscious conflicts, external reality, personal experiences, thoughts, wishes, or needs and the emotions that they may generate.
Undoing	A pattern of behavior in which something unacceptable and already done, wished, or fantasized is symbolically or physically acted out in reverse.
Repression	A process in which unacceptable unconscious conflicts, external reality, personal experiences, thoughts, wishes, or needs and the emotions that they may generate are eliminated from conscious thought or memory but may emerge in disguised or symbolic form.
Reaction formation	A process in which attitudes, beliefs, values, and behaviors are adopted that are the reverse of unacceptable unconscious conflicts, external reality, personal experiences, thoughts, wishes, or needs and the emotions that they may generate.

TABLE 8.1 continued

Definitions and Descriptions of the Major Psychological Defenses

Defense mechanism	Definition/Description
Displacement	A process through which unacceptable feelings are transferred or expressed toward a person, group, or organization different from the original one that generated the response.
Sublimation	A process in which unacceptable unconscious conflicts, external reality, personal experiences, thoughts, wishes, or needs and the emotions that they may generate are shifted into personally and socially acceptable and often productive activities, thoughts, or feelings.
Altruism	Behaving in ways designed to be of benefit to others that constructively express what may be unacceptable unconscious conflicts, external reality, personal experiences, thoughts, wishes, or needs and the emotions that they may generate.
Suppression	A conscious effort to control, regulate, or conceal unacceptable or unconscious conflicts, external reality, personal experiences, thoughts, wishes, or needs and the emotions that they may generate.
Anticipation	A process of using one's experience, training, or intuition to foresee possibilities, events, or potential consequences and take constructive or preventive actions.
Humor	The process of taking perspective on conscious experience, history, or unacceptable unconscious conflicts, external reality, personal experiences, thoughts, wishes, or needs and the emotions that they may generate and being able to appreciate and express them in ways that are funny to oneself or others.
Curiosity	The process of being mentally and emotionally inquisitive about conscious experience, history, or unacceptable unconscious conflicts, external reality, personal experiences, thoughts, wishes, or needs and the emotions that they may generate and being able to explore, appreciate, and potentially express them appropriately.
Work	The process of using time, energy, training, experience, intuition, creativity, knowledge, skills, and abilities to do real-world tasks that have meaning and value to oneself or others.
Play	The process of using time, energy, training, experience, intuition, creativity, knowledge, skills, and abilities to simply have fun or express oneself.
Love	The process of devoting oneself physically, emotionally, or spiritually to individuals, a family, groups, organizations, activities, tasks, professions, etc., that a person finds meaningful.
Wisdom	A complex expert knowledge system that integrates cognitive and emotional elements and enables a person to effectively manage the fundamental pragmatics of life through insight into human development and life matters, exceptionally good judgment, sound advice, and commentary about difficult and poorly defined problems.

As a child grows and develops cognitively, emotionally, physically, and spiritually, other capacities for defensive organizations present themselves. My experience has led me to believe that nearly everyone experiments with these forms of defense. So, each person possesses some capacity for projection, distortion, obsession, intellectualization, repression, displacement, and so forth. Depending on how traumatic and stressful life events become for individuals and on their sensitivities and proclivities, they seem to settle into a set or defensive pattern that largely works to perform the functions described above. In the world around us, it is fairly easy to see individuals who are organized around defenses such as intellectualization, rationalization, isolation, and undoing. These people tend to be obsessive–compulsive in their approaches to life, developing complex patterns and explanations for what they think, feel, and experience. Individuals who tend to use denial, repression, and displacement have less complicated ways of understanding and experiencing the world. They are able to keep the adverse aspect of the world comfortably outside of their normal experience. People who consistently use primitive denial, splitting, projection, distortion, and projective identification have very simple and extremely powerful ways of organizing experience. They create a world for themselves in which absolute categories help define everything and in which negative, adverse, painful, and traumatic events, thoughts, and feelings are kept away by not experiencing them at all or by seeing them in others. These simple explanations of complicated sequences of developmental events, processes, and structures help coaches know that each client will have such a defensive organization. These defensive patterns always affect coaching activities and the capacity of clients to grow.

At the other end of the continuum of defensive behaviors are such operations as sublimation; suppression; humor; and eventually, the rise of wisdom and its expression through altruism, love, reality testing, and problem solving with the mysteries and complexities of life. Individuals using these defenses are generally much more aware of their inner emotional lives. They process information using complex, parallel, relativistic strategies that permit the incorporation of both polarities and paradox. Their adaptive strategies tend to be much more subtle and sophisticated. They allow for the rise of truly creative expressions of themselves and new methods and means of interacting with other people and events in the world around them. More often than not these people demonstrate the capacity to use and dwell in Kegan's (1994) fourth and fifth levels of consciousness and use Kramer's (1990) intersystemic and integrated methods of thinking. They are most likely to rise to the highest levels of cognitive complexity described by Jaques and Clement (1991), using parallel processing of universals to understand and create strategies for being in the world. They become individuals who are capable of understanding environmental complexity, human conflict, and spiritual challenges and then of using their understanding to continuously recreate both who they are as people and how they develop meaning in life.

Anyone doing executive coaching would be wise to have at least some understanding of these forms of defensive behaviors. In almost any situation in which resistance to change becomes an issue, some of these defenses will be present. The case example opening this chapter illustrates this. Carl, the identified client and unit director, cooperated with the consultation and coaching project for nearly 2 years. He made some changes in his unit and his behavior that he could tolerate, changes that did not fundamentally challenge his defensive strategies. He tended to use a great deal of rationalization, intellectualization, isolation, and undoing, behaviors usually associated with patterns of obsessive–compulsive types of individuals (keep in mind that I am trying to use these terms descriptively and not in the formal sense of providing a psychological diagnosis). As discussed previously, coaching is not therapy, but I believe that it can be well informed by much of what has been learned clinically in the past 100 or so years about changing human behavior.

When confronted clearly and concisely with the need to move his controlling and sometimes invasive style of management into a more consultative and collaborative approach, Carl could not and would not consider a change or even a minor experiment. Any efforts by me or his two more mature colleagues to request, suggest, or challenge the need to do something different elicited the same convoluted, highly rationalized, and intellectual explanations. He made no conscious connection to the real pain and suffering that his behavior and management style caused his subordinates. Having agreed to try to change through coaching, he undid his contract and commitment. He was, in Kegan's terms, unable or unwilling to rise to the requirements of fourth- or fifth-level consciousness and use the full reaches of cognitive complexity that I would have wished. At his worst emotionally, he seemed to operate at the second level of Kegan's typology of consciousness, which involves the systematic use of categories to understand and organize the world. When mired there, he functioned as the manipulative, venomous spider so poignantly and frighteningly described by his colleague.

When working with these types of strong responses, coaches are often left with little maneuvering room, and they frequently fail. Unconscious operation of defensive behavior patterns is one of the most difficult problems coaches face with clients, because by definition, they are not readily apparent to either party. Defenses automatically rise to protect both client and coach when material becomes potentially threatening. Despite repeated reassurances and requests for only initial experiments and not wholesale changes, Carl buried his colleagues, the consultation project, our coaching efforts, and me as a coach beneath a blizzard of rationalization of the status quo.

When facing and working with such unconscious defensive routines, coaches are well advised to proceed slowly and carefully, remembering that the boundary between counseling and coaching can sometimes become blurry. Identifying the presence of unconscious defensive operations in a client provides any coach with a unique opportunity to maneuver in the sometimes tight psychic space in which change may be barely possible. The less mature defenses can and must be approached with care if major change is desired. Coaches must remember at all times that the self-protective mission of these behaviors gives them enormous power and that significant shifts in or challenges to them can generate strong anxiety even when the client may both want and need to modify the behavior.

Remember the previous descriptions and discussions of repulsors and attractors as they operate in emotion and development. We can apply the same concepts here and see them operate with defensive behaviors. As we grow and experiment with these various methods of self-protection, repeated trials and exposure create habituated response patterns, especially when the responses reward the person with improved short-term coping ability and anxiety reduction. The more practiced and rewarded the pattern becomes, the stronger and broader its appeal. In this way, defenses can become attractors into which individuals can instantly and catastrophically retreat in the face of external demands or internal pressures. As any human being then proceeds through daily life and confronts such forces and problems, defensive attractors present ready and seemingly reasonable opportunities to ensure comfort and survival. Difficulty occurs because most defenses are designed to minimize anxiety and maintain the status quo in some way and, therefore, offer limited opportunities for human growth and development. The less mature the level of defensive operations used, the less likely the person will be to achieve a creative solution to whatever problem is being confronted.

Higher level defenses such as sublimation, suppression, humor, problem solving, reality testing, and anticipation, although also operating unconsciously, offer increased possibilities for behavioral and emotional transformation. Levels of psychosocial awareness are usually higher for individuals who often use these operations. Alternatives, often quite creative, are invented, represented, and sometimes acted out when humor and sublimation are called on. Even the darkest, most difficult situations can be viewed and reframed with such methods.

Suppression keeps emotion, thoughts, wishes, and conflict just below the surface but not so far below that they become unaccessible. Anticipation allows for the possibility of examining behaviors or events for information and consequences that might happen in the future. The problem with using these defenses and becoming good with them is that they usually require the tolerance of higher levels of anxiety and the other strong disconfirming emotions. Even though virtually every human being has some experience with these mature types of defenses, I have come to believe that for many people they never really become attractors. Rather, they operate as repulsors, requiring a person to work harder to use them. This makes the evolution and use of wisdom very chancy at best. Kegan (1994), in a review of the empirical studies done with his subject–object conceptual approach, suggested that about 25% of the normal adult population may achieve fourth-level consciousness in which systemic thinking, the ability to consider and create new values, and the capacity to reauthor parts of the self are available. He also suggested that many tasks of normal adult living at work and in the home require such fourth-order capacity, thus providing an interesting hypothesis and potential explanation of why so many people struggle in their lives.

Despite the sometimes difficult work of supporting clients in using the higher order defenses, some of the features of the coaching containment and relationship naturally support their emergence. Coaches who have proceeded carefully with the coaching process have clarified expectations and established goals; set specific time to quietly and confidentially reflect on the organization; the client's role and performance in that enterprise; his or her inner experiences with those activities and events including emotions, thoughts, relationships, defenses, and conflicts; and agreed to practice new behaviors and ways of conceptualizing management and leadership. Each coaching session then becomes an opportunity to witness, explore, and potentially modify defensive routines, old ideas and behaviors, and vicious circles that can inhibit higher level performance. The natural pull in well-managed sessions is toward increased self-awareness, thus toward the higher level defenses and, it is hoped, toward increased executive wisdom. Coaches merely need to coach effectively with most clients to accomplish that shift. This conceptual material on defensive operations should help coaches to understand what happens in and between coaching sessions and how to productively maneuver when confronted with major resistance to change. The basic principle to keep in mind is as follows: Whenever and wherever possible, encourage, support, and coach clients toward engaging higher order defensive behaviors and be prepared to engage, work with, and confront the less mature defenses.

With Carl, most efforts on my part to use humor, suppression, anticipation, and sublimation; to encourage extending self-awareness; or to help him consider or practice other methods of coping and change led most often to his mantras and repetitive behaviors. On a number of occasions in individual sessions, we would have a good conversation, and I would walk out of his office believing that we had made progress. Then in the team sessions, I would find that he had just continued to respond the way he always had and often possessed no recollection of our conversations. My work with him and his team serves as a constant reminder to me of how defenses energize resistance to change.

In addition to the types of psychological defenses described in Table 8.1, self-protective patterns can also be seen operating in groups and organizations. Table 8.2 presents an abstracted and enhanced listing of some of the types that Argyris (1993) identified in his discussion of defensive routines as they manifest in work teams. I will not describe them in detail, because most of them speak for themselves; however, I will emphasize that when working with executives, coaches must remain alert for the presence of such defensive operations in the groups and organizations in which clients work. In coaching sessions, clients will often raise problems that they are having with their colleagues, in groups or teams to which they belong, or with their whole organization. At times, the client may also be using one or more of these defenses as he or she copes with problems in the organization. Helping them assess, diagnose, and creatively cope with and possibly change such defensive behaviors in themselves or in others with whom they are working can be of tremendous assistance. Most often these defenses operate in ways that make them difficult for an executive to bring to the surface and to manage in a straightforward way. Pushing these defenses into awareness—creating time and space to reflect on their origins, contents, processes, structures, and consequences—can help clients become more comfortable personally and professionally. Such reflective exercises can also relieve intense emotional pressures; decrease the likelihood of acting out; increase competence and self-efficacy; and, through the creative actions and new behaviors of the clients, help the organization eliminate regressive slides or problem behaviors.

Coaching To and Through Defenses

What follows illustrates the principles of coaching defensive behavior patterns with a more successful example than Carl. John was another

TABLE 8.2

Defensive Operations in Organizations

Alterations in work, task behaviors, and productivity in individual, group, and organizational performance

Engaging in goal-oriented behavior aimed at and interfering with the organization's or group's vision or mission.

Engaging in goal-oriented behavior aimed at and interfering with an individual's or subgroup's vision or mission.

Engaging in politically sophisticated behavior with negative goals, such as destroying the careers or performance of colleagues or other work groups within the organization.

Ignoring orders.

Cutting or substituting orders of which the supervisor is not aware.

Accepting neither organizational nor personal responsibility.

Remaining in a dependent position with the leader and refusing or neglecting to think for oneself.

Holding ritualized meetings that discourage reexamination and rethinking.

Engaging in "group think" in which deviant thoughts, different points of view, and creative alternatives are repressed or not permitted.

Doing the wrong thing and continuing to do it.

Increasing controls.

Trying to bypass controls.

Promoting a "can-do" attitude that ignores reality.

Focusing on operational objectives with no concern for values, vision, or goals.

Generating noncontroversial issues for discussion during meetings that enable one to avoid reality.

Protecting supervisors from having to choose sides or decide courses of action.

Creating a shadow organization that undercuts the formal organization.

Creating a powerful partnership or pair bond with one or more members of the work group or team that excludes others from entry, develops and advocates its point of view regardless of its effect on the rest of the organization, or uses some or all of these types of defensive behaviors to pursue its own goals and serve its own needs.

Avoiding orienting new staff members about how the organization works.

Altering political behavior. Placing or projecting the responsibility for problems on other individuals or forces in the organization's culture.

Developing professional arguments against proposed innovations that threaten one's territorial interests.

Losing work or recommendations from working parties, committees, or task forces by referring the recommendations or material to other groups, or by simply ignoring them.

Controlling and rigging agendas of meetings.

Massaging minutes of meetings so that they do not reflect reality.

Inventing consensus where consensus has not been tested or reached.

Going around regulations.

Giving staff menial tasks and "busy work" and communicating that it is very important to do.

Permitting subordinates very little choice in their work and no participation in decisions.

Making the schedule the key determinant in everything that happens.

Taking any action that inhibits cooperation or collaboration.

Favoring some employees over others, encouraging unnecessary rivalries.

Acting as if students, peers, or employees cannot be trusted.

Engaging in aimless, pointless, or disorganized behavior. Changing one's mind a lot with no true rationale.

Projecting a sense of futility about everything within the organization.

Engaging in hopelessness, learned helplessness, or other forms of dependent behavior.

(continued)

TABLE 8.2 continued

Defensive Operations in Organizations

Dominating colleagues.
Creating alliances and relating only to one's clique or subgroup.
Not setting high standards or expectations.
Not supporting subordinates that set high standards.
Being paranoid about lawsuits or about what others may be doing or thinking.
Creating and manipulating institutional privileges for one's own interest.
Creating and defending simplistic views of causality and reality.
Using intuition, wish fulfillment, and irrationality to explain what is happening.
Avoiding open-mindedness, reflection, or curiosity.
Engaging only in routine behavior.
Establishing task forces, committees, and teams and giving them leaders who cannot lead.
Acting as though one, a team or group, or the organization operates as the center of the universe and nothing else is important or that everything else remains in a subservient position at all times and in all ways—creating and enforcing a narcissistic position within the organization or between the organization and the rest of the world.
Failing to test reality.

Alterations in interpersonal behavior
Lacking trust in other people.
Being rigid in expectations and behavior.
Being insensitive to the needs and feelings of other people; not using empathy under any circumstances.
Creating behaviors that keep unnecessary distance or detachment between one, one's organization, and one's colleagues.
Eliminating all boundaries and limits between one, one's work, one's organization, and one's colleagues; enmeshing one's self in and overcontrolling everything that happens.
Engaging in distancing and enmeshment randomly, sequentially, or simultaneously.

Alterations in emotions and emotional expression
Engaging in vicious cycles/circles; attractors and repulsors.
Engaging in unnecessary shame and rage; anxiety and shame; anxiety and rage; sadness and rage; sadness and shame (desperation dynamics); and all combinations of powerful negative, repugnant emotion with peers, subordinates, or others.
Denying, suppressing, repressing, or other mismanagement of positive emotions such as joy, curiosity, humor, sex.

Acting-out behavior
Violating policy, procedures, ethics, or laws.
Sexually harassing colleagues or subordinates.
Sabotaging organizational goals, property, processes, or projects.
Deliberately engaging in overt or covert disobedience.
Deliberately engaging in unnecessary overt or covert fighting.
Losing one's temper publicly and unapologetically.
Engaging in public and private acts meant to bully, victimize, humiliate, or degrade colleagues.
Performing acts of oppression such as discrimination, colorism, racism, sexism, ageism, heterosexism, etc.

Distortions and deviations in conflict behavior in individuals, groups, and the organization
Retaliating against those who pay attention to reality by publicly humiliating them and constantly being angry at them.
Engaging in or experiencing manifest or latent conflict that is avoided, poorly managed, not managed, symptomatic, or out of control.

TABLE 8.2 continued

Defensive Operations in Organizations

- Deliberately playing one group or person against another.
- Acting as if one is not engaging in defensive or conflict operations.
- Fighting covertly with other people and acting as though one is not.
- Avoiding conflict at all costs with other people.
- Remaining inept at managing conflict with other people; doing nothing to learn or develop more skill.
- Causing mischief or trouble for the sheer delight of it or as a pattern that is never acknowledged or changed in any way.
- Not discussing conflict or covering up conflict or acting-out behavior.
- Blaming and shaming others for problems.
- Engaging in a pattern of fighting and then fleeing and refusing to deal with the consequences, causes, or process of a conflict.
- Scapegoating or stereotyping other members of the work team or organization.
- Behaving in an organizationally deviant fashion regardless of the consequences and remaining oblivious to or deliberately ignoring constructive feedback.
- Threatening violent behavior or actually committing acts of overt or covert violence.

Physical and health problems for individuals and work teams

- "Blue flu."
- Psychosomatic symptoms.
- Stress-related psychophysiological disorders (e.g., ulcers, migraines).
- Chronic fatigue.
- Back problems.
- Repetitive strain injuries.
- Drinking and drugging as an individual, group, or subgroup.
- Other physical and health problems.

Distortions and deviations in communications

- Engaging in lies or deceptions.
- Chronically complaining, whining.
- Engaging all meaningful conversation only on the grapevine or in triangulated relationships.
- Avoiding public discussion of anything that is threatening or embarrassing, curtailing inquiry.
- Deliberately or unintentionally misperceiving the communications of others; not clarifying encoding or delivering processes in communicating to others.
- Deliberately starting or spreading rumors or gossip.
- Treating the motives and behaviors of others with suspicion and paranoia.

Distortions and deviations in problem-solving behavior

- Doing anything to avoid discussion of important issues such as spending cuts, market and technology changes, forecasts of the future, interpersonal problems that impede performance, defensive operations, emotional injuries, and strategic planning.
- Inhibiting error detection; data collection, problem solving, and decision making.
- Avoiding meeting to discuss issues, or sabotaging meetings aimed at solving problems.
- Engaging in repetitively stupid behavior patterns, nonfunctional attractors, repulsors, or vicious circles with no efforts to reflect, assess, or change the behavior.
- Repetitively using the same approach or methodology to try to solve problems with no evaluation of its effectiveness or by ignoring adverse consequences.
- Delegating problem solving to subordinates without supporting their efforts and then blaming them for achieving inadequate results.
- Giving subordinates too much work to accomplish within reasonable timelines, telling them that everything is equally important, and refusing to prioritize assignments, or withholding adequate resources for accomplishing the work assigned while maintaining the same high standards.

client whom I had worked with for over 2 years. Initially, he had been referred by both of his supervisors after two of his subordinates had complained vigorously about his micromanagement, intrusiveness, lack of trust, and temper outbursts. Working in a complex, high-profile position that required him to report to two powerful leaders in a matrix management structure, John quickly responded to coaching and made major changes in his interpersonal behavior, methods, and ideas about management. Our sessions increasingly focused on improving his personal performance and the daily operations of his unit. Ordinarily, he came prepared to discuss specific issues that he had thought about and wanted to work on in the session. He used the reflective process well, and he had repeatedly demonstrated an interest in and willingness to explore his emotional responses to situations and the relationship of present work issues to past personal events. He also engaged constructively in assessing and trying to change his defensive behaviors. After the initial few months of coaching during which he had struggled with changing his behavior, I found it very easy to work with him. He repeatedly demonstrated a wonderful sense of mildly self-deprecating and insightful humor, easily anticipated events and explored potential consequences before they occurred, sublimated well, and most often suppressed his defensive anger, which routinely simmered close to the surface. In short, John had become a wonderful client.

In the session that follows, John came in uncharacteristically upset. He stripped off his jacket and sat down. He opened his notebook and flipped to a page at the back.

"Well coach, I really need help today," he said, with flushed cheeks and tension in his voice.

"So, tell me what's happening."

"You know I got a new boss named Michael. We've been talking about that for over 6 months. I've worked with my direct subordinates and my whole team on the succession management process. Everyone knows what's at stake, and we've been very successful. In fact, the new guy pointed us out to everyone as a model of how he wants his people to work. It's a little embarrassing how often he compliments us, but we've all worked hard at it, and we've produced. I'm trying to make sure he's kept informed, offer him options and choices and not just problems, stay out of defensive postures, you know, the whole nine yards. And, it's working, it's really working."

"What's so troubling?"

"This week he tells me something highly confidential that he wants to do in the organization."

"So?"

"So, he then tells me that he doesn't want anyone else to know, and it directly concerns my other boss Daniel. I've been just crazy ever since he told me what he wants to do. He's going over Dan's head and trying to pull off a coup to get more resources. He thinks he really can't accomplish what he wants to do without pulling an end run, and he explicitly told me not to tell Dan."

"What did you do?"

"I tried to reason with him. I did like we've talked about before. I described the conflict this would potentially produce, how it might undermine what Dan thinks of me and the trust that he places in me. I suggested that it might have long-term consequences for working with Dan's whole unit, which I can't do without, and that it might affect his reputation."

"And?"

"And, nothing. This guy doesn't care what Daniel thinks or what Daniel's boss thinks. I've come to believe he doesn't care what anyone thinks. He's a rogue, and he's going to cause me major problems if he follows through with what he's proposing to do."

"What consequences do you see?"

"That's easy. Daniel will never trust me again. I've worked so closely with him over the past 2 years. I never make a major move without informing him, consulting with him. I'm always so careful to follow the doctrine of "no surprises" with everyone now. But, Michael doesn't care. He only wants what he wants. He's an impulsive animal. He acts out all over the place. He threatens people, just tromps all over them. He says stupid stuff about how tight he'll run the place, how poorly it was run before, how only he can do what's necessary. I've heard him yell at someone, a very good staff member, 'if you don't like it you can leave.' I'm tired of it. In fact, I'm sick and tired of it. I hate being in this position. He's gonna get me fired if I'm not careful."

Listening carefully to John, I could tell by his tone of voice and demeanor how angry he was about the situation. I also noted that he had described Michael as a rogue animal, tromping all over people, refusing to heed advice, impervious to the injuries that he was piling up. John's language, usually rich with qualifiers and complex descriptors, was stripped down and full of negation, strong categorical adverbs, and adjectives that labeled his supervisor as stupid, threatening, and impulsive. Oozing through this depiction, John's underlying anxiety about job security and the potential for experiencing a humiliating public injury caused by his supervisor was palpable. I knew that one of my tasks was to move him away from the regressive slide into a split, projected attractor full of absolutist and categorical thinking into which the interactions with Michael had sent him.

"Are you aware of how you're describing Michael?" I asked.

"No. I just know that I hate what's happening."

"Take a second and try to connect with any other feelings you might be having," I suggested.

John stopped talking for a moment or two and turned inward. After the pause, he smiled.

"Well, my old friend anger is certainly here," he chuckled.

I smiled with him, trying to acknowledge the increased level of awareness of his emotional state.

"Now, we know that anger is usually produced by the need to protect oneself, so the next question is?"

"Why do I feel so threatened?" he asked.

"Exactly."

"Well, you know I don't feel so threatened personally by him. I mean I do a little, but he's responded so positively to how I've been handling the transition. We're talking about possible increases in staff resources for my unit. He compliments my staff and me all the time."

"So, he's never hurt you."

"No, but he can be so callous. I've watched him just destroy other people in public."

"How did he do that?"

"He's murderously critical. If people slip up, don't keep him informed, aren't prepared in meetings, he just jumps all over them."

"How do you think they feel after he does that?"

"He humiliates them."

"Do you worry he might do that to you?"

"You bet. That's why I stay so prepared, so on my toes."

"And, that's working."

"Yeah, but I gotta tell you, it's costly. I walk around tense all the time. I never know when he might explode."

"You mean criticize you."

"Yeah."

"So, if you came unprepared to a public meeting, didn't do your homework, made repeated mistakes, what would you expect him to do?"

"Criticize me of course, just like I'd do to my staff."

"But, you would do it differently."

"Of course I would. We talked so much about self-esteem and shame, I've stopped yelling at people. Privately, I would sure tell them that mistakes have been made and that performance would need to improve, but I wouldn't deliberately humiliate people in public."

"So, what do you think the anger you feel protects you from?"

"My other old friends, shame and anxiety."

With that admission, John smiled and relaxed visibly. He seemed to gather himself together inside, almost as though he was picking up discarded pieces of knowledge and skill.

"So, the interactions with Michael have put you into a defensive posture."

"Yep, they sure have. What he's doing scares me to death. It's countercultural and may lead to some pretty severe consequences, especially with Daniel and his boss."

"You're anticipating trouble."

"Of course."

"Has the trouble happened yet?"

"No, nothing's happened."

"So, you're really scared about something that might happen but that hasn't. You're angry at him and afraid that he'll publicly humiliate you for something that you don't do or something that you might say. Do you think that your ability to anticipate trouble may be getting you a little ahead of yourself here?"

"What do you mean?"

"Well, go back to what I asked before."

"What was that?"

"How did you describe Michael to me?" I said and ignored his lapse of memory.

"I don't remember."

"Yes you do. This stuff is really powerful and your feelings are running high. Try to recall how you described him," I challenged and encouraged him.

John paused and then smiled. "I called him a rogue, didn't I?"

"What other words did you use?"

"Let's see . . . animal . . . impulsive . . . dangerous."

"Threaten, tromp, fired, murderous . . ." I added.

John paused and then said, "I guess I am painting quite an extreme picture here."

"Has Michael done anything well?"

"Sure. He's getting rid of dead wood, pushing folks to work harder, setting a very clear agenda."

"In other words, taking charge."

"He sure is doing that."

"Would you behave differently than him?"

"Given what I know now, yes I would. I think that I could accomplish what he is trying to do and not cause so much damage to people."

"So, what you are objecting to seems to be some of his methods, not his goals."

"That's right. There I think he's right on target."

"OK, let's see if you can summarize what you've just explored."

John proceeded to pull together a succinct description of how he felt and how he was behaving in the situation. He also more accurately described Michael's behavior and managed to leave out most of the negative adjectives. I then asked him to shift his attention and focus on Michael's request to keep confidential what he was planning to do to advocate for increased resources. After exploring the details for several minutes, he summarized what he had said quite succinctly.

"You know, it's almost like this is a test, like he's set me up somehow."

"How would that work?"

"Well, he knows that I share most everything with Daniel. He's asked me specifically not to reveal this confidence to Daniel. If I tell, Dan will undoubtedly react to it, and Michael will know that I told."

"How will he know?"

"Michael and Daniel have really worked quite well together. Dan has been very supportive to him, and they meet quite often."

"So?"

"So, Michael probably thinks that Daniel would probe or raise the issue with him."

"And?"

"And, discover that I can't keep a confidence."

"Proving what?"

"I'm untrustworthy."

"With what consequences?"

"He'll place less trust in me."

"And?"

"He'll be less likely to support me and my unit."

"Exactly. So, he has you in a real bind, doesn't he?"

"He sure does."

"What are the consequences if you don't tell?"

"Potentially, a real loss of trust with Daniel."

"And, you have more than 2 years worth of political credit banked with him."

"Well, that's right. I'm pretty sure that Daniel would really understand if it came out that I knew what Michael was trying to do but kept quiet."

"So, there are risks on that front, but they are less than what you face with Michael."

"That's right."

"It sounds to me like Michael has set a real test for you to pass."

"You know, it's awful and really scary, but I can see the logic in it. He really is a pretty savvy operator."

"So, what do you think that you should do?"

"That's easy. Keep my mouth shut, control my anxiety and anger, and be prepared to do damage control with Daniel and his boss. Boy am I glad I had this coaching session today."

We went on to discuss several other issues that John faced in his unit. About a month later, he told me that Michael never did the end run around Daniel. He laughed about it when he described it to me, saying that it had been nothing but a test all along. His ability to reframe Michael's behavior as that of a savvy operator gave him a new metaphor with which to guide his interactions and within which to assess his emotional responses. John knew he had to be on his toes at all times with his new supervisor, and he took great pains with his staff and himself to make sure that he was always prepared. About 6 months into the transition, he told me that Michael had supported his requests for increased resources for his unit.

This short case example demonstrates clearly how emotion and defensive routines can combine into extraordinarily powerful chaotic attractors or vicious circles of behavior. John's initial logic, metaphor, and feelings had regressively pushed him far down the ladder of defensive operations and of consciousness. His ideas and responses had categorized Michael as a vicious, out-of-control animal, one who could and would destroy him. His anxiety and associated defensive anger had combined with categorical, absolutist thinking and language and left him with no place to go behaviorally except destructive self-defense. The containment of coaching, my questioning of emotion, exploration of his defensive routines, and appreciative challenges of his metaphor and language enabled him to break through the negation, splitting, and projection and to consider other ways of thinking about and behaving in the situation. By the end of the session, he had pulled himself into his more "normal attractor," using his sense of humor, his ability to suppress his anxiety and anger, and to pushing his powers of anticipation into more constructive uses. His emotional release and relief during the session were palpable. Even more important, John succeeded in assessing the situation correctly and in devising a strategy to adapt to it. Ultimately, he won exactly what he needed for his unit to improve its performance and thus enhance the functioning of both Michael's and Daniel's units.

By the end of the session, John demonstrated aspects of Kegan's fourth and fifth levels of consciousness. He could voluntarily remake his understanding of the situation and his response to it. He could see the need for behavior that supported his new supervisor, the organization as a whole, and his own unit; in other words, he could use a systemic point of view. He incorporated paradox, polarity, complexity, and a long-term time horizon (5 years or more) in the formulation of his approach. He behaved exactly as one would have any senior executive in a similar situation.

When coaching in these types of complicated circumstances, practitioners often rely on their own experiences and sense of human and organizational behavior. This was not an example of coaching for skill building or transfer of training. As many clients do, John had all of the requisite knowledge, skill, and ability to handle the situation. However, as is often the case, the dynamics of his own inner, psychological world interacted with his experience in this environment to prevent him from using most of these. In this situation, a skill- or knowledge-focused coaching session would not have been nearly as useful to John because he simply could not put what he knew or what he knew how to do into action. My coaching interventions helped John move into his higher level defensive operations and level of consciousness through which he better mastered his own emotional, cognitive, and behavioral states and created and implemented a winning strategy for himself, his unit, his supervisors, and the entire organization (see Exercise 8.1).

Guiding Principles

I end this chapter with a set of principles to further guide coaching work with client defensive operations:

1. Remember that defenses are always present and operating in everyone. Unless the defenses are interfering with the client's work and ability to learn and change, the activity of the session, or the coach's ability to help the person, it is generally best to not confront directly or focus on them. Doing so may have significant and unseen consequences for the coaching relationship and the client's progress.
2. Coaching on defensive operations can take practitioners into using counseling and psychotherapy methods, a most complicated territory. Caution is well advised here, and significant skill and expertise is required. A coach who has any doubt about his or her ability to handle the situation should consult with a colleague, seek some shadow consultation on the work, or consider referring the person to a therapist or coach with the appropriate skill and experience.
3. Try to take an educational rather than a confrontational approach when initially working on defensive operations. Try to expand the envelope of self-awareness and the zone of reflection to help the client stretch slowly into such a dialogue. Gauge carefully whether the client needs to do this work and the degree to which the person can tolerate the anxiety, shame, sadness, and anger that often are discovered, experienced, or expressed when working with defenses.
4. Direct confrontations of and with defensive routines are sometimes necessary when they are inhibiting the client's growth or

performance. Again, caution is warranted when using direct confrontations. Remember the case of Carl that opened this chapter; confrontations can clarify the situation and sometimes lead to client breakthroughs, but they can also lead to premature cancellation or termination of coaching contracts.

5. Expect defenses, resistance, regression, reinstatement of bad habits, overlearned behaviors, and vicious circles as a normal part of coaching work. A coach who has a sense of perspective and is able to access his or her own higher level defenses, such as a sense of humor, can cope with these most difficult times in coaching.
6. Remember defenses have fundamentally good purposes such as
   - regulating and controlling emotions, especially anxiety, shame, sadness, and anger
   - preventing, distorting, or blocking perception and awareness, or enhancing conscious or unconscious fantasies, needs, wishes, thoughts, and feelings that may underlie psychological, interpersonal, or organizational conflict
   - maintaining the psychological or organizational status quo
   - maintaining the perceived and largely unconscious integrity of both the person's unconscious ego or a group's or organization's identity and culture

Although the intentions underlying such behaviors may be good, too much of a good thing can result in a poor outcome. As we've seen, defenses can significantly inhibit or even completely prevent the emergence of wisdom and Kegan's highest levels of consciousness.

7. Finally, coaches should remember that their own defenses are always operating to protect them and may, therefore, interfere with their ability to coach in particular situations or with specific clients.

EXERCISE 8.1

Assessing Client Defensive Routines

Introduction

This exercise provides a framework within which any coach can assess the presence, degree of operation, and consequences of defensive routines in clients. It may be difficult to actually use during coaching sessions because of the fluidity and speed with which they often move. However, using it to think about client behaviors and actual sessions will improve the coach's familiarity and competence in thinking about how defensive routines influence coaching sessions and in creating strategies for managing them constructively. I encourage coaches to take examples from their own coaching or professional experience and think through the behaviors involved.

Instructions

Check the lists provided in Tables 8.1 and 8.2. Describe the actual behavior as best as you can, and then rate it on a 5-point scale from *low* to *high* for the degree of severity with which the defensive operation interferes with the individual's and the organization's performance. Try to examine some consequences of the self-protective routine, then use the techniques you have learned in this and other sources to map a plan to address the behavior that you've identified (see the lists of approaches provided in chapter 2, this volume, as well as the lists and exercises from other chapters).

Virtually any of the methods and techniques described in the previous chapters can be useful in helping clients address defensive operations. I encourage any coach to pay particular attention to maintaining the containment of the relationship and to consider using the circle of awareness, invitations to reflect together on and make objective the behaviors in evidence, and the language of *could, choices,* and *options*, rather than of should. Also try to use appreciative inquiry and good questioning, reframing, and finding and creating metaphors when working in this defensive zone.

This type of work requires the utmost skill and patience on the part of any coach, because most often clients' resistance to change and their naturally powerful self-protective mechanisms serve to defeat coaches' work with them and their growth and development.

EXERCISE 8.1

Framework for Assessing Defensive Routines

Defense(s) present (individual or organizational)	Description	Degree present (1 = *low*; 5 = ***high***)	Consequences for client, organization, or coaching process	Ideas for managing defensive routine in coaching session(s)

9 Working With Client Conflicts

The Case of Metastasizing Resentment

Rodney removed his coat and trudged over to the chair in my office. His shoulders slumped forward and his face seemed to be sucked toward the floor by the severe frown he wore. Impeccably dressed as usual, he nonetheless had a rumpled and "used-up" look to him. This stood in stark contrast to previous sessions in which he had appeared alive and vigorous.

"I think I may have to leave," he started in immediately with a soft, quaking monotone.

"What makes you think that?" I asked.

"Joan, my supervisor, has lost confidence in me. She used to tell me everything that she was doing, invite me into all of the key meetings, discuss long-term issues with me. Now, that never happens."

"Never?"

"Well, not as often. Not since the IS [Information Systems] revision started. God, I hate that project. I wish we'd never decided to change over to the new systems. It's been a complete nightmare."

Rodney went on to describe a decision that the organization had made to upgrade the software that helped his unit process a great deal of paperwork in the accounting department. The project had begun with high hopes and expectations, but at each turn in the road they encountered staff resistance, technical glitches in the new systems, major implementation issues, conflict with other organizational units, and political problems throughout the administration in the organization. Rodney bore the responsibility for managing the relationship with the software vendor that the company had selected. He really liked the people he worked with in his office, and he also got along well with the technicians and programmers who were helping install the systems.

On the other hand, Joan hated to deal with them. She had come to think of them as sleazy characters, only interested in the money that they were "gouging" from the company and not very helpful when it came to customizing their product for a complex organization like theirs. Over the past 6 months, she had to return repeatedly to her supervisors to explain delays, problems, and increased costs. Although they remained both supportive and upbeat about the project, Joan found the interactions stressful and ultimately humiliating. She was accustomed to delivering work on time and under budget. Normally, Joan was fairly easygoing because she kept the trains running. She had recruited a highly talented and energetic group of staff around her and supported them well. Rodney had become one of two key operations managers for her.

"What have you tried to change the situation?" I asked.

"Oh, the usual. I've ignored all the slights, tried to keep up appearances, focused on doing a good job, stayed out of her way as much as possible."

"Have you tried to talk to her?"

"Yep. I've approached her three or four times and asked her if there was anything wrong. She denied having any reactions to me and said I was imagining everything. I even took her out to lunch to talk."

"How did that go?"

"Actually, it went quite well. She loosened up. We talked about our kids and all the stresses of working as hard as we do and still make time for families. I think it's especially hard on her with four little ones and a busy husband."

"So, she goes home at night to another full-time job?"

"Absolutely! I don't know how she does it."

"Does she have any history of implementing projects like this current IS one?"

"Oh yeah. Our boss asked her to implement some godforsaken system a couple of years ago before I got there. It was an absolute disaster. They spent about a million dollars with nothing to show for it. There was even a story in the company newspaper about how badly that system had performed. They ended up in a lawsuit that was settled out of court."

"Sounds pretty traumatic."

"It was, and I try to take that into account. I really do. But when she goes into a meeting that I know I should be in, ignores what I say when I am in a meeting, and doesn't even say hello in the morning, it's very upsetting. I'm really starting to resent her treatment of me, and if it continues, I'm going to leave no matter how badly it hurts to go."

As he described the effect of Joan's behavior on him, Rodney's face flushed and he grimaced as though someone had his hand in a vise and was slowly turning the screw. It was obvious that he was having intense emotional reactions to the situation he faced. Despite good efforts to cope constructively with both the stresses and the inherent conflicts in the situation, he was losing the battle with his own feelings.

"Where do you experience conflict in this situation?" I asked him directly, knowing that we had done some conflict-oriented work in the past. He sat pensively for several moments while I waited for his response.

"God, there's a lot of it. I'm in conflict with myself because I really like my job and I like Joan. I don't want to leave, but I hate what is happening to me and to the unit in this implementation. There's conflict with the vendors, with other units, with other staff, with the system itself. There's what is happening between Joan and myself."

As he described these complexities, I could sense Rodney breathe a little easier. The flushing in his face decreased somewhat, and he leaned back in his chair.

"Can you see anything else by way of conflict in the situation?"

He shook his head.

"What about for Joan?"

"What does that have to do with me?"

"Well, you're responding to how she's treating you, right?"

Rodney nodded.

"What if she's responding out of her own conflicts in the situation, and it has little or nothing to do with you?"

"What do you mean?"

"Stick with me for a moment. What do you think Joan might be experiencing by way of conflict?"

"That's simple. She hates this new system, she doesn't want to be responsible for implementing it, and she's ticked off at our boss for making her do it."

"Anything else?"

"She's tired all the time from working so hard at home, and she still has her normal job to do, which gets harder all the time."

"If you were in her shoes, how do you think you'd feel?"

Rodney stopped cold and looked straight at me.

"I'd resent almost every moment of every day. I'd be angry all the time. I'd want to run away from all of it."

"So, both you and Joan have a variety of things and situations that you want to avoid."

"Oh yeah."

"And, there are other preferences, other choices, you both would make in this situation if you could?"

"Definitely!" Rodney almost shouted at me.

"What would you want different in the situation?" I asked.

"I want Joan to treat me like she used to. Like she did at lunch a couple of weeks ago. I'd want the project to be completed successfully. I'd want to stop being between Joan and the vendor."

"Can you get any of these things to happen?"

"Not likely. Not any time in the future."

"So, what can you do to change the situation?"

"I don't have any idea."

"What about how you are framing the experience?"

"What do you mean?"

"How you see and experience all of your interactions with Joan. For example, if you say to yourself every time you interact with her negatively on the project, 'I resent this, I hate this, I want to run away,' you're likely to build up a pretty big load of resentment aren't you?"

"Yeah, just like I have been doing."

"Reframing something allows you to see a situation more creatively, get a different perspective, and perhaps then relate differently to it."

Rodney shifted forward in his chair and his eyes lit up. "So, how could I reframe this thing?"

"What do you want to avoid?"

"Resenting Joan and feeling so hurt."

"And seeing her as the person who's responsible for hurting you."

"Oh yeah!"

"What if you interpreted these events in terms of the project?"

"Like how?"

"Well, in the next staff meeting, what if Joan says something sarcastic to you about the vendor or your work with them. How could you experience that differently?"

Rodney pondered for a moment. "Well, it's all just bullshit anyway," he said.

"So, when Joan makes a crack, instead of feeling resentful of what she says, getting mad, and feeling like you must leave your job, you could say something like 'look out below, another load of project bullshit coming in for a landing.' "

Rodney let out a loud, long laugh. "You know, that's what it's really like. You're just sitting there minding your own business and a pigeon flies over and craps on you."

"And, what if elephants fly?" I asked and we both laughed heartily together.

Rodney and I spent the rest of the session discussing ways he could creatively cope with this complicated set of conflicts. As the session progressed, he became increasingly more active and interested in what he might do differently. He was able to acknowledge that the lunch with Joan had signaled to him that she did not hate him or disrespect his work. He spontaneously thought of several additional steps he could take to inhibit his resentment and anger. At the end of the session, he thanked me and said that it had really given him a constructive way of looking at the situation and working with it.

Coaching Executives on Human Conflict in Organizations

Rodney's experience demonstrates the complexity of what underlies many situations that executives encounter in their daily organizational lives. It is rare for any person holding a leadership role in an enterprise to go through a day without conflict. In a sense, I have come to believe that leaders and management teams function as human shock absorbers for organizations. Coping with internal and external problems forms the foundation of managerial work, and these problems almost always consist of some form of human conflict. Adding the internal dynamics and personal histories of everyone involved, the complexity and difficulty of managerial work should cease to surprise anyone.

Starting with chapter 1, this volume has repeatedly emphasized the importance of executive coaches being aware of and savvy within this world of human conflict. The models of systems and psychodynamics; the coaching definitions, psychodynamic processes, and problems; and the organizational structures, processes, and regression presented in previous chapters highlight the central message that coaches must have some understanding and competence in assessing and maneuvering in these worlds. Simultaneously, I have emphasized that coaching, although often having and creating therapeutic value for clients, is not and should never be considered psychotherapy. Whenever a coach feels that he or she is being dragged into such a role, referrals are in order. Nevertheless, in my experience, it is rare to be in a coaching session and not be confronted with either implicit or explicit conflict in the client's life.

As discussed in chapter 5, human conflicts are usually managed through a complex process leading to a compromise formation that may be dysfunctional and regressive, homeostatic, or creative and emergent. Rodney's description of his initial response to the complex situation he faced with Joan and the new IS implementation can be thought of as having creative, homeostatic, and regressive features. Indeed, Rodney did his job with the vendor team, his colleagues, and his supervisor, trying to bring the new system on-line. He searched for creative solutions to the conflicts he experienced externally with the various people and problems and to the challenges he encountered in the working relationship with Joan. He demonstrated flexibility in trying different strategies with Joan and courage in talking directly to her about his experience. Fundamentally, he sought a homeostatic solution that would leave the relationship with Joan unchanged and a simultaneously creative solution in trying to implement the new software.

However, the situation proved overwhelming for him and led to a regressive slide into a vicious circle of shame, sadness, anxiety, and defensive rage. Rodney felt close to a decision to leave a job that he loved and an organization to which he had become attached. In this case, the desire to escape, to flee the tensions in the moment, were, in my judgment, largely reactive and far less than the creative responses that I knew he was capable of inventing as adaptive strategies in managing these conflicts. Our discussion and exploration, or reframing, succeeded in helping him break through the negative attractor and his vicious compromise to see that despite his complex and intense feelings and responses to the situation, the relationship with Joan was in no real jeopardy. His laughter at the metaphor of flying elephants pulled him into a higher level of defensive operations from which he proceeded to engage in better reality testing and effective problem solving. In breaking through the defensive logjam of obsessive, absolutist, categorical thinking, he went forward to describe how he planned to support Joan, to try to remain nondefensive and reactive when she vented long-standing frustrations on him, and to maintain harmonious and productive working relationships with the vendor and implementation team.

Focusing on conflict within a coaching session can often have liberating effects on clients. In my experience, they usually know some of the sources of their troubles and most often find it helpful, if somewhat anxiety arousing, to explore their situations in more depth. This is also true when coaching clients regarding the development of new knowledge and skills with which they may have some difficulty. Table 2.6 presented a summary of conflict problems and types that executives often face in their daily work in organizations. The astounding array of issues and problems that can produce conflict is immediately obvious. Looking both at the table and at some of the other models in this book should make manifest that a substantial portion of the work of any executive involves the management of conflict. In a sense, it constitutes the core of the adaptive work of management. Heifetz (1994) suggested that the adaptive work of leadership consists of trying to bridge the gap between what can be identified as reality and other values that often transcend issues of personal or organizational survival including the management of aspirations. Problems arise whenever individuals or groups perceive or even unconsciously experience such gaps, and voids always exist in and for organizations.

Conflicts faced by executives such as Rodney often are the most difficult type, namely multiple approach–avoidance. In these, there are usually multiple outcomes or situations that are desired or aspired to in the situation and, simultaneously, multiple events or circumstances that an individual wishes to avoid. In Rodney's case, he wanted a restoration of his excellent working relationship with Joan, a significant decrease in negative emotional experiences, maintenance of harmonious relationships with his colleagues and the vendor, success in managing the IS implementation, and a return to a feeling of being in control and having power in his life. Simultaneously, he wanted to avoid Joan's continuing criticisms, her differential and disrespectful treatment of him, the implementation problems for the new IS system, losing his job, and so forth. These issues can readily be identified in Table 2.6. Figuring out how to obtain the positives and avoid the negatives eluded Rodney when his emotions and defenses pushed him away from wisdom, Kegan's (1994) fourth- and fifth-order consciousness, and into a regressive slide. The coaching containment, working relationship, and his productive work in the session enabled Rodney to restore his emotional equilibrium and think creatively, positively, dialectically, and more wisely about what he wanted to do in his situation.

Table 2.6 should be useful to any coach confronting a conflicted executive client in that it provides a map of conflict situations. Alert coaches should be able to identify quickly the underlying themes in the material their clients present. Framing them as tasks of internal integration or external adaptation can orient coaches to the nature of the conflict work facing the individual. Looking for what the client wants to approach or avoid can help significantly in the work of assisting clients to craft strategies to access their adaptive capacity for wisdom and determine how they wish to solve the often highly unstructured problems that they face.

Exercise 9.1 provides coaches with a generic approach to help clients identify, explore, and creatively invent revised ways of managing conflicts. Approaching this type of material with clients usually cannot be avoided by coaches because the majority of the truly troubling or challenging issues and situations facing executives are usually full of conflict. Although Table 2.6 (chapter 2, this volume) identifies some of these likely themes, coaches must keep in mind that the manifestations of such conflict issues are always unique to the individual client and his or her situation. Using the general method outlined in the exercise also presupposes the competence of the coach; the motivation, reasonable maturity, and health of the client; that the coach probably has a working agreement if not formal contract with the client; and that the containment and coaching relationship are well established. I would also hope that the client has demonstrated some interest and ability in expanding his or her self-awareness and implementing more reflective approaches to thinking and acting.

In keeping with the material presented in chapters 5–8, I am advocating coaching on this conflict material as one of the central avenues to assist clients to further develop and advance their wisdom as people and executives. Conflict situations and issues often present just the kind of highly unstructured, complex, paradoxical, and challenging problems that stubbornly resist other problem-solving, decision-making, and behavioral approaches. In a sense, any executive who improves his or her ability to work with these types of issues and problems automatically becomes wiser by increasing both personal and professional competence. This provides more value to the organization for which the executive works, and it ultimately leads to better personal adaptation and more growth for the individual.

In the example opening this chapter, Rodney's improved ability to cope with his resentment and to modify his approach to a difficult and challenging set of interpersonal and organizational issues kept him in the organization and producing effectively. Ultimately, the IS system was successfully and fully implemented. Eventually, his supervisor relaxed and received major rewards for managing the changes. She was extremely grateful to Rodney for his steadfastness and competence in getting the job done. Rodney was also rewarded and felt more confident and competent as he managed the situation through to its logical conclusion. My role in coaching Rodney required several additional sessions as the IS implementation rolled forward. However, these sessions were, on the whole, much easier to manage and maneuver than the one described here. As demonstrated in this case example, the general method outlined in Exercise 9.1 can have powerful and long-lasting positive effects for clients when used correctly by an experienced coach.

Readers should also be aware by now that much of this book has been devoted to improving their ability to assess and intervene in these seemingly complex, unstructured, and difficult situations with clients. In the following section, a few unique conflict issues and situations that are likely to confront any coach are presented.

Special Conflict Situations for Coaching

EFFECTING CHANGE

The first and perhaps the trickiest conflict situation to highlight here involves the executive who believes that he or she should, or must, act in a deliberately deviant way in the organization. The most obvious case happens when the individual comes to understand that some sort of change is required in the organization and that he or she must exercise some leadership to ensure that the change takes place. The position occupied by the executive makes a great deal of difference as to how such situations can be managed. Obviously, a leader with the authority, knowledge, and skill necessary to make the changes represents the most desirable and simplest of these circumstances. Coaching these individuals can be fun and rewarding even if the most valuable service a coach offers is a safe and confidential place to reflect on, challenge, and explore circumstances, issues, alternatives, and outcomes. This "haven" can be valuable for a senior executive, because often they feel strongly that they have limits on whom they can talk to and what they can say.

More complicated situations arise when the executive is lower in the hierarchy, does not have the formal authority to initiate change, or lacks sufficient knowledge or skill. In these circumstances, coaching will move beyond the simple construction and implementation of a reflective, supportive, and challenging containment for the client. The coach may need to add knowledge and skill in assisting the client to conceptualize, implement, and evaluate change. In organizations with reasonably healthy and supportive cultures that encourage executives to grow, challenge, and take on new initiatives, this can be rewarding even if difficult work. However, in severely regressed organizations, those with rigid, inflexible structures and leaders who resist change advocated from below or in the middle, or those with compromised or ineffective leadership, such change initiatives can be threatening to one's job, career, and even life. Coaches must be prepared to support clients in these situations. In particular, political- and power-based maneuvering can become important to success or failure. Coaches should have a good sense of their own limitations in such organizational settings and, where experience or expertise is insufficient, referrals or shadow consultation can be vitally important to ensuring the quality of the coaching work and, ultimately, positive outcomes for clients.

In these situations, beginning coaches especially must remain vigilant at all times to the fact that the advice that they give and the directions that they take in coaching can have huge costs for clients if they are wrong. Clients sometimes lose power, prestige, and jobs; permanently injure careers; and suffer personal losses when they cannot properly manage conflict situations. Coaching that contributes to such negative outcomes should be avoided at all costs, including resigning from or refusing assignments for which there may be insufficient experience and expertise. Although I firmly understand that it is impossible to succeed with every client or in every situation that may face a client, I believe strongly that coaches have ethical, moral, and personal responsibilities to know their limitations and to practice within them.

Finally, there are situations in which executives must be able to pick a fight or defend themselves against attack or incompetence in order to survive in their positions, careers, and organizations. Depending on the culture of the group, subunit, or organization as a whole, these behaviors can be considered either normal and in the mainstream of experience or extremely deviant and in violation of the implicit norms, values, and assumptions of the enterprise. Coaching can be valuable to managers in these situations, because it usually slows them down, making them more reflective, creating options to consider, and providing opportunities to invent strategy and practice the behaviors that they want to use. It becomes important to help clients understand the concepts of behavior outside the norm and the defensive routines that individuals and groups can use against such deviance, however creative and well intended (see Heifetz, 1994). Here again, the experience, knowledge, and skill of the coach can be severely tested by clients and their organizations; however, helping clients with these issues creates some of the most rewarding work that coaches do because it often makes a significant impact on careers and quality of work life. The information, concepts, and skills provided in this book can help coaches work in these situations.

MANAGING BOUNDARIES AND LIMITS

A second difficult conflict situation involves the continuous need to identify, set, reinforce, maintain, or renegotiate interpersonal and organizational boundaries and limits. Tools such as organizational charts, policies, procedures, job descriptions, contracts, agreements, and memoranda of understanding are used by almost every organization to deal with the formal boundaries and limits that they require. Roles, interpersonal relationships, physical space markers, dimensions of diversity, nonverbal communication, and personal preferences also play a significant part in delineating the bounded and limited spaces in human organizations. Leaders are often called on to negotiate and renegotiate boundaries between themselves and others, peers, subordinates, their organizations and other enterprises, work and family life, and so forth. Boundaries and limits are also all around us, and the ability to identify, set, and maintain them can be a crucial determinant in the success of an executive.

Working with executives on the subjects of boundaries and limits requires coaches to be knowledgeable about these issues and comfortable in the dynamics of how they are structured and with the processes and contents that drive them into disarray. Leaders confronted by subordinates inappropriately ambitious for their supervisor's job, who are displaying out-of-control, acting-out, or regressive behavior and who are refusing to comply with policies, procedures, or work orders; by colleagues invading their organizational domains or inappropriately refusing to collaborate; or by superiors who pile on unreasonable work expectations and demands while providing insufficient resources will by definition be in a conflict or will need to start one. Everyone's experience with limits and boundaries begins with very early childhood and stretches through formal education and virtually every type of interpersonal relationship. This history informs people's attitudes, values, beliefs, and behaviors whenever we bump into boundaries. Executives play special roles in these matters because they have formal responsibility for defining and maintaining them. It goes without saying, then, that all of the conflict associated with these issues will confront the responsible individual. However, if the client struggles with establishing boundaries, reinforcing limits, or challenging others when violations have occurred, then major trouble usually follows.

Reassuring clients that such limit-setting and boundary maintenance activities are both legitimate and necessary and helping them conceptualize and implement approaches to such problems often are critical for the success of a coaching engagement. This type of conflict work often requires the courage of a warrior in battle; the interpersonal adroitness of a foreign-service professional; and the cognitive, emotional, and verbal dexterity of escape artists and magicians. Proper implementation can require clients to confront their own longstanding attitudes and values that may be incongruent with the demands of the executive role or organizational situation. These circumstances often create multiple approach–avoidance scenarios in which the client may be emotionally, historically, and cognitively troubled about the boundary and limit conflicts themselves. Sorting through such complexity and helping a client discriminate job duties from personal history and inner psychodynamics is very rich and difficult coaching work.

DEALING WITH SPIRITUAL AND MORAL ISSUES

A third conflict topic concerns situations in which spiritual and moral questions arise for clients. These are also very delicate and tricky; they require careful and respectful work on the part of the coach because of the level of power and significance that they usually have for clients and their complex and frequently unconscious components. Questions and challenges about what is socially, personally, and professionally right and wrong and the creation of meaning in life form the core of the inner experiences of many adults. Organizations and the situations that they confront or create will often push executives to face and question these central elements of their true identities. Yet, few, if any, enterprises possess the necessary foresight to have established resources or mechanisms through which executives can confront and work through such questions and issues. The legal and ethical challenges of the modern corporation are complex. Gilligan (1984), Gowans (1987), Lowman (1998), Mann and Roberts (1999), Pearce and Littlejohn (1997), Velasquez (1992), and many others offer a great deal of insight and information on these moral, ethical, and legal issues. However, even these resources are often insufficient when helping clients confront basic questions that arise in how they construct the very meaning of their lives. When working in these close spaces with individuals, it often can be helpful to be familiar with the Old and New Testaments of the Jewish and Christian Bible, the Koran, the Bhagavad Gita, and other sources of religious and moral beliefs and practices. Other contemporary sources of information and insight on these issues can be obtained through such authors as Barks (1990), Buber (1970), Dass and Gorman (1988), Eisler (1987), James (1961), Moody and Carroll (1997), and Moore (1992).

Coaches must be exceedingly circumspect when working on these issues with clients. Careful exploration of the moral and religious training, personal beliefs, key moral challenges or experiences in life, and professional ethics of individuals before providing any insight or advice can often assist the coach in avoiding harmful or simply stupid mistakes. For example, offering a client who is a practicing Orthodox Jew a metaphor or explanatory parable from the New Testament of the Christian Bible could create unnecessary tension and defensiveness when similar parallels may exist in sections of the Old Testament. Other types of moral and ethical mistakes can be avoided through such careful explorations and through the continuous education of the coach.

It is also useful to remember that conflicts of these types will always involve the conscience of the client. Along with what has been said above, I have come to understand that conscience evolves in unique ways for every individual and that this inner voice of moral authority plays an incredibly powerful role in everyone's life. I have found many individual clients well versed with the functions, demands, and structure of their own conscience, and with them I have had some of the most remarkable dialogues and meaningful exchanges of my personal and professional life. Similarly, I have had interactions with some individuals for whom a question such as "What might your conscience think about that?" elicits only nervous laughter or a questioning frown. Yet, I am often drawn into working with clients on these issues because they face decisions or situations with enormous moral implications such as firing one individual or a thousand or more people; dealing with a key organizational performer who has been found guilty of sexual harassment, discrimination, or other wrongdoing; or such deceptively simple issues as how much vacation to take and spend with family as opposed to staying at work to oversee a critical piece of business. In my experience, being able to help a client explore his or her basic values and beliefs in such situations constitutes a key aspect of executive coaching.

VALUING DIVERSITY

The final special conflict topic I want to address briefly concerns an expansion of the previous one. Moral and religious experiences are just one dimension of diversity that any client brings to coaching. Katz and Miller (1996) discussed coaching executives on diversity issues and offered a variety of models, methods, and issues for consideration. I realize that I have mostly skipped over such considerations in the material previously covered in this book. However, as stated in chapter 1, I set out to address a set of issues with this volume that other authors and resources have not sufficiently considered. Page limitations have forced me to make a number of critical choices and compromises; to cover adequately the psychodynamic and coaching issues, I have had to leave out other material.

With regard to working diversity issues in conflict situations, I know that coaches must understand the dynamics of diversity and inclusion in the modern organization. Dimensions of diversity include race, gender, age, ethnicity, physical and mental ability, sexual orientation, religion, and many others. Coaches must have an awareness of the dynamics of such dimensions and how they are treated in client organizations. It has become routine to see newspaper headlines dealing with racial discrimination and sexual harassment in the workplace. These heinous practices must be confronted and fought vigorously whenever encountered. Consultants must remain vigilant on the subjects of racism, sexism, and other forms of human oppression that can surface often in the most insidious and devious ways in human organizations. The tendency to collude with clients when they deliberately or unconsciously ignore the fact that their management team has no racial or gender diversity is but one small example of these issues operating in an organization and in coaching relationships. However, coaches must remain aware of many of the other issues involving inclusion and how they can affect clients even unconsciously. The best way to address these issues is to make them a part of the formal and informal assessment with clients. Asking a few questions about how the client's organization manages diversity and inclusion; deals with issues of racism, sexism, discrimination, harassment, sexual orientation, ageism, and disabilities; and structures its personnel policies around things like religious holidays, flex time, and medical leave can provide a coach with a great background against which to assess the particular issues that arise in a session.

These issues cut across all types of clients. The coaching experience of the problems and conflict issues may change depending on whether the coach is dealing with a 50-year-old White male CEO of a company or with a 28-year-old African American lesbian who works as a first-line supervisor. Similarly, the approach of the coach may also need to change with these dimensions of diversity. Helping a middle-aged, White male CEO manage inclusion across a whole organization will be different than assisting an entry-level African American female supervisor deal with overt and covert fears, unconscious oppression, and at times formal discrimination that are often present in many organizations. Again, coaches must push themselves to explore these problems and issues and how they affect themselves and their clients. Education about diversity and inner psychological and moral development regarding one's personal experience and perspectives on human oppression are lifelong propositions, and work on the issues in our own lives as professionals and individual human beings is required if we are to be of assistance to clients in modern organizations.

Final Words on the Attention and Wisdom of the Coach

Training as a psychotherapist teaches practitioners that the crucial ability or tool required to do the work competently consists of a well-educated and disciplined capacity to pay attention. Gray (1994) provided a wonderful exploration of these issues based on his psychoanalytic education and experience. I have come to believe that consultants can profit greatly from these insights and perspectives when doing executive coaching. Keep in mind that throughout this book I have argued that coaching should be considered and practiced differently than psychotherapy. However, the boundaries are not crisply drawn lines, and many of the examples, case studies, tools, and concepts provided in the previous chapters demonstrate the complexity of coaching in situations and with clients that are not conflict free and in which the insights and experience of psychotherapy can inform the work of coaching. The attention of coaches is another of these areas.

I believe the therapeutic literature can offer the following pieces of advice to practitioners of coaching:

- Be aware of how and to what you pay attention. This requires some skill and training, but the ability to track how your own attending behavior can both focus on and avoid different topics and issues is the best protection against our own and client defensiveness and resistance to change. In a sense, this means applying Schon's (1987) three levels of reflection to the coach's attention and learning how to do so in a seamless fashion.
- Engage empathic listening. Literally trying to put yourself in the client's shoes and attempting to understand emotionally, cognitively, and socially what he or she experiences can take you quickly to the heart of what troubles him or her.
- Be friendly, respectful, and curious in how you attend. Remember that attention is a two-edged sword. Humans thrive when attended to properly. However, attention based on voyeurism, an unconscious desire to demonstrate superiority, needs for power and control, and a host of other motivations can ultimately destroy a client's willingness to participate in coaching.
- Try to direct your attention evenly throughout the domains described in the 17-dimensional model (see chapter 2, this volume) that forms one of the conceptual bases for this book. If you find yourself focusing exclusively on one dimension over another, ask yourself how the other 16 might be playing in the situation. For example, a coaching session focusing exclusively on elements of the group process of a management team can be positively informed by some questions concerning structures such as boundaries, roles, limits, and jobs.
- Be aware of trying to remain emotionally neutral to the material that the client presents. Empathic listening does not require coaches to take sides in the lives of our clients. Even when we are hearing horrifying information, the discipline of being a helping professional requires us to first attempt to understand what may be happening and not to rush to judgment. This can be critically

important when working with the emotional, defensive, and conflict issues described in the past several chapters. Emotional neutrality does not require a coach to divorce him- or herself from feelings about the client and his or her life. In fact, those emotions and the insights they provide are some of the best tools a coach can have for helping clients. However, clients can slant their presentations, withhold critical pieces of information or details, or be unaware of their true reactions to a situation, so it is important that coaches are aware that this happens and not to leap in one direction or another until completing a more thorough exploration.

- Finally, it takes practice and experience to be able to listen empathically in this multidimensional way. Humans do it all the time, possessing a natural ability to track both consciously and unconsciously. However, being able to willfully redirect one's attention in different directions, often at moments of high emotional tension, is not easy or simple. Training, practice, supervision, and providing yourself with opportunities to reflect on your work can be extremely important to growing as a coach.

Becoming an expert in maneuvering coaching attention is central to working successfully with clients. As implied in most of the above points, the development of this skill does not happen naturally for most people. It is vital that we remain vigilant about the important contribution that coaching attention plays in work with clients. Doing so will lead to greater satisfaction as a coach and to improvement for clients.

Similarly, one of the major themes of this book has focused on the idea that executive coaching, when done well, deliberately facilitates the continued emergence of wisdom in clients. The definition of wisdom and the various ways in which coaching activities can be directed to support its development should be part of the key learning you take from exploring this material. One additional point to keep in mind as you move forward in providing these services to clients is that you must intensely push the evolution of your own wisdom as a human being and as a coach if you are to truly help clients in the ways described in the previous chapters. The wisdom of the coach cannot be taken for granted. It requires continual nurturance on every conceivable front. Those consultants who do coaching know that the challenges are enormous and unpredictable. The definition of wisdom as consisting of the cognitive and emotional capacities to identify and solve highly unstructured, complex, and challenging problems applies just as much to the activities of the coach as to the client who is leading a large, modern organization.

If you have had the patience and curiosity to read all the way through this book, then I hope and believe that some of the ideas and techniques presented here will be of value to you. The work of coaching individual executive clients and teams of managers requires a great deal of courage because you never know what situation you will face when you sit down with your client and begin to talk. The pathways to explore in coaching are nearly infinite in number and incredibly rich in their complexity. Your ability to help clients on their journeys will be greatly aided if you remember that coaches are tested just as much by the situations that they face. The courage, humanity, experience, skill, and wisdom that you bring into each coaching session are critical if your clients are to survive and grow.

I sincerely hope that the problems and challenges outlined in chapter 1 of this book have been addressed by what has followed. I realize fully that the material here varies significantly from that presented in virtually every other book currently available about coaching executives. The fact that I have chosen to emphasize systems and psychodynamics does not invalidate the approaches and contributions of other authors and coaches. Rather, I hoped to enrich readers and open their eyes to other useful ideas and methods that can be used in this work. I know that what I have described in this book has been of enormous value to me and to my ability to help my clients. I will be curious if my readers find the material equally valuable. I wish you good luck and much wisdom in your coaching efforts.

EXERCISE 9.1

Identifying and Creatively Assisting Clients in Managing Conflicts

Introduction: Tuning Into Conflict

Assume that any coaching session will automatically involve you in the process of trying to identify, assess, and help executive clients manage the adaptive conflict work in their lives. Always attune yourself to listening to the material produced by the client for its conflict themes and types; it is there if you simply tune into it. Metaphorically, human conflict can be seen as something akin to the now constant bath of electromagnetic radiation in which the world is immersed in the form of radio, cell phone, and television transmissions. You cannot readily see or hear these transmissions unless you have the proper receiving equipment. Coaches must develop and constantly refine their receivers for conflict information.

Once you make this assumption and begin to tune in, you will face your own emotional and defensive responses to what you hear and see. You will need to understand the biases, history, strengths, growth edges, and diversity dynamics that you bring to the work of conflict. Understanding your own filters, attractors, repulsors, and vicious and virtuous circles will assist you in exploring the material that you are receiving. As you move into the conflict domain of the client, consider taking some or all of the following coaching steps:

Coaching Steps

1. Using the models presented in this book and those you bring from other training, education, or your own experience, try to identify the types and nature of the conflict issues; the parties or psychic structures involved; the emotions being produced by, contributing to, or generating the conflict; and any defensive operations present. Write them down as they come to you.
2. Look for the compromise formation that the client may be considering or has formulated. Be especially attuned to formations that seem to consist of long-standing patterns even if they have usually worked well, namely the client's strengths. Listen carefully for historical antecedents in previous situations or relationships that may have shaped or currently inform the compromises and the way in which the client may think, feel, and otherwise construct both the conflict and the compromise solution. Family history and early interactions with parents, other authority, religious, or educational figures, and peers, and dimensions of diversity are often rich sources of such long-standing compromise patterns and will most often be at least partially unconscious in clients. See if you can understand the adaptive value of the compromise. Namely, is it creative, homeostatic, or regressive? If homeostatic or regressive, what does it help the client potentially maintain, approach, or avoid? If creative, consider how the compromise was reached and how and why the client may not be responding in the same innovative fashion in the present situation.
3. Map the parties involved—individuals, groups, organizations. Again look for and explore historical antecedents or situations or relationships outside of the immediate work environment that may be implicated.
4. Explore the identified goals, objectives, needs, wants, values, attitudes, beliefs, aspirations, and desires of the client both in the situation and laterally in terms of life course and career planning.
5. Try to identify the outcomes and consequences of the conflict and the compromise formation for the client.
6. Use empathic listening, appreciative inquiry, and coaching questions to help in these explorations.
7. State explicitly in a tactful and diplomatic fashion that you believe that conflict is present in the situation, and invite the client to reflect on it with you. As the client explores, use the work that you have already done to help him or her press toward a fuller appreciation of the complexity, history, and dynamics of how the conflict operates.
8. Push the client to identify what he or she wants to be different or to change in the conflict that has been identified. Be sure to state these desired outcomes and new goals clearly and distinctly as significant shifts from the present situation.
9. Push the client to try to identify defenses, barriers, resource problems, and so forth that may prevent him or her from making changes. Also explore what supports, strengths, and other assets can help to make and sustain the changes.
10. Consider using reframing, new or revised metaphors, humor, storytelling, and other techniques to help the client deepen the understanding of the conflicts and compromises and to begin to create some detachment and objectification of the situation.
11. Use any of the coaching techniques and methods to help the client begin to construct a revised meaning for the conflict that allows a cognitive, emotional, or behavior shift to begin. Brainstorming, "what if" scenarios, role playing, modeling, role reversals, model building, and developing new strategies are some of the methods that can be helpful.
12. Push the client to develop concrete plans to continue the shift into a revised approach to the conflict. See the exercise on gaps analysis (Exercise 7.1, this volume) for some ideas about what to do. Set goals and timelines; think through additional resources

needed; create activities that will develop new knowledge, skills, or relationships that will assist in changing the approach to the conflict.

13. The client may need to create additional conflict to respond more creatively in some situations. These circumstances could include setting limits, establishing or reaffirming boundaries; confronting bullies; defending oneself; advocating for needs, resources, and positions; negotiating for needs, demands, ideas, or values; managing the performance of an underdeveloped, incompetent, or malignant person or system; working with psychopathological or "evil" behavior in an organization or person; or initiating major changes that may not be desired or expected by subordinates, colleagues, or others. Be conscientious in helping the person to assess the situation as completely as possible, develop plans and fallbacks, and consider the long-term personal, organizational, and political consequences of engaging, creating, and increasing conflict.
14. Assist the client to create a strategy and method for evaluating the effects of trying to create, modify, or manage the conflict. Make additional changes based on the results of the evaluation.

Appendix

MODEL AGREEMENT FOR COACHING SERVICES

AGREEMENT FOR COACHING SERVICES

CLIENT NAME ______________________ DATE ______________

ADDRESS ______________________

HOME PHONE NUMBER ______________ WORK PHONE NUMBER ______________

FAX NUMBER ______________ E-MAIL ADDRESS ______________

COMPANY (IF APPLICABLE) ______________________

COMPANY ADDRESS ______________________

CONTACT PERSON ______________________

HOME PHONE NUMBER ______________ WORK PHONE NUMBER ______________

FAX NUMBER ______________ E-MAIL ADDRESS ______________

SERVICE AGREEMENT

Duration of Agreement From: ____________ To: ____________

Frequency of Coaching Sessions

As Needed	___	Bimonthly	___
Weekly	___	Quarterly	___
Biweekly	___	Semiannually	___
Monthly	___	Annually	___

Goals of Coaching

1. ______________________
2. ______________________
3. ______________________
4. ______________________
5. ______________________

Services to Be Rendered

1. ______________________
2. ______________________

3. ______________________________

4. ______________________________

5. ______________________________

Consultant Fee: $______________

Resources Provided by the Client (and the Client's Organization)

1. ______________________________

2. ______________________________

3. ______________________________

4. ______________________________

Resources Provided by the Coach-Consultant

1. ______________________________

2. ______________________________

3. ______________________________

4. ______________________________

Type of Confidentiality to Be Observed

Completely confidential	___
Limited disclosure with prior agreement	___
Service delivery accountability	___
Full disclosure	___

Notes on confidentiality: ______________________________

____

COMPLIANCE AGREEMENT

By negotiating and signing this service agreement, both the client and the coach-consultant commit to following through with all of the major components specified. In addition, any homework assignments or reasonable requests that are mutually agreed on will be honored to the best of the parties' abilities. Both the client and the coach-consultant agree to communicate clearly and address openly any problems, disagreements, or questions that arise during the duration of this coaching project.

____

COACH-CONSULTANT DATE

____

CLIENT DATE

____

CLIENT'S SPONSOR/SUPERVISOR (if appropriate) DATE

References

Acosta-Amad, S. (1992). Training for impact: Improving the quality of staff's performance. *Performance Improvement Quarterly, 5*(2), 2–12.

Allenbaugh, G. E. (1983). Coaching a management tool for a more effective work performance. *Management Review, 72,* 21–26.

American Psychiatric Association. (1980). *A psychiatric glossary* (5th ed.). Boston: Little, Brown.

American Psychiatric Association. (1994). *Quick reference to the diagnostic criteria from* DSM–IV. Washington, DC: Author.

Argyris, C. (1993). *Knowledge for action: A guide to overcoming barriers to organizational change.* San Francisco: Jossey-Bass.

Arlin, P. K. (1990). Wisdom: The art of problem finding. In R. Sternberg (Ed.), *Wisdom: Its nature, origins, and development* (pp. 230–243). Cambridge, UK: Cambridge University Press.

Aurelio, S., & Kennedy, J. K., Jr. (1991). Performance coaching: A key to effectiveness. *Supervisory Management, 36,* 1–2.

Bandura, A. (1977). Self-efficacy: Toward a unifying theory of behavioral change. *Psychological Review, 84,* 191–215.

Bandura, A. (1982). Self-efficacy mechanism in human agency. *American Psychologist, 37,* 122–147.

Barks, C. (1990). *Delicious laughter: Rambunctious teaching stories from the Mathnawi.* Athens, GA: Maypop Books.

Barnett, W. P., & Carroll, G. R. (1995). Modeling internal organizational change. *Annual Review of Sociology, 21,* 217–236.

Barratt, A. (1985). Management development: The next decade. *Journal of Management Development, 4*(2), 3–9.

Barron, J. W. (Ed.). (1993). *Self-analysis: Critical inquiries, personal visions.* Hillsdale, NJ: Analytic Press.

Baum, H. S. (1987). *The invisible bureaucracy: The unconscious in organizational problem solving.* New York: Oxford University Press.

Beck, A. T., Rush, A. J., Shaw, B. F., & Emery, G. (1979). *Cognitive therapy of depression.* New York: Guilford.

Beckhard, R. (1969). *Organization development: Strategies and models.* Reading, MA: Addison-Wesley.

Bedian, A. G., & Zammuto, R. F. (1991). *Organizations: Theory and design.* Chicago: Dryden.

Bell, C. R. (1987). Coaching for high performance. *Advanced Management Journal, 52,* 26–29.

Berne, E. (1964). *Games people play: The basic handbook of transactional analysis.* New York: Ballantine.

Bielous, G. A. (1994). Effective coaching: Improving marginal performers. *Supervision, 55,* 3–5.

Bion, W. R. (1961). *Experiences in groups and other papers.* London, UK: Tavistock.

Birdi, K., Allan, C., & Warr, P. (1997). Correlates and perceived outcomes of four types of employee development activity. *Journal of Applied Psychology, 82*(6), 845–857.

Bosserman, R. W. (1982). The internal security subsystem. *Behavioral Science, 27,* 95–103.

Brenner, C. (1976). *Psychoanalytic technique and psychic conflict.* Madison, CT: International Universities Press.

Brown, T. L. (1990). Boss or coach? It's not what works for you—it's what works for your team. *Industry Week, 239*(8), 4.

Buber, M. (1970). *I and thou.* New York: Charles Scribner's Sons.

Butz, M. R. (1997). *Chaos and complexity: Implications for psychological theory and practice.* Washington, DC: Taylor & Francis.

Cafferata, G. L. (1982). The building of democratic organizations: An embryological metaphor. *Administrative Science Quarterly, 27,* 280–303.

Cameron, K. (1978). Measuring organizational effectiveness in institutions of higher education. *Administrative Science Quarterly, 23,* 604–633.

Caporael, L. R. & Brewer, M. (1991). Issues in evolutionary psychology [Special issue]. *Journal of Social Issues, 47*(3), 187–195.

Carver, C. S., & Scheier, M. F. (1998). *On the self-regulation of behavior.* Cambridge, UK: Cambridge University Press.

Case, T. L., Vandenberg, R. L., & Meredith, P. H. (1990). Internal and external change agents. *Leadership and Organization Development Journal, 11*(1), 4–15.

Chiaramonte, P. (1993). Coaching for high performance. *Business Quarterly, 58,* 1–7.

Child, J., & Kieser, A. (1981). Development of organizations over time. In W. Starbuck & P. Nystrom (Eds.), *Handbook of organizational design.* New York: Oxford.

Church, A. H. (1997). Managerial self-awareness in high-performing individuals in organizations. *Journal of Applied Psychology, 87*(2), 281–292.

Coggins, M. F. (1991). Facilitating change through peer coaching (Doctoral dissertation, University of Georgia, 1991). *Dissertation Abstracts International, 52*(4-A), 1209.

Cohen, S. L., & Cabot, L. (1982). Managing human performance for productivity. *Training and Development Journal, 36*(12), 94–100.

Collins, J. C., & Porras, J. I. (1994). *Build to last: Successful habits of visionary companies.* New York: HarperCollins.

Conte, J. R., & Plutchik, R. (Eds.). (1995). *Ego defenses: Theory and measurement.* New York: John Wiley & Sons.

Cooper, R. K., & Sawaf, A. (1997). *Executive EQ: Emotional intelligence in leadership and organizations.* New York: Grosset/Putnam.

Cooperrider, D. L. (1996). The child as agent of inquiry. *OD Practitioner, 28*(1 & 2), 5–11.

Cowen, E. L., & Work, W. C. (1988). Resilient children, psychological wellness, and primary prevention. *American Journal of Community Psychology, 16,* 591–607.

Cunningham, S. (1991). Coaching today's executive. *Public Utilities Fortnightly, 128,* 22–25.

Czander, W. M. (1993). *The psychodynamics of work and organizations: Theory and application.* New York: Guilford.

Darling, M. J. (1994). Coaching people through difficult times. *HR Magazine, 39,* 70–73.

Dass, R., & Gorman, P. (1988). *How can I help: Stories and reflections on service.* New York: Alfred Knopf.

Davanloo, H. (Ed.). (1980). *Short-term dynamic psychotherapy.* New York: Jason Aronson.

de Bono, E. (1973). *Lateral thinking.* New York: Harper & Row.

Decker, P. J. (1982). The enhancement of behavior modeling training of supervisory skills by the inclusion of retention processes. *Personnel Psychology, 35*(2), 323–332.

Deepose, D. (1995). *The team coach.* New York: Amacom.

Diamond, M. A. (1993). *The unconscious life of organizations: Interpreting organizational identity.* Westport, CT: Quorum Books.

Douge, B. (1993). Coach effectiveness. *Sport Science Review, 2*(2), 14–29.

Dougherty, D. C. (1993). Peer coaching: Creating a collaborative environment for change. (Doctoral dissertation, University of Oregon, 1993). *Dissertation Abstracts International, 54*(1-A), 71.

Duffy, E. M. (1984). A feedback-coaching intervention and selected predictors in out placement (Doctoral dissertation, Hofstra University, 1984). *Dissertation Abstracts International, 45* (5-B), 1611–1612.

Eisler, R. (1987). *The chalice and the blade: Our history, our future.* New York: Harper & Row.

Ericsson, K. A. (Ed.). (1996). *The road to excellence: The acquisition of expert performance in the arts and sciences, sports and games.* Mahwah, NJ: Erlbaum.

Evered, R. D., & Selman, J. C. (1989). Coaching and the art of management. *Organizational Dynamics, 18,* 16–32.

Ferguson, C. K. (1986). Ten case studies from an OD practitioner's experience: Coping with organizational conflict. *Organizational Development Journal, 4*(4), 20–30.

Ferrari, M., & Sternberg, R. J. (1998). *Self-awareness: Its nature and development.* New York: Guilford.

Fineman, S. (Ed.). (1993). *Emotion in organizations.* London, UK: Sage.

Finke, R. A., & Bettle, J. (1996). *Chaotic cognition: Principles and applications.* Mahwah, NJ: Erlbaum.

Flay, B. R. (1978). Catastrophe theory in social psychology: Some applications to attitudes and social behavior. *Behavioral Science, 23,* 335–350.

French, W. C., & Bell, C. H. (1990). *Organization development: Behavioral science interventions for organization improvement.* Englewood Cliffs, NJ: Prentice-Hall.

Freud, A. (1966). *The ego and the mechanisms of defense.* Madison, CT: International Universities Press.

Freud, S. (1893). The neuro-psychoses of defense. In J. Strachey (Ed. and Trans.), *The standard edition of the complete psychological works of Sigmund Freud* (Vol. 3, pp. 45–61). London: Hogarth.

Freud, S. (1916). Introductory lectures on psychoanalysis. In J. Strachey (Ed. and Trans.), *The standard edition of the complete psychological works of Sigmund Freud* (Vol. 16, pp. 3–239). London: Hogarth.

Freud, S. (1923). The ego and the id. In J. Strachey (Ed. and Trans.), *The standard edition of the complete psychological works of Sigmund Freud* (Vol. 19, pp. 19–27). London: Hogarth.

Freud, S. (1933). New introductory lectures on psychoanalysis. *The standard edition of the complete psychological works of Sigmund Freud* (Vol. 22, pp. 7–182). London: Hogarth.

Freud, S. (1937). Analysis terminable and interminable. In J. Strachey (Ed. and Trans.), *The standard edition of the complete psychological works of Sigmund Freud* (Vol. 23, pp. 209–253). London: Hogarth.

Freud, S. (1964). Introductory lectures. In J. Strachey (Ed. and Trans.), *The standard edition of the complete psychological works of Sigmund Freud* (Vol. 23, pp. 1–137). London: Hogarth.

Fromm, E. (1941). *Escape from freedom.* New York: Holt, Rinehart, & Winston.

Garmezy, N., & Masten, A. S. (1986). Stress, competence, and resilience: Common frontiers for therapist and psychopathologist. *Behavior Therapy, 17*, 500–521.

Giacalone, R. A., & Greenberg, J. (1997). *Antisocial behavior in organizations*. Thousand Oaks, CA: Sage.

Gilley, J. W., & Boughton, N. W. (1996). *Stop managing, start coaching! How performance coaching can enhance commitment and improve productivity*. New York: McGraw-Hill.

Gilligan, C. (1984). *In a different voice: Psychological theory and women's development*. Cambridge, MA: Harvard University Press.

Gleick, J. (1987). *Chaos: Making a new science*. New York: Viking.

Goldberg, C. (1993). The unexplored in psychoanalysis. *Psychotherapy, 30*(1), 159–161.

Goldberg, T. E. (1994). Schizophrenia, training paradigms, and the Wisconsin Card Sorting Test redux. *Schizophrenia Research, 11*(3), 291–296.

Goleman, D. (1995). *Emotional intelligence: Why it can matter more than IQ*. New York: Bantam Books.

Goleman, D. (1998). *Working with emotional intelligence*. New York: Bantam Books.

Good, D. J. (1993). Coaching practice in the business-to-business environment. *Journal of Business and Industrial Marketing, 8*(2), 53–60.

Goodman, P. S., & Associates. (1982). *Change in organizations: New perspectives on theory, research, and practice*. San Francisco: Jossey-Bass.

Gowans, C. W. (Ed.). (1987). *Moral dilemmas*. New York: Oxford University Press.

Graham, S., Wedman, J. F., & Garvin-Kester, B. (1993). Manager coaching skills: Development and application. *Performance Improvement Quarterly, 6*(1), 2–13.

Gray, P. (1994). *The ego and analysis of defense*. Northvale, NJ: Jason Aronson.

Greenspan, S. I. (1989). *The development of the ego: Implications for personality theory, psychopathology, and the psychotherapeutic process*. Madison, CT: International Universities Press.

Greiner, L. E. (1972, July–August). Evolution and revolution in organizations. *Harvard Business Review, 50*, 37–46.

Guastello, S. J. (1987). A butterfly catastrophe model of motivations in organizations: Academic performance. *Journal of Applied Psychology, 72*(1), 165–182.

Guastello, S. J., & Guastello, D. D. (1998). Origins of coordination and team effectiveness: A perspective from game theory and nonlinear dynamics. *Journal of Applied Psychology, 83*(3), 423–437.

Hall, C. S., & Lindzey, G. (1970). *Theories of personality* (2nd ed.). New York: John Wiley & Sons.

Hall, D. T., Otazo, K. L., & Hollenbeck, G. P. (1999, Winter). Behind closed doors: What really happens in executive coaching. *Organizational Dynamics*, 39–53.

Hamel, G., & Prahalad, C. K. (1994). *Competing for the future*. Boston: Harvard Business School Press.

Hammer, M., & Champy, J. (1993). *Reengineering the corporation: A manifesto for business revolution*. New York: HarperCollins.

Hammond, S. A. (1996). *The thin book of appreciative inquiry*. Plano, TX: Kodiak Consulting.

Hammond, S. A., & Royal, C. (1998). *Lessons from the field: Applying appreciative inquiry*. Plano, TX: Practical Press.

Handy, C. (1994). *The age of paradox*. Boston: Harvard Business School Press.

Hannan, M. T., & Freeman, G. R. (1977). The population ecology of organizations. *American Journal of Sociology, 82*, 926–964.

Hannan, M. T., & Freeman, G. R. (1984). Structural inertia and organizational change. *American Sociological Review, 49*, 149–164.

Hargrove, R. (1995). *Masterful coaching: Extraordinary results by impacting people and the way they think and work together*. Johannesburg, South Africa: Pfeiffer.

Harvey, D. F., & Brown, D. R. (1992). *An experiential approach to organization devel-*

opment (4th ed.). Englewood Cliffs, NJ: Prentice-Hall.

Heifetz, R. A. (1994). *Leadership without easy answers.* Cambridge, MA: Harvard University Press.

Hein, H. R. (1990). Psychological type, coaching activities and coaching effectiveness in corporate middle managers (Doctoral dissertation, University of Bridgeport, 1990). *Dissertation Abstracts International, 50*(10-A), 3293.

Hekelman, F. P. (1994). Peer coaching in clinical teaching: Formative assessment of a case. *Evaluation and the Health Professions, 17*(3), 366–381.

Hemfelt, R., Minirth, F., & Meier, P. (1991). *We are driven: The compulsive behaviors America applauds.* Nashville, TN: Thomas Nelson.

Herring, K. (1989). Coaches for the bottom line. *Personnel Administrator, 34,* 22.

Hersey, P., & Blanchard, K. (1977). *Management of organizational behavior: Utilizing human resources* (3rd ed.). Englewood Cliffs, NJ: Prentice-Hall.

Hillman, J. (1992). *Emotion: A comprehensive phenomenology of theories and their meanings for therapy.* Evanston, IL: Northwestern University Press

Himes, G. K. (1984). Coaching: Turning a group into a team. *Supervison, 46,* 14–16.

Hirschhorn, L. (1988). *The workplace within.* Cambridge, MA: MIT Press.

Hogan, R., Curphy, G. J., & Hogan, J. (1994). What we know about leadership: Effectiveness and personality. *American Psychologist, 49*(6), 493–504.

Horney, K. (1937). *The neurotic personality of our time.* New York: W. W. Norton.

Horney, K. (1942). *Self analysis.* New York: W. W. Norton.

Howard, A., & Bray, D. W. (1988). *Managerial lives in transition.* New York: Guilford Press.

Howe, B. (1993). Psychological skills and coaching. *Sport Science Review, 2*(2), 30–47.

Hunt, J., & McCollom, M. (1994). Using psychoanalytic approaches in organizational consulting. *Consulting Psychology Journal, 46*(2), 1–11.

James, W. (1961). *The varieties of religious experience.* New York: Collier Books.

Jaques, E., & Clement, S. D. (1991). *Executive leadership: A practical guide to managing complexity.* Arlington, VA: Cason Hall.

Katz, J. H., & Miller, F. A. (1996). Coaching leaders through cultural change. *Consulting Psychology Journal: Practice and Research, 48*(2), 104–114.

Keen, S. (1986). *Faces of the enemy: Reflections of the hostile imagination.* San Francisco: Harper & Row.

Keeys, G. (1994). Effective leaders need to be good coaches. *Personnel Management, 26,* 52–54.

Kegan, R. (1982). *The evolving self: Problem and process in human development.* Cambridge, MA: Harvard University Press.

Kegan, R. (1994). *In over our heads: The mental demands of modern life.* Cambridge, MA: Harvard University Press.

Kelly, P. J. (1985). Coach the coach. *Training and Development Journal, 39*(11), 54–55.

Kernberg, O. F. (1978). Leadership and organizational functioning: Organizational regression. *International Journal of Group Psychotherapy, 28,* 3–25.

Kernberg, O. F. (1979). Regression in organizational leadership. *Psychiatry, 42,* 24–39.

Kernberg, O. F. (1998). *Ideology, conflict, and leadership in groups and organizations.* New Haven, CT: Yale University Press.

Kets deVries, M. F. R. (Ed.). (1984). *The irrational executive: Psychoanalytic explorations in management.* Madison, CT: International Universities Press.

Kets deVries, M. F. R., & Miller, D. (1987). *Unstable at the top: Inside the troubled organization.* New York: New American Library.

Kiechel, W., III. (1991). The boss as coach. *Fortune, 201,* 201.

Kiel, F., Rimmer, E., Williams, K., & Doyle, M. (1996). Coaching at the top. *Consult-*

ing Psychology Journal: Practice and Research, 48(2), 67–77.

Kilburg, R. R. (1991). *How to manage your career in psychology.* Washington, DC: American Psychological Association.

Kilburg, R. R. (1995). Integrating psychodynamic and systems theories in organization development practice. *Consulting Psychology Journal: Practice and Research, 47*(1), 28–55.

Kilburg, R. R. (Ed.). (1996a). Executive coaching [Special issue]. *Consulting Psychology Journal: Practice and Research, 48*(2).

Kilburg, R. R. (1996b). Toward a conceptual understanding and definition of executive coaching. *Consulting Psychology Journal: Practice and Research, 48*(2), 134–144.

Kilburg, R. R. (1997). Coaching and executive character: Core problems and basic approaches. *Consulting Psychology Journal: Practice and Research, 49*(4), 281–299.

Kilburg, R. R., Nathan, P. E., & Thoreson, R. W. (1986). *Professionals in distress: Issues, syndromes, and solutions in psychology.* Washington, DC: American Psychological Association.

Kilburg, R. R., Stokes, E. J., & Kuruvilla, C. (1998). Toward a conceptual model of organizational regression. *Consulting Psychology Journal: Practice and Research, 50*(2), 101–119.

Kimberly, J., & Miles, R. H. (1980). *The organizational life cycle.* San Francisco: Jossey-Bass.

Kimble, G. A. (1961). *Hilgard and Marquis' conditioning and learning* (2nd ed., rev.). New York: Appleton-Century-Crofts.

Kirchhoff, B. A. (1977). Organizational effectiveness measurement and policy research. *Academy of Management Review, 1,* 347–355.

Kitchener, K. S., & Brenner, H. G. (1990). Wisdom and reflective judgement: Knowing in the face of uncertainty. In R. Sternberg (Ed.), *Wisdom: Its nature, origins, and development* (pp. 212–229). Cambridge, UK: Cambridge University Press.

Knippen, J. T. (1990). Coaching. *Management Accounting, 71,* 36–38.

Kramer, D. A. (1990). Conceptualizing wisdom: The primacy of affect-cognition relations. In R. Sternberg (Ed.), *Wisdom: Its nature, origins, and development* (pp. 279–313). Cambridge, UK: Cambridge University Press.

Kreitner, R. (1992). *Management* (5th ed). Boston: Houghton Mifflin.

Kuhn, A. (1974). *The logic of social systems.* San Francisco: Jossey-Bass.

Lacy, A. C. (1994). Analysis of starter/nonstarter motor-skill engagement and coaching behaviors in collegiate women's volleyball. *Journal of Teaching in Physical Education, 13*(2), 95–107.

Lakoff, G., & Johnson, M. (1980). *Metaphors we live by.* Chicago: University of Chicago Press.

Langs, R. (1973). *The technique of psychoanalytic psychotherapy* (Vol. 1). New York: Jason Aronson.

Langs, R. (1974). *The technique of psychoanalytic psychotherapy* (Vol. 2). New York: Jason Aronson.

Lawler, E. E., III, Nadler, D. A., & Cammann, C. (1980). *Organizational assessment: Perspectives on the measurement of organizational behavior and the quality of worklife.* New York: John Wiley.

Lawrence, P. R., & Lorsch, J. W. (1969). *Developing organizations: Diagnosis and action.* Reading, MA: Addison-Wesley.

Lazarus, R. S. (1991). *Emotion and adaptation.* Oxford, England: Oxford University Press.

Leibowitz, A. B., Kaye, B., & Farren, C. (1986). Overcoming management resistance to career development programs [Special Issue: Communications]. *Training and Development Journal, 40*(10), 77–81.

Levinson, H. (1972). *Organizational diagnosis.* Cambridge, MA: Harvard University Press.

Levinson, H. (1981). *Executive.* Cambridge, MA: Harvard University Press.

Levinson, H. (1991). Counseling with top management. *Consulting Psychology Bulletin, 43*(1), 10–15.

Lewin, K. (1997). *Resolving social conflicts and field theory in social science.* Washington, DC: American Psychological Association.

Lewis, M., & Haviland, J. M. (1993). *Handbook of emotions.* New York: Guilford.

Likert, R. (1967). *The human organization: Its management and value.* New York: McGraw Hill.

Lippitt, G. L. (1969). *Organization renewal: Achieving viability in a changing world.* Englewood Cliffs, NJ: Prentice-Hall.

Lowman, R. (1993). *Counseling and psychotherapy of work dysfunctions.* Washington, DC: American Psychological Association.

Lowman, R. L. (1998). *The ethical practice of psychology in organizations.* Washington, DC: American Psychological Association.

Lucas, R. W. (1994). Performance coaching now and for the future. *HR Focus, 71,* 13.

Lukaszewski, J. E. (1988). Behind the throne: How to coach and counsel executives. *Training and Development Journal, 42*(10), 32–35.

Luthar, S. S., Doernberger, C. H., & Zigler, E. (1993). Resilience is not a unidimensional construct: Insights from a prospective study on inner-city adolescents. *Development and Psychopathology, 5,* 703–717.

Maccoby, M. (1976). *The gamesman: The new corporate leaders.* New York: Simon & Schuster.

Maccoby, M. (1988). *Why work? Motivating and leading the new economy.* New York: Simon & Schuster.

Mann, R. A., & Roberts, B. S. (1999). *Business law and the regulation of business.* Cincinnati, OH: West Educational Publishing.

Marks, M. L., & Mirvis, P. H. (1998). *Joining forces: Making one plus one equal three in mergers, acquisitions, and alliances.* San Francisco: Jossey-Bass.

Martin, I. (1996). *From couch to corporation: Becoming a successful corporate therapist.* New York: John Wiley & Sons.

Masterpasqua, F., & Perna, P. A. (Eds.). (1997). *The psychological meaning of chaos: Translating theory into practice.* Washington, DC: American Psychological Association.

Maurer, T., Solamon, J., & Troxel, D. (1998). Relationship of coaching with performance in situational employment interviews. *Journal of Applied Psychology, 83*(1), 128–136.

Maxwell, J. C. (1995). *Developing the leaders around you.* Nashville, TN: Nelson.

Meissner, W. W. (1996). *The therapeutic alliance.* New Haven, CT: Yale University Press.

Miller, D. J. (1990). The effect of managerial coaching on transfer of training (Doctoral dissertation, United States International University, 1990). *Dissertation Abstracts International, 50*(8-A), 2435.

Miller, J. B., & Brown, P. B. (1993). *The corporate coach.* New York: Harper Business.

Miller, S. G. (1972). Living systems: The organization. *Behavioral Science, 17*(1).

Miller, W. C. (1984). The value of nonsupervisory feedback in coaching sessions. *Supervisory Management, 29,* 2–8.

Minor, M. (1995). *Coaching for development: Skills for managers and team leaders.* Menlo Park, CA: Crisp Publications.

Mohr, D. C. (1995). Negative outcome in psychotherapy: A critical review. *Clinical Psychology: Science and Practice, 2*(1), 1–27.

Moody, H. R., & Carroll, D. (1997). *The five stages of the soul: Charting the spiritual passages that shape our lives.* New York: Doubleday.

Moore, T. (1992). *The care of the soul: A guide for cultivating depth and sacredness in everyday life.* New York: HarperCollins.

Morgan, R. B. (1989). Reliability and validity of a factor analytically derived measure of leadership behavior and characteristics. *Educational and Psychological Measurement, 49*(4), 911–919.

Morgan, R. L. (1994). Effects of peer coaching on the acquisition of direct instruction skills by low-performing preservice teachers. *Journal of Special Education, 28*(1), 59–76.

Murphy, K. (1994). Coaching socially rejected early adolescents regarding behaviors used by peers to infer liking: A dyad specific intervention [Special Issue: Canadian research on early adolescence]. *Journal of Early Adolescence, 14*(1), 83–95.

Musgrave, J., & Anniss, M. (1996). *Relationship dynamics: Theory and analysis.* New York: Free Press.

Nathanson, D. L. (Ed.). (1987). *The many faces of shame.* New York: Guilford.

Neisser, U. (1967). *Cognitive psychology.* New York: Appleton-Century-Crofts.

Nicholson, N. (1998, July–August). How hardwired is human behavior? *Harvard Business Review,* 138–147.

Obholzer, A., & Roberts, V. Z. (Eds.). (1994). *The unconscious at work: Individual and organizational stress in the human services.* London: Routledge.

O'Connell, J. J. (1990). Process consultation in a content field: Socrates in strategy. *Consultation: An International Journal, 9*(3), 199–208.

O'Neil, J. R. (1993). *The paradox of success: When winning at work means losing at life.* New York: G. P. Putnam's Sons.

O'Reilly, C. A. (1991). Organizational behavior: Where we've been, where we're going. *Annual Review of Psychology, 42,* 427–458.

Orth, C. D., Wilkinson, H. E., & Benfari, R. C. (1987). The manager's role as coach and mentor. *Organizational Dynamics, 15*(4), 66–74.

Overholser, J. C. (1993). Elements of Socratic Method: I systematic questioning. *Psychotherapy, 30*(1), 67–74.

Parsons, R. D., & Meyers, J. (1991). *Developing consultation skills.* San Francisco: Jossey-Bass.

Pascual-Leone, J. (1990). An essay on wisdom: Toward organismic processes that make it possible. In R. Sternberg (Ed.), *Wisdom: Its nature, origins, and development* (pp. 212–219). Cambridge, UK: Cambridge University Press.

Pearce, W. B., & Littlejohn, S. W. (1997). *Moral conflict: When social worlds collide.* London: Sage.

Peli, G., Masuch, M., Bruggerman, J., & Nuallain, O. B. (1994). A logical approach to formalizing organizational ecology. *American Sociological Review, 59,* 571–593.

Peterson, D. B. (1993). Skill learning and behavior change in an individually tailored management coaching and training program (Doctoral dissertation, University of Minnesota, 1993). *Dissertation Abstracts International, 54*(3-B), 1707–1708.

Peterson, D. B. (1996). Executive coaching at work: The art of one-on-one change. *Consulting Psychology Journal: Practice and Research, 48*(2), 78–86.

Peterson, D. B., & Hicks, M. D. (1996). *The leader as coach: Strategies for coaching and developing others.* Minneapolis, MN: Personnel Decisions.

Piaget, J. (1971). *Biology and knowledge: An essay on the relations between organic regulations and cognitive processes.* Chicago: University of Chicago Press.

Popper, M., & Lipshitz, R. (1992). Coaching on leadership. *Leadership and Organization Development Journal, 13*(7), 15–18.

Pratt, S. R., & Eitzen, D. S. (1989). Contrasting leadership styles and organizational effectiveness: The case of athletic teams. *Social Science Quarterly, 70,* 311–322.

Rancourt, K. L. (1995, April). Real-time coaching boosts performance. *Training and Development, 49,* 53–56.

Robinson, J. (1996). *Coach to coach: Business lessons from the locker room.* Johannesburg, South Africa: Pfeiffer.

Roskies, E. (1987). *Stress management for the healthy Type A: Theory and practice.* New York: Guilford.

Rousseau, D. M. (1997). Organizational behavior in the new organizational era. *Annual Review of Psychology, 48,* 515–546.

Saporito, T. J. (1996). Business-linked executive development: Coaching senior executives. *Consulting Psychological Journal: Practice and Research, 48*(2), 96–103.

Sawczuk, M. P. (1991). Transfer-of-training: Reported perceptions of participants in a coaching study in six organizations (Doctoral dissertation, University of Minnesota, 1991). *Dissertation Abstracts International, 51*(12-A), 4195.

Scandura, M. P. (1992). Mentorship and career mobility: An empirical investigation. *Journal of Organizational Behavior, 13,* 167–174.

Schein, E. (1990). Organizational culture. *The American Psychologist, 45*(2), 109–119.

Schermerhorn, R. J., Hunt, J. G., & Osborn, R. N. (1994). *Managing organizational behavior* (5th ed.). New York: John Wiley.

Schneider, C. D. (1992). *Shame, exposure, and privacy.* New York: W. W. Norton.

Schon, D. A. (1987). *Educating the reflective practitioner.* San Francisco: Jossey-Bass.

Schunk, D. H., & Zimmerman, B. J. (1998). *Self-regulated learning: From teaching to self-reflective practice.* New York: Guilford.

Schwartz, H. S. (1990). *Narcissistic process and corporate decay: The theory of the organization ideal.* New York: New York University Press.

Senge, P. M. (1990). *The fifth discipline: The art and practice of the learning organization.* New York: Doubleday.

Sheehan, D. V. (1983). *The anxiety disease.* New York: Bantam Books.

Shore, L. M. (1986, August). Developing employees through coaching and career management. *Personnel, 63,* 34–38.

Shula, D., & Blanchard, K. (1995). *Everyone's a coach.* New York: Harper Business.

Singh, J. V., House, R. J., & Tucker, D. J. (1986). Organizational change and organizational mortality. *Administrative Science Quarterly, 31,* 587–611.

Smith, L. (1993). The executive's new coach. *Fortune, 203*(12), 126–134.

Socarides, C. W. (1977). *The world of emotions: Clinical studies of affects and their expression.* New York: International Universities Press.

Sperry, L. (1993). Working with executives: Consulting, counseling, and coaching. *Individual Psychology: Journal of Adlerian Theory, Research, and Practice, 49*(2), 257–266.

Spinner, E. M. (1988). The relationship between selected prescribed leadership behavior variables and self-reported measures of coaching leadership behavior (Doctoral dissertation, Temple University, 1988). *Dissertation Abstracts International, 48*(7-A), 1702.

Stacey, R. D. (1992). *Managing the unknowable: Strategic boundaries between order and chaos in organizations.* San Francisco: Jossey-Bass.

Stacey, R. D. (1996). *Complexity and creativity in organizations.* San Francisco: Berret-Koehler Publishers.

Steers, R. M. (1975). Problems in the measurement of organizational effectiveness. *Administrative Science Quarterly, 20,* 546–558.

Steers, R. M. (1977). *Organizational effectiveness: A behavioral view.* Santa Monica, CA: Goodyear.

Stern, D. N. (1985). *The interpersonal world of the infant: A view from psychoanalysis and developmental psychology.* New York: Basic Books.

Sternberg, R. (Ed.). (1990). *Wisdom: Its nature, origins, and development.* Cambridge, UK: Cambridge University Press.

Stowell, S. J. (1987). Leadership and the coaching process in organizations (Doctoral dissertation, University of Utah, 1987). *Dissertation Abstracts International, 48*(2-B), 589.

Stowell, S. J. (1988, June). Coaching: A commitment to leadership. *Training and Development Journal, 42,* 34–38.

Tavris, C. (1982). *Anger: The misunderstood emotion.* New York: Simon & Schuster.

Thom, R. (1972). *Structural stability and morphogenesis: Essay on a general theory of models.* Reading, MA: Benjamin.

Thompson, A. D. (1987). A formative evaluation of an individualized coaching program for business managers and professionals (Doctoral dissertation, University of Minnesota, 1987). *Dissertation Abstracts International, 47*(12-A, Pt. 1), 4339.

Thompson, J. G. (1988). *The psychobiology of emotions.* New York: Plenum.

Thorndike, R. L. (1949). *Personnel selection: Test and measurement techniques.* New York: Wiley.

Tichy, N., & Charan, R. (1995, March–April). The CEO as coach: An interview with Allied Signal's Lawrence A. Bossidy. *Harvard Business Review,* 68–78.

Tomkins, S. S. (1962, 1963). *Affect, imagery, and consciousness (Vols. 1 & 2).* New York: Springer.

Tsui, A. S., & Ashford, S. J. (1994). Adaptive self-regulation: A process view of managerial effectiveness. *Journal of Management, 20*(1), 93–121.

Tyson, L. (1983, September). Coaching: A tool for success. *Training and Development Journal, 37,* 30.

Vaill, P. B. (1991). *Managing as a performing art: New ideas for a world of chaotic change.* San Francisco: Jossey-Bass.

Valliant, G. E. (1977). *Adaptation to life.* Boston: Little, Brown.

Valliant, G. E. (1993). *The wisdom of the ego.* Cambridge, MA: Harvard University Press.

VandenBos, G. R., & Bulatao, E. Q. (1996). *Violence on the job: Identifying risks and developing solutions.* Washington, DC: American Psychological Association.

Velasquez, M. G. (1992). *Business ethics: Concepts and cases* (3rd ed.). Englewood Cliffs, NJ: Prentice Hall.

Von Bertalanffy, L. (1968). *General systems theory.* New York: Braziller.

Voss, T. (1997). *Sharpen your team's skills in coaching.* New York: McGraw-Hill.

Wallach, E. J. (1983, November). Performance coaching: Hitting the bull's-eye. *Supervisory Management, 28,* 19–22.

Weinberger, J. (1995). Common factors aren't so common: The common factors dilemma. *Clinical Psychology: Science and Practice, 2*(1), 45–69.

Weisinger, H. D. (1985). *Dr. Weisinger's anger work out book: Step-by-step methods for greater productivity, better relationships, healthier life.* New York: Quill.

Weisinger, H. (1998). *Emotional intelligence at work.* San Francisco: Jossey-Bass.

Wheatley, M. J. (1992). *Leadership and the new science: Learning about organization from an orderly universe.* San Francisco: Berrett-Koehler.

Wheatley, M. J., & Kellner-Rogers, M. (1996). *A simpler way.* San Francisco: Berrett-Koehler.

Whitmore, J. (1994). *Coaching for performance.* San Diego, CA: Pfeiffer.

Winnicott, D. W. (1965). *The maturational processes and the facilitating environment.* New York: International Universities Press.

Witherspoon, R., & White, R. P. (1997). *Four essential ways that coaching can help executives.* Greensboro, NC: Center for Creative Leadership.

Wohlers, A. J., & London, M. (1989). Ratings of managerial characteristics: Evaluation difficulty, co-worker agreement, and self-awareness. *Personnel Psychology, 42,* 235–261.

Wolff, M. F. (1993, January–February). Become a better coach. *Research Technology Management, 36,* 10–11.

Woodlands Group. (1980). Management development roles: Coach, sponsor, and mentor. *Personnel Journal, 59*(11), 918–921.

Wurmser, L. (1981). *The mask of shame.* Baltimore: The Johns Hopkins University Press.

Yammarino, F. J., & Atwater, L. E. (1993). Understanding self-perception accuracy: Implications for human resource management. *Human Resource Management, 32* (2–3), 231–247.

Zeeman, E. C. (1976, April). Catastrophe theory. *Scientific American, 234,* 65–83.

Zeeman, E. C., Hall, C. S., Harrison, P. J., Marriage, G. H., & Shapland, P. H. (1976). A model for institutional disturbances. *British Journal of Mathematics, Statistics, and Psychology, 28,* 66–80.

Index

About the Author

Richard R. Kilburg received his PhD in clinical psychology from the University of Pittsburgh (Pittsburgh, PA) in 1972. He attended a postgraduate program in mental health administration at the Community Psychiatry Laboratory at Harvard University (Cambridge, MA) and obtained a master's degree in professional writing from Towson University (Towson, MD) in 1992. He has held positions in the Department of Psychiatry of the University of Pittsburgh as an assistant professor, as the director of the Champlain Valley Mental Health Council (a community mental health center in Burlington, VT), at the American Psychological Association's (APA's) Offices of Professional Affairs and Public Affairs, and in private practice as a clinician and consultant. Currently, he is the senior director of the Office of Human Services, a multiprogram service component of human resources that meets the developmental needs of the faculty and staff of Johns Hopkins University (Baltimore, MD). He has published widely in the fields of management, professional impairment, and executive coaching. His two previous books, both published with the APA, are *Professionals in Distress: Issues, Syndromes, and Solutions in Psychology* (1986) and *How to Manage Your Career in Psychology* (1991). He was the founding president of the Society of Psychologists in Management and is a Fellow of APA's Division 13 (Consulting Psychology). He has one son, Benjamin, and currently lives in Towson, MD.